DATE DUE

BRODART, CO.   Cat. No. 23-221

ACC Libraries

All Rise

NUMBER SIXTY-TWO:
*The Centennial Series
of the Association of Former Students,*
Texas A&M University

All
Rise

REYNALDO G. GARZA,
the First Mexican American Federal Judge

by Louise Ann Fisch

Texas A&M University Press
College Station

The paper used in this book meets the minimum requirements
of the American National Standard for Permanence
of Paper for Printed Library Materials, Z39.48-1984.
Binding materials have been chosen for durability.

Library of Congress Cataloging-in-Publication Data

Fisch, Louise Ann, 1967–
    All rise: Reynaldo G. Garza, the first Mexican American federal
judge / by Louise Ann Fisch.
        p.   cm.— (The centennial series of the Association of Former
Students, Texas A&M University ; no. 62)
    Includes bibliographical references and index.
    ISBN 0-89096-713-X
    1. Garza, Reynaldo G. 2. Mexican American judges—Texas—
Biography. I. Garza, Reynaldo, G. II. Title. III. Series.
KF373.G35F57   1996
347.73'01089'6872073—dc20
[B]
[347.30710896872073]
[B]
                                          96-5453
                                          CIP

Contents

Illustrations

Preface

Reynaldo G. Garza's place in history rests in his status as the first Mexican American federal judge.[1]

In March, 1961, through the urging of Vice President Lyndon B. Johnson and Attorney General Robert F. Kennedy, President John F. Kennedy nominated Garza to the United States district court.[2] Neither Johnson nor the Kennedy brothers would have predicted that more than thirty-five years later, the ground-breaking appointee would remain an active federal judge. Garza's tenure was not only lengthy but also filled with many other firsts. He became the first Mexican American chief judge of a federal district court. Except for his refusal of President Jimmy Carter's offer to become United States attorney general, he would have become the first Mexican American in a presidential cabinet. In 1979 Garza also became the first Mexican American appointed to the United States Court of Appeals.

Tracing the life's path of this pioneering man offers a true sense of American possibility. It further reveals one man's ability to retain essential tenets of his heritage while seizing success within the surrounding dominant culture. Garza's ability to succeed in the American

Establishment while maintaining his ethnicity represents an enigma to many who study minority populations. These scholars teach that upwardly mobile Mexican Americans generally abdicate their ethnic identity and completely assimilate to the prevailing American culture.[3] A similar melting-pot phenomenon was first advanced by French expatriate St. John de Crèvecoeur.[4] In reaching the federal bench, Garza neither betrayed nor melted his ethnicity, rather he balanced his Mexican and American identities, retaining key aspects of his Mexican culture while integrating himself into American life.[5] This biography details the events, activities, and decisions that created the dichotomy.

Garza's life is also characteristic of the influential college-educated Mexican Americans of his generation and class, who ranked highly in both the Democratic party and the Mexican American community. Historians Arnoldo De León and Richard A. Garcia, who have examined the middle-class Mexican American, embodied by Garza's life accomplishments, have argued that this cadre developed a class consciousness in the 1930s that created the way for the Chicano revolt of the 1960s. This book aids in personalizing one of the participants in the broad social class De León and Garcia so keenly defined.

The primary goal of this biography is to document and thereby inform. Historian David Brion Davis cogently presented the benefit of teaching cultural history through the medium of biography. Davis explains that "by showing how cultural tensions and contradictions may be internalized, struggled with, and resolved within actual individuals, biography offers the most promising key to the synthesis of culture and history."[6] Capturing Garza's life story and consequently giving voice to his cultural struggles is a task no other scholar has undertaken. This lack of coverage represents a significant void in the body of modern American history. This biography seeks to fill that void.

The biography's desired secondary goal is to encourage research into the lives of other barrier-breaking Mexican Americans. Although there are a number of general works on Mexican Americans by authors such as Rodolfo Acuña, Arnoldo De León, Mario T. García, Richard A. Garcia, Benjamin Márquez, David Montejano, and David J. Weber, there is a paucity of scholarship specifically detailing individuals ascending to the ranks of the American Establishment. The number of Mexican Americans reaching Garza's heights may be few, but unearthing these few stories is vital to amplifying Mexican American history.

Acknowledgments

A number of people and institutions helped advance my work. I am indebted to the librarians at the Library of Congress, specifically reference librarians at the law division and Everette E. Larson of the Hispanic division. Roger Karr and Matt Sarago at the Federal Judicial Center aided in my research on the Southern District of Texas Court and the Fifth Circuit Court of Appeals. The cooperation of the following libraries also aided the research process: the Amistad Research Center in New Orleans; the Arnulfo L. Oliveira Memorial Library in Brownsville, Texas; the Center for American History at the University of Texas at Austin; the Lyndon B. Johnson Presidential Library in Austin; the Perry-Castañeda Library at the University of Texas at Austin; the Sterling C. Evans Library at Texas A&M University in College Station; and Tulane University's Howard-Tilton Memorial Library.

Tulane Law Library government documents librarian Katherine B. Nachod and assistant librarian Luis Castrillo were especially helpful in locating federal documents. I also appreciate the efforts of librarians June Payne and Ronald Whealan at the John F. Kennedy Library in Boston, and Claudia Anderson, senior archivist at the Lyndon B. Johnson Presidential library in Austin.

University of Texas at Brownsville President Juliet García and her assistant, Letty Fernandez, provided valuable insights regarding Judge Reynaldo G. Garza that greatly influenced my work. I have also benefited from the knowledge of Brownsville Historic Museum director Bruce Aiken and Brownsville historian and University of Texas at Brownsville history professor Milo Kearney. Both men were kind enough to sit with me for hours, giving me the benefit of their wisdom concerning their beloved city. Archivist Letty Mansano at the archdiocese of Corpus Christi also provided useful information.

Nancy Kocurek, executive council assistant at the University of Texas Ex-Students' Association and Tony Turner of the University of Texas Law School provided me with various laudatory materials reflecting Garza's college and law school years.

University of Texas at San Antonio Professor Félix D. Almaráz, Jr., gave methodically detailed comments regarding the manuscript that helped strengthen the final work. Tulane history professors Patrick Maney, Bill C. Malone, and Ralph Lee Woodward, Jr., offered insight into the historical nature of my project.

The project could not have been completed without the cooperation of Reynaldo G. Garza and his wife Bertha. The judge made time in his crowded judicial schedule for extensive interviews. He endured questions that at times probed into his personal life, responded patiently and candidly, and never suggested that he see or review the manuscript. Mrs. Garza equaled her husband's cooperation and candor. She supplied details of their life together and was a valuable source of emblems of the half-century they have shared.

The judge's family and friends were also eager to aid in my efforts to piece together his early years. I am especially grateful to Judge Garza's sisters María Rosa Dosal and Argentina Garza as well as Judge Garza's children, Rey, Jr., David, Nacho, and Bertita. Judge Garza's eldest grandchild, Jessica, and youngest daughter, Monica, generously gave of their time to assist in finding family photographs. All illustrative material has been provided courtesy of the Garza family. The recollections of the judges on the Southern District of Texas Court and the Fifth Circuit Court of Appeals and Judge Garza's former law clerks also served to guide my research.

Tulane Law School professor and Fifth Circuit historian Harvey C.

Couch provided me valuable information on the Fifth Circuit and on judicial selection procedures.

Eric A. Fisch, my brother-in-law, provided much needed technical support.

Alan M. Fisch, my husband, maintained a keen interest in my work and helped me through the rough periods to sustain me as the rock he has always been. Alan wholeheartedly gave me his interest, his brilliant intellect, and his enduring encouragement. He discussed my ideas, repeatedly read my manuscript with the greatest care, and made invaluable suggestions that have enriched the final product.

All Rise

CHAPTER 1

Heritage and Youth
1901–35

Reynaldo G. Garza's ascendancy to the upper echelons of the federal government began in the modest surroundings of Brownsville, Texas. This southern community played a crucial role in Garza's life, helping him to develop a unique bicultural identity. It fortified in Garza a sense of self-worth, not only by giving him a regional culture imbued with small town values and a Mexican orientation but also by insulating him from the discrimination rampant in Texas. Garza's roots lay in Brownsville, and he carried his hometown with him throughout his life, ever proud of his birthplace.

Nestled at the southernmost tip of Texas, Brownsville rests at the intersection of the Rio Grande and the Gulf of Mexico. The yearlong sweltering climate of this city in the Rio Grande Valley makes it a subtropical region, adorned with rows of palm trees and numerous small lakes termed *resacas*. Brownsville's climate and fertile soil encouraged northern United States farmers to migrate to the city, creating an agricultural-based society by the turn of the twentieth century. As the city proper developed into a service center for the surrounding agricultural community, the outskirts of Brownsville brimmed with farmland. Citrus and cotton crops became the mainstays of the South Texas area, which by the early 1900s was described as the "most intensively developed agricultural community in the nation." Yet, acts of nature, including fierce hurricanes and hard freezes, at times tempered the economic development of this ever-struggling region.[1]

Despite Mother Nature's fury, agricultural development continued unabated, creating an economic bonanza in the Southwest. To meet the labor needs induced by the mushrooming growth, farmers recruited workers from nearby Mexico. Thousands of Mexican nationals welcomed the opportunity to leave their country, finding the South Texas farming environment an attractive alternative to the vile surroundings and harsh treatment present in Mexican farming. Accordingly, constant waves of Mexican nationals streamed across the border during the turn of the twentieth century.[2]

Along with economic opportunities, Mexico's civil unrest, which eventually led to the Mexican Revolution, prompted many Mexican nationals to immigrate to the United States. In contrast to the unskilled immigrants enticed by farming opportunities, the vast majority of these political refugees arrived with sufficient capital to establish businesses in their new South Texas communities. These immigrants intended to return to Mexico after the conclusion of hostilities, but the prolonged Mexican Revolution, beginning in 1910 and lasting until the 1930s, would frustrate their plans. Their presence in South Texas immediately swelled the population of the middle class of Mexican descent.[3]

One of the political refugee families who came to Texas and remained was that of Reynaldo G. Garza. Prior to coming to the United States, Garza's parents, Ygnacio Garza and Zoila Guerra, who were then courting, lived across the Rio Grande from Brownsville in Matamoros, Tamaulipas, Mexico.[4] In 1894, while living in Matamoros, Ygnacio began working in Brownsville at the Yturria bank, the first American financial institution established south of San Antonio.[5] Francisco Yturria, owner of the bank, was a successful Brownsville merchant and one of the wealthiest men in the area. Within a few years of starting at the Yturria bank, Ygnacio rose to a trusted accounting position, giving him an increased income.[6]

Ygnacio's additional salary provided him the opportunity to escape the political unrest of Mexico and immigrate to Brownsville. On September 22, 1901, Ygnacio married seventeen-year-old Zoila Guerra. Two weeks later, he moved himself and his new bride into a Brownsville house owned by Yturria. The two-bedroom home rested along the banks of the Rio Grande and overlooked the international bridge, which linked the two border cities. Like other political refugees, Ygnacio never moved back to his native land, nor did he or his wife become American citizens.[7]

A few months after arriving in Brownsville, Ygnacio was overjoyed to learn that Zoila was pregnant. On October 11, 1902, she gave birth to a son named Ygnacio, Jr. Nearly two years later, on August 12, 1904, Zoila gave birth to another son, christened Leonel. With two young babies to fill her time, Zoila kept busy at home while Ygnacio continued working at the Yturria bank. The small family that had moved to a new country just three years before easily settled into their new life in Brownsville, Texas.[8]

By the early 1900s Brownsville was a small rural community of approximately ten thousand residents, of whom over eight thousand were born in Mexico. The majority of these citizens had Spanish surnames, making the Rio Grande Valley one of the few areas in the United States where the names García and Martínez were more common than Smith and Jones. An 80 percent Mexican American majority in Brownsville resulted in a predominantly Mexican life-style that often ignored American cultural traits such as the English language. Not surprisingly, interest in Mexican affairs often superseded attention to American events. This included Brownsville citizens' focus on Mexico's political revolution rather than America's pre-industrial revolution.[9]

In the Rio Grande Valley, citizens referred to Matamoros and Brownsville as the Twin Cities, because the regions, separated only by a narrow river as the international boundary, shared a symbiotic relationship. Residents of each city freely crossed the wooden, two-lane bridge linking Brownsville and Matamoros, making the two areas virtually indistinguishable. In a region where barbecue and *menudo* were equally popular cuisine, citizens conducted business and social conversations in English and Spanish. Spanish signs lined downtown Brownsville advertising for such items as *ropa de damas,* as Spanish-speaking people from both sides of the border shopped in the flea market–like environment.[10]

The Mexican influence of Brownsville represented an anomaly to the city's visitors. Notably bewildered by the Rio Grande Valley's culture at the turn of the century, a *Harper's* reporter commented on the area, "The majority of those who live along the Rio Grande River, even on the Texas side, are very different from any other population in this country." The reporter cynically added, "[T]he people . . . are almost as much an alien race as the Chinese and have shown no disposition to amalgamate with the other Americans."[11]

The lack of amalgamation, the reporter observed, grew from Brownsville's geographic proximity to Mexico and its isolation from other American population centers. Brownsville entrepreneurs, including Ygnacio's employer, Yturria, eventually grew tired of Brownsville's provincialism and in 1904 funded the St. Louis, Brownsville, and Mexico Railway. The introduction of the railroad transformed the area's existing agricultural and commercial growth into a full fledged boomtown, encouraging not only Mexicans but also Americans from the North to move to Brownsville.[12]

Because the majority of landowners were Anglo, though their laborers were Mexican, to an outsider ethnicity appeared to dictate relations in the city. Economics, not ethnicity, however, guided relations in Brownsville in the 1900s, as evidenced by the acceptance of upper middle-class Mexican Americans, such as Yturria. Thus, divisions in the city arose between upper middle-class and lower-class lines instead of between Anglo and Mexican lines.[13] The city's economic hierarchical system would eventually play a major role in Garza's developing identity.

Brownsville's unique class structure, based predominantly on wealth, not ethnicity, faced disruption early in the twentieth century. City residents remained intolerant toward non-Hispanic or non-Anglo groups.[14] The most infamous example of the community's general disdain towards these groups occurred in 1906. In that year, African Americans clashed with local residents, resulting in one of the most tragic events in Brownsville history—the Brownsville affair.

The Brownsville affair had its genesis with the arrival of 175 African American soldiers to the local United States army base, Fort Brown. The soldiers arrived in a city where African Americans comprised less than 1 percent of the population. Local intolerance led many of the citizens to scrutinize the actions of the soldiers. Within days after the troops' arrival, residents reported cases of assault and disorderly conduct by the soldiers. In turn, the soldiers protested their exclusion from local establishments throughout Brownsville, as they were unaccustomed to being barred from off-base facilities because of their race. Friction between the two groups resulted in daily confrontations.[15]

The situation climaxed on a balmy summer evening. At midnight, on August 13, 1906, assailants fired gunshots into local homes and businesses situated near the fort, which was adjacent to the international bridge to Matamoros. One Brownsville man died and a few citizens were injured. Shots hit the Garza home, located only two hundred feet from Fort Brown. The noise awakened the Garza family. Garza's older brothers Ygnacio, Jr., and Leonel, four and two years old, respectively, nearly became victims of the errant shots. "My mother put my two oldest brothers under the bed and put the enamel night potties over their heads like a helmet," recalled Garza, who heard the story hundreds of times during his childhood.[16]

While Zoila shielded her two young sons, Ygnacio watched the incident unfold. Fearing for his family's safety, he cautiously peered out one of his windows. But because of the darkness of the midnight sky, Ygnacio could not see the gunmen; he heard only recurring gunshots fired from the direction of Fort Brown.[17]

The Brownsville newspaper and the United States War Department averred that the soldiers committed the crime. The *Brownsville Herald* accused the soldiers, stating, "It is estimated that anywhere between 100 and 200 shots were fired by the Negroes during this raid." Three months after the Brownsville affair, President Theodore Roosevelt, acting on the Inspector General's conclusions about the soldiers' guilt, dismissed the entire battalion of African American troops "without honor." After the dismissal of the soldiers, controversy surrounded the affair. None of the witnesses to the affair, including Ygnacio, positively identified any of the perpetrators. Additionally, one historical account suggested that Brownsville citizens armed themselves and shot at homes in the city to force the troops out of Brownsville. In the city, a majority of citizens firmly believed in the soldiers' guilt.[18]

Because his home was targeted by the assailants, Ygnacio served as a witness to the U.S. Senate investigation of the incident in Washington, D.C. In late May, 1907, Ygnacio traveled for three days by train to the nation's capitol. Accompanying him were a dozen other Brownsville witnesses, all testifying about their recollections of the Brownsville affair. It was a rare event for any Brownsville resident to leave the Rio Grande Valley area, much less the state of Texas. Zoila, pregnant with her third child, was extremely proud of her husband's efforts on behalf of their adopted country.[19] It would not be until a half-century later that another Garza would distinguish his family by appearing before the United States Senate—this time in preparation for a federal judicial appointment. For the young Garza family, Ygnacio's appearance before the U.S. Senate helped mold a strong patriotic mentality.

On June 4, 1907, the morning after Ygnacio's arrival in Washington, D.C., the Brownsville affair witnesses were escorted to a Senate meeting room. Once Ygnacio took the witness stand, he testified about his recollection of the previous year's tragic event. He stated that the shooting sounded like high-powered rifles and further testified that at the conclusion of the shooting he heard several persons running back to Fort Brown. A day later Ygnacio began his three-day journey back to Brownsville. Although Garza was not yet born during the incident, the countless accounts of Ygnacio's Senate testimony and of the Brownsville affair itself developed Garza's first sense of racial awareness. "There were no blacks in Brownsville, and hearing the story of the Brownsville affair first sensitized me to the fact that blacks were just not accepted in my hometown in the early twentieth century," said Garza.[20]

Although the Brownsville affair temporarily affected daily life, a sense of normalcy rapidly returned. In the Garza household the routines of daily life included following their deep religious beliefs. One teaching they followed was God's command to "be fruitful and multiply" (Gen. 1:28). The Garzas' decision to have a large family was further influenced by the high infant mortality rate present in Brownsville in the early 1900s. Garza's sister Zoila, the third child, was born soon after Ygnacio's return from Washington, D.C., in the summer of 1907. Two other children, Lucila and María Rosa, followed in 1910 and 1913, respectively.[21]

On July 7, 1915, during the explosive blasts of the Mexican Revolution across the river, Reynaldo Guerra Garza was born in the family home. Ygnacio could not locate the family's doctor when Zoila went into labor, but he knew that a new doctor had just arrived in town and was staying at the Miller Hotel a block away from the Garza home. Ygnacio rushed to the hotel and introduced himself to Dr. Bill Wertz as he rushed the doctor to Zoila's side. It was an easy delivery. Finding no complications after examining the robust eight-pound, twelve-ounce boy, Wertz pronounced the baby in perfect health. Although he was baptized Reynaldo José Garza, he kept his mother's maiden name, Guerra, as his middle name.[22]

The sixth baby, like his siblings, shared many of his father's features, including the lightly tanned skin. Garza's deep green eyes, however, set him apart from his brothers and sisters. The young baby grew rapidly and became an active and curious child, warranting his mother's close attention. By the age of two, Garza's parents translated his inquisitive nature into a sign of a budding genius. The precocious child began speaking Spanish and English at an early age, often mixing the two, thus displaying his first signs of an emerging bicultural life-style.[23]

In 1917, at the age of two, Garza lost his status as the baby of the home. Younger sister Argentina was born in June of that year. A year later Zoila became pregnant again, and Ygnacio decided to move to a three-bedroom home that would better accommodate the family. In August, 1919, a few weeks after the move, Zoila gave birth to the last child, her eighth, a baby boy named Osbaldo. At first, jealousy set in for Garza as he competed for attention with two younger siblings. To mitigate the impending sibling rivalry, his wise parents gave four-year-old Garza some minor responsibilities caring for his younger sister and brother. Zoila directed him to sing songs for his siblings and rock them to sleep, and soon Garza took on the role of the protective big brother.[24]

The Garza family organization, which existed along patriarchal lines, reflected a Mexican cultural pattern that mirrored American culture. Like most Mexican American and American families, the father personified authority. During Garza's boyhood, Ygnacio was typically the disciplinarian. At over six feet tall, Ygnacio's stout frame, striking mustache, large head with ample brown hair, and ever-present cigarette, presented an imposing figure for the Garza children.[25]

Conversely, Zoila assumed the traditional Mexican mother's role of the sympathizer. The children regarded Zoila as a saintly, patient woman who showered them with affection. Since religion was the core of Zoila's existence, she was a deeply spiritual woman who saw in her Catholic faith the answers to any contemporary problem. She kept a Bible close to her side and adorned her home with spiritual symbols. She was a conservative woman, who always wore her coal black hair back with a small wooden barrette and refrained from using cosmetics. Most of Zoila's energies were concentrated on her children and her husband. Zoila spoke only Spanish, even though her father, who attended a Jesuit school in Ohio in the late 1800s, taught her some English. She understood the language but rarely needed to speak it, since most of her friends and neighbors, including her Anglo friends, conversed with her in Spanish.[26]

The family conversed in English and Spanish, and Ygnacio, who was thoroughly bilingual, encouraged his children to master both languages. Because of the large population of Mexican descent in Brownsville, a majority of citizens, including the Garza family, spoke a heavily accented English. Many Anglos in the city, whose first language was English, also integrated a heavy Spanish accent when speaking English. When Brownsville children left the city, their heavy accent remained embedded in their speech patterns. Accordingly, from an early age, Garza, like many members of his ethnic group and generation, was immersed in a bilingual environment.[27]

Garza's eldest sisters helped his mother care for the younger children, attempting to create a serene environment. Four protective females hovered over Garza and his two younger siblings. Doting family friends treated the youngsters to strolls through Market Square where children Garza's age played together in the lush green grass surrounding the square. Market Square, four blocks from the Garza home, was the center of commerce and social interaction in the city. At the square, farmers parked their wagons to sell fresh fruit, vegetables, and handmade Mexican candies. Zoila and the children walked to the square daily to buy food and converse with the many men and women who congregated in the area. In the afternoon Garza's busy father joined the family, amusing the smaller children with games of catch or with humorous Mexican tunes. On the weekends the family attended church bazaars where Garza and his siblings frolicked with the neighboring children as their parents played card games of bridge or canasta.[28] It was an idyllic childhood for Garza, filled with the memories of playful children and pampering parents.

Like most American families in the early 1900s, many of the Garzas' activities revolved around the home. The Garzas were a spirited, animated family who participated in frequent songfests, a favorite form of entertainment. "My oldest sister played the piano beautifully," Garza fondly recalled. "I remember rolling up the rug in our living room and my sister playing and my daddy dancing. He loved to dance. Everyone would join in the singing." The family enjoyed both American and Mexican music, a factor that entered into Garza's developing bicultural identity.[29]

In September, 1922, Garza began his first day of school at West Brownsville Elementary, later renamed Russell Elementary School. The eight-room schoolhouse was only six blocks from his home, and Garza, along with other neighborhood children, walked to classes daily. As with other city public schools, West Brownsville Elementary was plagued with poor attendance, primarily because in the 1920s a majority of school-age Mexican American children failed to attend classes since their labor was vital to their family's financial stability. To compound the problem, education was not encouraged by many Brownsville families. "Students went to school because their families wanted them to be educated; there was a desire, not like today where attendance is mandatory," stated Bruce Aiken, a past staff administrator for the Brownsville Independent School District. As a result, Garza's fellow students at West Brownsville Elementary were upper middle-class Mexican Americans and a few Anglo children.[30] Immersed in this environment from an early age, Garza was shielded from discriminatory treatment. Simultaneously, he acclimated to a dual cultural society whose members came from the upper social and economic strata of the community. He became acutely aware of these defined divisions in his city and eventually developed a world view that sought to maintain this economic status quo.

Unlike many Texas schools where the tendency was to suppress the Mexican American culture, in Brownsville schools cultural symbols were encouraged—except the Spanish language. During Garza's early school years educators did not permit students to speak Spanish in school, and those who violated the rule received a paddling in the principal's office. Although the public school system prohibited the use of the Spanish language, it did encourage popular Mexican music, art, and dances.[31] Through these cultural features, Brownsville schools offered Garza special Mexican traditions that helped him maintain a distinct collective identity.

The Brownsville Independent School District also differed from many Texas schools as it did not practice segregation, attributable to the substantial Mexican American majority.[32] Although many Mexican Americans in other areas of Texas were precluded from attending Anglo schools, Garza never experienced this type of overt discrimination. As a middle-class Mexican American, he was treated by Anglo teachers no differently than Anglo students, allowing him to develop his potential at a young age.

In 1923, by the close of Garza's first year in school, educators became keenly aware of Garza's intellect and ability to learn. He impressed teachers with his photographic memory and his ability to recall large sections of prose and poetry after only glancing at books for short intervals. Consequently, teachers consulted with his parents and decided to allow him to pass over the second grade and enter the third grade. In the third grade he continued to excel, especially in math. His excitement over school projects occasionally manifested itself in rambunctious behavior, yet he was easily calmed by a stern look from a teacher.[33]

Garza's boisterous nature as a young boy was rarely displayed at his family's church, Immaculate Conception. Undoubtedly, the imposing surroundings of the church intimidated Garza. Immaculate Conception was massive in appearance. It was a Gothic Revival–style church structure with a bell tower rising to eighty-eight feet. Garza and his family were regularly greeted by the resonant notes of the pipe organ, and the priests, in their liturgical vestments, conducted church services in the family's native Spanish. The centuries-old ceremonies and rituals helped to enhance Immaculate Conception's solemn, yet majestic, atmosphere. Much like the grand churches found in Mexico, Immaculate Conception symbolized Mexican Americans' religious devotion. As a young boy, Garza felt as if the Immaculate Conception blanketed the entire city. Garza could see the cross-shaped church from his home, as the nave stood 150 feet high. The family often awoke to the chimes of one of three church bells, which parishioners named Jesus, Mary, and Joseph.[34] With the church's seemingly omnipotent presence it was not surprising that Garza formed a deep reverence for the structure as well as for his Roman Catholic faith.

Most of Garza's early memories revolved around Immaculate Conception, as his family actively participated in the church. His sisters attended private school at the church, which often held bazaars, picnics, and dances. The entire family, with the exception of brothers Ygnacio, Jr., and Leonel, who pursued accounting degrees at the University of Texas at Austin in the early 1920s, helped organize Immaculate Conception events. Church dances were especially memorable occasions for Garza. Ygnacio and Zoila were traditional parents and did not allow their daughters to go out unescorted to these festivities. On many occasions Garza would serve as his sisters' escort.[35] As a result, he was able to attend social events normally reserved for older children.

By the time Garza turned ten in 1925, he reached a level of intellectual maturity such that sermons challenged his critical thinking. During one Sunday morning Mass, the priest taught the Biblical story about an adulterous woman. When the townspeople asked Jesus's advice regarding the woman's punishment, which included stoning, Jesus replied, "He that is without sin among you, let him first cast a stone at her" (John 8:7). To Garza this was a thought-provoking story symbolizing the ease with which people condemned others. "I think it was that day that I started thinking that I was going to be a lawyer," stated Garza.[36]

After the experience, Garza pursued his interest by learning about the legal field. He began to spend time after school in Market Square listening to local curmudgeons discuss trials at the courthouse. He found these discussions intriguing and was often most concerned with the relationship between crime and punishment. Within a few months he announced his desire to become an attorney. The professionals of the Garza family were his two eldest brothers, both close to graduation with accounting degrees. Garza's siblings teased the young attorney-to-be that he would become the black sheep of the family. But Garza searched through his family's lineage and found one attorney, a great grand-uncle who was governor of Tamaulipas, Mexico. He became determined to follow this ancestor's career path.[37]

Ygnacio and Zoila strongly believed in encouraging all their children's professional pursuits. Ygnacio delighted in Garza's career aspirations and nourished his young son's interest by occasionally ac-companying Garza to city court trials. The visits captivated Garza, and he would discuss every detail of the trials during family dinners. Ygnacio remained the wellspring of encouragement, urging his children to excel in education. He constantly preached to his sons about the virtues of education, regularly quizzed Garza on his school subjects, and supported his academic and cultural interests. To Ygnacio education was the key to a bright future for his children. By 1925 eldest son Ygnacio, Jr., was about to graduate from the university with a double degree in accounting and foreign trade. Second son, Leonel needed only two more semesters to earn a similar degree. For most Brownsville citizens in the early 1900s, a college education seemed unattainable; in the Garza household, a college education was expected. Advised of the importance of education as a young boy, Garza resolved to excel in academic pursuits, a resolution that would thrust him into a predominantly Anglo culture, yet it by no means fostered a loss of ethnic identity.[38]

By the spring of 1925, Ygnacio, Jr., graduated, and in August, 1925, with the aid of his father, the two opened the Garza Hardware Store in downtown Brownsville. The Garza family patriarch retired from managing the Yturria family businesses, which had now grown to include vast real estate holdings, and now devoted most of his energies to helping his son run the new business. For Garza's part, he assisted his brother and father by working on weekends as a stock boy. In 1926 Leonel also returned from Austin after graduating and became Ygnacio, Jr.'s business partner. A year later, through the efforts of the entire Garza family, the Garza Hardware Store turned its first year's profit, and Garza began working more frequently as a stock boy after school. Although Garza enjoyed assisting the family, he did not want to join his elder brothers in the partnership, as his legal aspirations continued to blossom. With the success of the store, however, Garza did garner an appreciation for his brothers' entrepreneurial spirit.[39] By 1927 the elder brothers' business enthusiasm reflected the degree to which the Garza family had embraced America's free enterprise system.

One especially memorable outcome of the family's financial success was the purchase of a radio. The Garza family, like most American families, was enamored with this new medium of mass communication. In recalling the family's first radio, Garza remembered that "it required one to put a hearing aid in your ear to listen. Because there were eight of us, and I [was] one of the youngest, you can imagine I heard the radio very little." Even an innocuous invention such as the radio reinforced Garza's bicultural existence: the Garzas enjoyed both American and Mexican music, but listened to news reports from Mexico.[40]

As the elder Garza brothers achieved economic success, civic involvement became the new family concern. The family patriarch, Ygnacio, was appointed to the Brownsville Development Committee, which in later years became known as the Chamber of Commerce. Ygnacio, Jr., and Leonel joined the Brownsville Businessmen's Club, organized to promote city and civic involvement. The Garza men's civic affiliation was uncommon for a majority of Mexican Americans in the early 1900s. Social and class restrictions prevented most from participating in civic life during this period. But Ygnacio, Ygnacio, Jr., and Leonel lived in Brownsville, Texas, where their Mexican ancestry favored, instead of forfeited, their chances for success. The three eldest Garza men made a strong impression on Garza; they were individuals he admired and sought to emulate. In later years Garza mirrored the family's community-minded orientation, a focus that helped him capture a firm footing in both the Anglo and Mexican American society.[41]

In August, 1927, Garza entered Brownsville Junior High School. By the age of thirteen, Garza's height had reached five feet seven inches, but his build remained slim and lanky. Nevertheless, he was determined to play football. Garza played, and although not exceptionally skilled, he supplemented his ability with generous amounts of spirit. In 1928, however, he suffered an athletic setback while playing the game. A large lineman struck Garza a bruising blow, aggravating an earlier wound from an appendectomy. Coaches rushed Garza to the hospital, where doctors informed him his football playing days were over. Undaunted, he returned to athletics by participating in sports requiring less physical contact, such as baseball.[42]

In August, 1929, Garza entered Brownsville High School and began a serious focus on future academic goals. Although he maintained his active involvement in extracurricular activities such as sports, he began to direct his attention more toward academic success. But his dream of becoming an attorney had remained. Garza continued to visit the city courthouse to listen to trials and during these visits became acquainted with a few Brownsville attorneys, who advised Garza of the importance of strong verbal and written English skills. Consequently, Garza worked tirelessly in high school to develop these skills, knowing that his efforts would be rewarded. In turn, Garza consistently ranked in the top ten percent of his class. In a city where close to 80 percent of the total population ten years old and older was illiterate in English,[43] Garza took his first steps toward defying the norm. It would be a practice he would continue for the rest of his life.

By his junior year in high school, sixteen-year-old Garza assumed the pose of big man on campus. He was a member of the baseball team, a top scholar, and had developed a charming personality that created enduring friendships. Garza enthusiastically led most of the activities he joined. His keen wit and confident stride attracted many female classmates, but he did not develop any serious relationships in high school. Although he became socially and academically successful in high school by acclimating to Anglo institutions, Garza continued his association with Mexican cultural institutions such as the Catholic church.[44]

In the fall of 1932, Garza attempted to reach his goal of becoming an attorney by applying to the University of Texas at Austin. Because of Garza's stellar academic record, the university accepted Garza. Ygnacio and Zoila enthusiastically celebrated the prospect of having another son attend UT. By 1933 few seventeen- and eighteen-year-olds in Brownsville had graduated from high school, much less attended college. In May, 1933, Garza graduated from high school with honors and began preparing for his fall departure to Austin.[45]

By June, 1933, the family's joy at Garza's impending university attendance soon turned to frustration after Ygnacio sadly informed Garza that he could not afford to send him to college in Austin. The Garzas' finances began to suffer under the growing national economic weakness of the Great Depression. Eventually, the deteriorating financial conditions forced the Garza Hardware Store to close. Ygnacio had counted on the income from the hardware store to send Garza to the university, but with the uncertain economic climate, the family could not part with the funds. The family patriarch promised Garza that he would continue saving and within two years he hoped he could send Garza to the university. Garza saw the somber look in his father's eyes and told Ygnacio that he would defer his admission for a two-year period. In that time Garza would attend junior college while working to fund his tuition.[46]

In September, 1933, Garza entered Brownsville Junior College. Students of Mexican American descent, most of whom could have never afforded schooling away from home, constituted the majority of the enrollment at the junior college. Not until Garza attended his first class at Brownsville Junior College did the reality of his situation overcome him. Since he had been a young boy he had dreamed of attending the University of Texas at Austin to become an attorney. Garza had watched his eldest brothers graduate from the university, hoping that one day he too would be able to fulfill his professional goal. He had honed his reading and writing skills in preparation for the college degree plan needed to become an attorney. Instead of beginning the path needed to achieve his goal, Garza would have to spend the next two years hoping for an upswing in the economy.[47]

At the junior college, Garza worked fervently to maintain the grades required for readmission to the University of Texas, while simultaneously holding a variety of jobs. One of his positions was working as an assistant football coach with Maurice Pipkin, Garza's former athletic coach in high school and now coach of the junior college football team. He became good friends with Garza and helped him find employment on the coaching staff to earn funds for to his planned move to Austin. "He was eager to work as many hours as he could to earn tuition for the university," stated Pipkin, who in later years served as a Texas state representative.[48]

In 1935, with the creation of the Works Progress Administration (WPA), new employment opportunities arose for Garza. The WPA, one of President Franklin D. Roosevelt's New Deal programs, provided federal relief through public works such as the building of schools and hospitals. The majority of work in Brownsville was in the construction field, and Garza helped build some of the government buildings going up throughout the city. Through the WPA, he worked twenty hours a week, making one dollar an hour—a substantial amount in the early 1930s. He saved half of his earnings for his future expenditures in Austin. The other half he gave to the family fund, as economic conditions in Brownsville continued to deteriorate.[49]

In November, 1935, although busy juggling academic and work activities, Garza began courting a young Brownsville native, Bertha Champion. Garza met his soon-to-be sweetheart, Bertha, through his position as editor of the junior college yearbook. The 1935–36 school year was marked by continuing dwindling funds precipitated by the Depression, which caused the high school and junior college yearbooks to be combined. While looking for candid scenes in the halls of Brownsville High School to include in yearbook photos, Garza noticed sixteen-year-old Bertha chatting with a couple of girlfriends. He asked a mutual friend to introduce them. Once they met, Garza offered to walk her the few blocks home from school. But Bertha informed him that her parents were very strict, and her two girlfriends would have to accompany them. Garza agreed, and from that day the four teenagers began walking home from school regularly.[50]

Bertha was three years younger than Garza and lived at home with her parents María and José Angel Champion. The Champions belonged to one of Brownsville's pioneer families and socialized with members of the elite of both Brownsville and Matamoros. They attended Sacred Heart Catholic Church, the first English-speaking parish in Brownsville. As members of Sacred Heart, the Champions were one of only seventy-five families in the city that attended the English-speaking service.[51] Like the Garzas, the Champions valued education and applauded Garza's enrollment at Brownsville Junior College and future plans to attend the University of Texas.

Garza and Bertha made a handsome couple. Garza's tall stature, dark brown hair, and penetrating green eyes complemented Bertha's slender build, elegant stance, and long wavy locks. On Saturdays the couple sat for hours talking at a nearby drugstore that doubled as a malt shop. Garza enjoyed making Bertha laugh. She captivated Garza both by her exquisite looks and her charming personality. The two developed an extremely close relationship, and Garza often told his friends, "That's the girl I'm going to marry."[52] His statement at the age of nineteen was truly prophetic but was not fulfilled until almost ten years later. For the time being, this lengthy courtship was only in its early stages. Garza's relationship with a Mexican American teenager like himself enhanced his dual cultural identity. Bertha shared many of his experiences and encouraged his desire to succeed in the Anglo culture. Simultaneously, though, because of her similar cultural roots, she kept Garza focused on his Mexican heritage.

As his friendship with Bertha blossomed, Garza continued to hold on to his goal of attending the university and becoming an attorney. In the winter of 1935, he reapplied to the university, and a few months later he received his acceptance letter. The university accepted Garza into a pre-law program consisting of three years of undergraduate studies and two years of law school. Since Garza's junior college credits were accepted in transfer, his five years would be trimmed to four. Garza had saved enough funds to attend the university for two semesters, but he was hoping to obtain a part-time job in Austin to complete his degree.[53]

With the preliminary financial matters settled, Garza readied himself to leave his hometown and move to Austin. He sought his brothers' advice on living in the larger Texas city. Ygnacio, Jr., and Leonel described to Garza their experiences as two of the few Mexican Americans at the university. Spanish was rarely heard on the campus, they cautioned Garza. They also advised him to join religious and student organizations. But the most important point Garza's brothers stressed was the importance of creating disciplined study habits. Brownsville High School had not fully prepared Ygnacio, Jr., and Leonel for the university's demanding curriculum, and they warned Garza that academics should be his main priority.[54] As he prepared to leave his bicultural city of Brownsville to attend the University of Texas, Garza decided to embrace the Anglo culture for the moment so as to survive the more mainstream populated climate of Austin, Texas.

CHAPTER 2

The Longhorn Years
1935–39

By the 1930s a large portion of the Mexican American population embraced American culture, yet they tempered their acceptance with a strong loyalty to their Mexican heritage. Dominance of the English language in the home and changes in ideas about marriage and religion, for instance, marked the process of Americanization begun by Mexican Americans in the 1930s. Geographic proximity to Mexico, along with the constant influx of new Mexican immigrants, however, helped reinforce their ethnicity, most notably demonstrated in their celebration of cultural fiestas, such as the Cinco de Mayo.

Anglos responded unfavorably to this strong Mexican ethos, believing instead that all Americans should demonstrate their complete allegiance to cultural institutions, such as the English language or the Protestant faith. Accordingly, many Anglos misperceived Mexican Americans as unassimilated and as a people clinging to backward traditions.[1] Garza defied assimilation misconceptions during his years as a student at the University of Texas. In fact, throughout his university experience he continued to challenge Mexican American stereotypes by retaining key aspects of his ethnic heritage and still achieving cultural solidarity with Anglos.

In August, 1935, Garza left Brownsville for the university, armed with the lessons of his heritage. He had absorbed personality traits commonly associated with small-town Texas: hospitality, graciousness of manner, and a strong attachment to home and roots. His religious beliefs strengthened these views. He also arrived at the university determined to maintain his bicultural identity, thus hoping to bridge any gaps existing between Anglos and Mexican Americans in the more racially intolerant Austin climate.

For his four years in Austin, Garza's life would center around the school's forty acres in the Texas Hill Country. Regal fountains and antebellum statues adorned the campus. From the school, students could view the pink granite dome of the state's capital. University students frequently congregated along Guadalupe Street, a five-block street adjacent to the campus. Known as the Drag, Guadalupe Street housed restaurants, movie theaters, barber shops, and bookstores. The wide variety of goods and services offered on the Drag and at the university created a small city within the environment of Austin.[2]

Wealth emanated from all areas of this self-contained city. Many of Texas' elite families sent their children to the University of Texas. Yet, the university was not solely a bastion for Southern aristocracy. Because of the university's relatively low cost, middle- and low-income families could afford to send their children to this educational mecca. Additionally, UT was the recipient of a major source of wealth that had resulted from a 1923 oil discovery on university-owned land in West Texas. For the university and the rest of the state, this oil find helped mitigate the economic depression facing other reaches of the nation.[3]

Through the university's wealth the campus swelled in students and buildings. Its undergraduate population doubled from approximately 5,000 undergraduate students for the academic year 1928–29 to approximately 10,000 students in the academic year 1938–39. The university also constructed nine new buildings between 1932 and 1934—an unprecedented level of construction for an established university. This growth created a dynamic, vibrant environment in the 1930s.[4] The wealth and vibrance of the university contrasted with Garza's sedate, poverty-ridden small town of Brownsville.

Garza began the process of assimilating into university life even before he registered for his first class. Based on discussions with his eldest brothers, Garza began mentally preparing for the task of being a minority at one of the nation's premier, and virtually all-Anglo, educational institutions. By the late 1930s only 1.5 percent of the undergraduate student body, approximately 150 students, bore Spanish-surnames. In the graduate school during this period, there were only three Spanish-surnamed students.[5]

The racial composition of Austin, like the university, consisted of an Anglo majority. Anglos composed 70 percent of Austin's population, unlike Brownsville, a city with an 80-percent Mexican American majority. Racial segregation was also commonplace in Austin. African Americans and Mexican Americans lived in the eastern portion of the city, known as East Austin, and Anglos frequently excluded both minority groups from shopping or loitering in other regions of the city. In response to the segregation, East Austin became an ethnically dominated section.[6]

The practice of racial segregation in Austin did not affect Garza's opportunity to find adequate housing near the university. He easily found a room within walking distance of the campus, undoubtedly because the supply of available housing exceeded the demand as a result of the Depression. The university student newspaper did not publish its first article describing ethnically biased renting practices near campus until 1940,[7] when the supply of nearby housing dipped below the demands brought by a swelling student population.

Garza rented a room in a two-story, red brick home belonging to the Westes, an Anglo couple. The home was on Nueces Street, three blocks west of campus. He shared the rented room with Joe Ramírez, a Mexican American student from the predominantly Mexican American town of Hebronville, Texas. The Garza family knew the Ramírez family prior to each son's attendance at college, and the families arranged for the two students to live together.[8]

Rooming with a Mexican American student was one way Garza maintained his cultural identity during his university years; another method was the church. As a devout Catholic, Garza's next task after securing a room was finding a house of worship. Again, Garza followed his two eldest brothers' advice and sought out Our Lady of Guadalupe Catholic Church. Like the priests at Immaculate Conception in Brownsville, priests at this church also conducted services in Spanish. Garza soon established a close personal friendship with the pastor. But the Catholic institution was as much a social outlet as a religious one. Garza attended Mass regularly and occasionally donated his time to church functions.[9] Regardless of the university's predominantly Anglo environment, Garza continued to retain the deep spirituality found in his heritage through his church affiliation.

With the first day of the fall, 1935, semester approaching, Garza was filled with nervous anticipation. Concerned over his brothers' warnings about the academic rigors of the university, he wondered whether his high school and junior college instruction would be sufficient training to prepare him to compete with students from wealthier areas and better preparatory schools. As classes began, Garza shunned many of the exciting extracurricular offerings at the school and for the entire semester channeled his energy into studies. His only diversion was weekly correspondence with Bertha Champion. His diligence paid off, and by the end of his first semester Garza had mustered a B average, particularly excelling in economics and government.

By January, 1936, at the start of his second semester, Garza had adjusted to university life. He was now ready to experience more of what the university had to offer. Confident that he could compete academically, he sought social outlets. Because he wished to socialize with people sharing his beliefs and attitudes, Garza's pious convictions attracted him to the university's Catholic student organization, the Newman Club. For Garza, the Newman Club, composed primarily of Anglo students, provided one means to become part of the Anglo community. He was an active participant in both the altruistic and social functions of the group. He also joined the Latin-American Club, formerly the Alba Club, and the newly created Rio Grande Valley Club. Fewer than a dozen Mexican American students from the Rio Grande Valley comprised the latter group.[10] Through membership in these mostly Mexican American organizations, Garza was able to cling to a strong Mexican ethos, much like many other members of his generation, class, and ethnic group.

By the end of the spring semester, Garza became acquainted with a warm group of friends and established himself as a solid student. He also began dining within a few blocks of campus at a boarding house owned by the Mexican American Saldívar family. The more than dozen patrons of the Saldívar house were from Texas cities with large Mexican American populations and, as such, shared both Garza's background and his Spanish accent. More notably, a small number of the Saldívar diners rose to great heights. Among Garza's co-diners were Henry B.

González, who in 1956 became the first Mexican American in the Texas Senate in modern times, and in 1961 became a United States congressman; Julian Saldívar, who later became a physician and survivor of World War II's tragic Bataan Death March; and Joe Alamía, a future Texas state district judge.[11] Garza befriended most of the regular diners and established friendships that would last a lifetime. Most of his friends at the Saldívar house represented members of the middle- to upper-economic strata, who, like Garza, were drawn together by a similar ideology based on a desire to succeed in Anglo institutions without losing a connection to their Mexican past.

During his second semester Garza continued to study diligently and showed his greatest talent in accounting. Within a few days after his accounting final examination, Professor C. August Smith, who had also taught Garza's brothers, informed him that he had received the highest score in the course and encouraged the pre-law student to switch majors. Although flattered by his professor's suggestion, Garza remained adamantly set on his longtime legal career goal.[12]

With his newly learned academic and social lessons, Garza returned to Brownsville for the summer. Back in his hometown, Garza carried himself with a new assurance. But despite his confidence, he never became so arrogant that he could not still enjoy the company of his childhood friends. He also basked in the loving environment of his family and enjoyed his dates with Bertha. Most of all, he used the summer to earn funds for his next term at the university. He immediately started working as a temporary bookkeeper in his brother Ygnacio, Jr.'s recently opened accounting practice. Time quickly passed and soon he was ready to begin another semester at the university.[13]

In August Garza returned to Austin for his second year at the university, the last required for his undergraduate degree. Garza moved into a boarding house owned and operated by the Hamiltons and only four doors down from Garza's old boarding house.[14]

Garza's favorite course during his second year was economics, taught by a popular professor, Robert H. Montgomery. Known as the Doctor, Montgomery taught students a liberal brand of philosophy that fascinated Garza. The professor favored Roosevelt's social reforms but refused to idealize them. More than Montgomery's teachings, the Doctor's classroom presentation enthralled Garza. Held in the largest university auditorium, Montgomery's classes attracted as many spectators as students. With his long sideburns and fiery red hair, Montgomery paced the stage as he lectured. His allusions to the King James version of the Bible especially intrigued Garza. Endowed with a near-photographic memory, the undergraduate rarely forgot a detail of Montgomery's economics lectures.[15]

By winter Garza began expanding his social network. He befriended students in his courses, and his circle of Anglo friends quickly grew. One person Garza met at the university was J. J. (Jake) Pickle, a personable West Texas native and future United States congressman. As an active campus politico, Pickle knew hundreds of students and was happy to introduce Garza to them. Through Pickle, Garza met John V. Singleton, Jr., a gifted scholar and future United States District Court judge, and Homer Thornberry, an outgoing university leader, future United States congressman from Texas, and later a federal judge on the Fifth Circuit Court of Appeals.

One of Pickle's closest friends was John B. Connally, a charismatic law student and future Texas governor, United States Treasury secretary, and one-time Republican presidential nomination hopeful. Pickle introduced Connally and Garza during a university football game, and the two became fast friends.[16] Undoubtedly, Garza, with his imposing six-plus-feet frame, handsome features, and outgoing personality, carried himself with such a confident stride that young men like Connally and Pickle disregarded any inherent prejudice they may have felt towards Garza's Mexican American heritage. Garza's confidence stemmed from his upbringing. Never having experienced discrimination and encouraged to flourish to his fullest potential, Garza naturally became self-assured. Although he easily socialized and befriended popular Anglos, he was far from assimilated into the dominant Anglo culture. He continued to speak Spanish, especially with his Mexican American friends, and retained his deeply religious beliefs. He often boasted to both his Anglo and Mexican American friends of his pride in his cultural roots. Garza was indeed an enigma in the 1930s; as close as thirty years before the Chicano movement began, he was expressing the movement's basic tenets: pride in ethnicity and a positive self-identity.[17]

Many of Garza's new Anglo friends were actively involved in campaigning for the 1936 United States presidential election, and Garza soon became interested in the race. In November, 1936, while studying for classes, attending church, and writing letters to Bertha, he took time out to cast his first presidential election vote. The national campaign pitted Democratic party nominee Franklin D. Roosevelt against Republican candidate Alf Landon. Like most college students of the 1930s, Garza had been a benefactor of Roosevelt's New Deal programs such as the WPA, which had allowed Garza to earn funds for his college tuition. Accordingly, Garza's allegiance to Roosevelt was strong. He voted for the first time by means of an absentee ballot, sent by his family from Brownsville. Garza voted a straight Democratic ticket, as did a majority of Americans.[18] In November, 1936, Roosevelt gained his second presidential term.

As his university peers continued to be galvanized by Roosevelt and his New Deal, Garza, too, developed an interest in social reform through politics. He found a natural outlet in Austin's Mexican Chamber of Commerce. The chamber worked for the benefit of the Mexican American community in the area, holding rallies and meetings to address both cultural and political issues.[19]

As Garza spent much of his time in the university community or at church in East Austin, he rarely felt a victim of Austin's racial intolerance. Yet, through the chamber of commerce, he became involved in working to solve problems of Mexican Americans in the capital city. In East Austin, police regularly harassed Mexican Americans when they strayed from their community. Additionally, the board of education relegated Mexican American youths in Austin to segregated schools. For his part, Garza attempted to publicize the Mexican American plight to Anglo community leaders.[20]

One month after Roosevelt's presidential victory, in an effort to aid the East Austin community, Garza spoke at a Mexican Chamber of Commerce meeting attended by Texas legislators, including Texas Governor James V. Allred. Garza outlined the problems faced by Mexican Americans and asked Texas leaders to encourage legislation aimed at outlawing segregation. His deep booming voice and powerful rhetoric captured audience members' attention, and legislators such as Allred later praised Garza for his eloquent speech. Praises, however, did not produce results, and it was not until almost thirty years later that Texas enacted legislation to end segregation. Like many Mexican Americans of his class and generation, Garza was concerned about the plight of the majority of his people. He believed one way discrimination could be abolished was by challenging racist ideas. Thus, he spent weeks writing his speech, hoping that not only by his status as a Mexican American college student but also through his proficiency for verbal communication could he help erase some common misconceptions regarding

Mexican Americans. The speech endeared Garza to both Texas legislators and Austin's Mexican American community.[21]

Garza employed his verbal skills once again in November, 1936,
when he ran for president of the Newman Club. Members voted for
Garza by a large margin. His election as head of a predominantly Anglo
organization was a harbinger of Garza's skill in moving easily between
the Anglo and Mexican American communities, given that many
Newman Club members lived in cities that practiced segregation towards Mexican Americans.

After his Newman Club election, final examinations began. Although
he maintained a passing average throughout the semester, he harbored
a natural concern about his performance on the tests. For three weeks
prior to the exams, Garza curtailed his social activities to devote himself to studying. Long nights and strong coffee were the norm. Garza's
preparation proved adequate, and he was rewarded with a slight increase in his grade point average. When the exams concluded, he returned to Brownsville for the winter vacation and enjoyed a festive
Christmas and New Year's celebration with his family. Winter vacation
was no different than the previous years, except that the family now
discussed graduation ceremonies.[22]

A few days before Garza returned to Austin, he received a letter
from John Barron, superintendent of public schools in Garza's home
county. Since few Brownsville citizens attended college in the 1930s,
those who excelled academically and attended universities were well
known to Barron. The superintendent had learned of Garza's active
participation in Austin's Mexican American community. To Barron, well
aware of Garza's charismatic personality, Garza's influence on Austin's
Mexican Americans seemed like an ideal opportunity to gain the minority group's support for Barron's college classmate, Lyndon Johnson.
In the letter Barron told Garza that Johnson was attempting in a special election in 1937 to fill the seat vacated by a recently deceased congressman. Barron asked Garza to help Johnson in his campaign. Garza
replied to Barron that he would be delighted to meet Johnson in Austin and gave the superintendent his university address.[23]

In February, 1937, more than a month after responding to Barron's
letter, Johnson visited Garza in Austin. "This tall, lanky young man
knocked on my room while I was studying," recalled Garza. As the
preoccupied college student glanced up to see Johnson walking briskly
through his door, Garza could feel the young candidate's pulsating

energy. The vivacious Texan complemented Garza's reserved nature with a sort of boisterous, sometimes profane, personality that enthralled Garza. Johnson first asked the Brownsville native about himself and his political beliefs. Once Johnson learned of Garza's allegiance to President Roosevelt and the New Deal, he enthusiastically spoke of his many plans to continue the president's programs in the Texas Hill Country area after he won the election.[24]

Impressed by Johnson's determination and caught up in the office seeker's fervor, Garza invited Johnson to a bazaar at Our Lady of Guadalupe Catholic Church. "I told him there would be a few hundred people out there, and I was going to have the microphone, and I'd be glad to introduce him." Johnson thanked Garza for the opportunity to speak at his church, and after chatting for a few minutes, the two drove in Johnson's car to the bazaar. During the car ride, Garza learned more about the boastful twenty-eight-year-old and his lofty goals. More than anything else, he discovered that Johnson enjoyed talking, especially about himself.[25]

At the church bazaar, Johnson soon became a popular figure among the Mexican Americans attending the event. Speaking in both English and Spanish, Garza introduced Johnson as a young New Dealer hoping to make sweeping changes in the Austin area. Johnson then began outlining his political platform, speaking, as usual, in his colloquial style. After the brief address, Garza translated Johnson's words into Spanish. As the crowd roared with applause, Garza knew Johnson had won the allegiance of the Mexican Americans, especially the church pastor. "The pastor was very enthused about Lyndon running for Congress. He had never been involved in politics, and he went all out for Lyndon," said Garza. No other political figure had ever approached Austin's Mexican American community with the perceived concern about the group as Johnson had. Undoubtedly, Garza, who had become a respected representative of the Mexican American citizenry, helped endear Johnson to the community. As the applause died down, Johnson thanked the crowd with a warm *gracias,* and then roamed through the bazaar speaking to many of the attendees. Garza watched Johnson and smiled to himself, admiring the campaigner's political expertise. As Johnson left the bazaar, he again thanked Garza for the opportunity to address such an enthusiastic crowd.[26]

After the young politician's departure, Garza began promoting Johnson's candidacy throughout East Austin. During the election Garza worked with his university friends, including John B. Connally and Jake Pickle, two of the most influential members of what later became known as the Johnson circle. Years later, men involved in this fledgling political group became influential national figures. Garza's early association with the Johnson circle became the first step in propelling him toward national heights.[27]

Garza handed out flyers and placed campaign posters on campus. Because Texas instituted a poll tax, and only a few Mexican Americans could afford to pay the fee, Garza also helped organize committees designed to gather funds for citizens. On election day he stood by the East Austin church rotunda and reminded all passers-by to go to the polls and cast their vote for Johnson. By mid-afternoon on election day, he learned of Johnson's victory.[28]

Garza was aware that the new congressman had recently undergone surgery for appendicitis. Consequently, he sent a congratulatory telegram to the hospital where Johnson was recuperating. Thereafter, he occasionally visited Johnson in Austin, where the two men discussed Johnson's two favorite topics—politics and himself.[29]

Garza's initial interest in politics motivated him to learn more about the political process, so he began regularly attending legislative sessions at the state capitol, ten blocks south of the university campus. He often sat in the capitol's oval balcony, witnessing the sometimes entertaining displays by solons attempting to pass bills or filibuster legislation. He also witnessed firsthand the debates. The same policies debated at the capitol also permeated discussions at the university, a place in the 1930s where academics and politics merged. The university and the state capital's ties were so close that the strikingly handsome Governor Allred routinely entertained UT professors and their students in the governor's mansion.[30] Impressed with Garza's speech a year earlier to the Mexican Chamber of Commerce, Allred invited the young man to a meeting attended by a dozen other university students and his economics professor, Robert H. Montgomery. It was during one of these roundtable discussions that Garza, enjoying the lively debate between his university peers and his favorite professor, learned of the problems plaguing Texas oil men. In later years Garza frequently crossed paths with Allred, who would become an overwhelmingly popular federal judge in South Texas. In the meantime, Garza was allowed to participate in an intellectual sphere from which most non-Anglos were excluded.

In May, 1937, Garza completed all requirements for his undergraduate degree and earned a bachelor of arts. Because of continued economic restraints, only Garza's parents, not the remaining seven siblings, could attend spring graduation ceremonies. Ygnacio and Zoila drove to Austin the day of the event and sat proudly in the stands waiting patiently for Garza to receive his diploma. When their son's name was read, Garza looked out into the crowd to see that both his parents were wiping away tears. The family capped off the impressive day with a dinner out.[31]

The following fall, Garza began working on a law degree at the University of Texas School of Law. Situated atop a hill on the northwest side of the university, the law school provided a picturesque view of the Texas Hill Country sunset. Along with its location, the educational institution benefited from the same oil money that helped finance the rest of the university. The law school used its portion of the oil funds, much like all the other university departments, to attract nationally acclaimed faculty, increase library collections, and provide a comfortable teaching facility. All of this activity resulted in the creation of a nationally acclaimed law school.[32]

Reflecting the tradition of legal studies in the 1930s, the UT law school required successful completion of a two-year course of study—different from the modern three-year course. The law school also adhered to traditional aspects of instruction, including the standard fare of required courses, such as torts and contracts; course grades based on a single examination given at the conclusion of each semester; and heavy reliance on the Socratic method of teaching.[33]

The law school's student body in 1937 was almost entirely from Texas. Of the approximately 175 students, 3 were female and 2 were Hispanic. Additionally, all the law school professors were Anglo males.[34] African Americans were prohibited from entry by state law. The practice continued until the 1950 landmark Supreme Court decision in *Sweatt v. Painter* (339 US 629 [1950]), which forced the law school to accept African Americans.

During his first year of law school, Garza continued to live at the Hamilton House, but his new roommate was Joe Champion, Bertha's brother. Champion was an undergraduate studying geology, and the Champions visited Joe every few months, enabling Bertha and Garza to see each other often. The two corresponded regularly and Garza began keeping a framed picture of Bertha on his desk.[35]

Academically, Garza spent his first year of law school adjusting to the Socratic method. Like all first-year law students, Garza found the material challenging, the professors intimidating, and the work load overwhelming. Garza coped as well as any of his peers with the hours of preparation required for each class. Fellow classmate Joe Greenhill, who later became chief justice of the Texas Supreme Court, remembered that Garza "was like everyone else; he didn't volunteer. You spoke only when you were called upon." Typically, the classroom remained deathly quiet, except for the stern voice of a law school professor discussing cases and the quivering voice of a student attempting to answer the lecturer's queries.[36]

Garza's law school experience not only enhanced his life educationally but socially and politically as well. Many of his strongest and most powerful ties in later years resulted from the friends he made while at the law school. Of the many notable students there, Greenhill was one of Garza's closest friends. The two met in Garza's first law school class because seating was alphabetical, and the professor assigned them to adjoining seats. Coincidentally, more than thirty years later, Garza and Greenhill's sons would also sit next to each other at the University of Texas School of Law, as seating remained alphabetical.[37]

Greenhill was an exceptional and popular student and a member of some of the most prestigious organizations at the law school, including the *Texas Law Review,* where he served as editor. Greenhill led a successful legal career, highlighted by his election to the Texas Supreme Court in 1957 and his ascendance to the position of chief judge in 1972. Garza's friendship with Greenhill was a result of their many commonalities. They were both raised in middle-class homes where their families encouraged education and civic service.[38] Both were highly motivated individuals and their career paths paralleled each other in later years. The cultural solidarity Garza attained in his law school years was evident by his friendship with such popular Anglo students as Greenhill.

Although Garza greatly curtailed his extracurricular activities during his first law school semester to focus entirely on studies, he made two exceptions. First, he continued to worship at the Catholic church; second, he attended to his father, Ygnacio, who had developed a serious case of shingles. After numerous treatments in Brownsville, Ygnacio's condition only worsened. Believing that his father could receive more advanced medical care in Austin, Garza brought Ygnacio from Brownsville to the larger city to undergo treatment. Ygnacio's wife,

Zoila, and youngest daughter, Argentina, joined him in Austin. The four stayed in Garza's boarding house room for three days while Ygnacio received medical attention. When Ygnacio's condition appeared to improve, the family returned to Brownsville.[39]

In the winter of 1937, as Garza prepared for first year final examinations, he received a distressing call. His father was gravely ill. Ygnacio's shingles had not improved, even after his care in Austin. Garza returned home at once. His immediate departure meant not only that he was foresaking his law school examinations but also the opportunity to become an attorney, for missing an examination meant an automatic failing grade. On January 22, 1938, three and a half weeks after Garza's arrival, fifty-three-year-old Ygnacio died at home, with his eight children at his bedside. For the entire family, the loss was devastating. For Garza, the new year of 1938 became one of personal grieving.

Confident that his eldest brothers would tend to the needs of his mother, Garza, two weeks after his father's death, was convinced by his family to return to Austin and inquire about taking the missed exams. The law school administration, though sympathetic with his unfortunate situation, would not permit him to take the same examinations other students had previously taken. Instead, Garza was allowed to remain in the law school, provided he retake the examinations with the following year's first-year class. Thus, he would have to take two sets of final examinations during the first semester of his second year.[40]

Garza soon began searching for part-time employment. His father's death had limited the Garza's family income, and, although Ygnacio had purchased life insurance, the insurance benefits and other family assets were insufficient to support Garza's tuition and living expenses. To remain in school, Garza found odd jobs in Austin. He worked for Repp Cleaners, a dry-cleaning business, where he earned a commission by bringing in new customers, and he occasionally tutored university sorority members who needed assistance in their Spanish language courses. Both activities demonstrated the ease in which Garza acclimated to the still racially intolerant Austin climate.[41]

In March, 1938, although preoccupied with his law school studies and his many jobs, Garza found time to become involved in campus politics. When his friend John B. Connally decided to run for student body president, Garza was one of the lead campaign organizers, responsible for delivering the undergraduate vote. Connally was attempting to defeat the fraternity clique, a powerful political faction at the university. A year earlier, Garza's friend and Connally's primary campaign manager, Jake Pickle, had, in fact, defeated the fraternity element, becoming the first nonfraternity member to do so in the history of the university.[42]

As a campaigner for Connally, Garza organized students opposed to the Greek fraternity and sorority system. Armed with Connally's leaflets and position papers, Garza regularly campaigned in campus thoroughfares. His efforts paid off. In April, 1938, Connally won a runoff election and all of his supporters, including Garza, gathered at the Varsity Inn to celebrate the victory.[43] In later years, students working in the 1938 student government elections would reappear in Connally's future Texas political races. After the experience of Johnson's campaign and now Connally's runoff election, Garza began to view political participation as an effective conduit to upward mobility as well as social power. But the importance of political participation was a lesson that greatly influenced not only Garza's history-making appointment but also the future careers of others influential in his generation, class, and ethnic group.

As the summer break approached, Garza made the decision to stay in Austin. He continued to live at the Hamilton House, and now, as manager, he received a rent-free furnished room. His duties included enforcing basic living rules and collecting the rent.[44] Obviously, Garza had gained the confidence and trust of Anglos—no easy task in the segregation-minded South. But the benefits also included earning a higher wage, and, given his free rent, he would make more money over the summer by staying and working in Austin rather than returning to Brownsville.

During Garza's second year in law school, pre–World War II tensions on campus began to surface. Students organized peace rallies to protest possible United States involvement in the European war. They gathered at the foot of the hill in which the law school rested, and law school students could easily hear the antiwar speeches from their classrooms. Although many undergraduate students participated in the peace rallies, most of the law school students remained in their classrooms. Dean of the law school, Ira Hildebrand, refused to allow law school students to attend the rallies and expressed his antidemonstration viewpoint in class lectures during the noisy protests. In a thick Texas drawl, Hildebrand often said: "I am a rancher, and when I go to check my cattle, I always know that if I'm carrying my thirty-one Winchester, I never run into a snake. But when I leave it at home, I run into all kinds of snakes." The dean staunchly believed that American troops should prepare for war and used this analogy to express his sentiments. The lesson was not lost on Garza.[45]

Garza and his fellow classmates had grown up with strong patriotic beliefs, and they agreed with Hildebrand. Garza himself was not a radical. He supported the Allies, and he applauded the possibility of America's entry into World War II. He also knew he would readily enlist if the United States entered the European war. Aware that enlistment would not likely be mandatory for a man over twenty-four with a professional degree, Garza, nevertheless, committed himself to serving his country.[46]

Part of Garza's ideological commitment to supporting the war was his deep sense of duty. For Garza, duty was a concept that captured the core of social obligations. But he was also in a precarious position as a member of an ethnic group that was often discriminated against. Although he never experienced overt discrimination, Garza was well aware of the racist stereotypes prevalent in the country. Much like others of his generation, class, and ethnic group, he believed that one way of challenging the stereotypes, especially those alluding to un-American sentiments, was to display his strong sense of patriotism.[47]

As America's entry into World War II neared, newspaper headlines detailed the war daily, making it difficult for many Americans to focus on little else. Yet, the life of a law school student allowed for few other distractions. School and work were still Garza's main preoccupations. By the end of the fall semester, Garza now prepared for two sets of law school final examinations, a total of twelve subjects—the six he had missed from the first fall semester, because of his father's death, and six for the current term. To overcome the pressures of such a heavy test load, Garza created an hourly calendar designating which subjects he would study every few hours. For two weeks before his exams, he awoke every morning at dawn, ate a small breakfast, and cradled a coffee mug while he studied until noon. He then took a half-hour lunch break and studied again until dinnertime. During dinner he relaxed for an hour, then went back to his study schedule until midnight, when he got ready for bed. The grueling schedule resulted in a passing score for all of Garza's law school tests. He was both elated and exhausted after he received his examination grades.[48]

With exams over, Garza decided to stay in Austin during the winter break, and he began working for the Texas Department of Public Safety Commission. This organization ran the state police and the famed Texas Rangers. One of the highlights of Garza's work for the Department of Public Safety was doing traffic duty for Governor W. Lee "Pappy" O'Daniel's inauguration. O'Daniel was an eccentric politico who invited the entire state of Texas to attend the gubernatorial inauguration held in January. The event was held at Memorial Stadium on the University of Texas campus, and over 65,000 people accepted O'Daniel's invitation. Garza helped direct the traffic jam caused by the rowdy crowd.[49] Already enthralled by other political activities, Garza found that attending the inauguration reinforced his love of politics.

In January, 1939, his last semester at the university, Garza's mastery of the law school process permitted him more time for nonacademic pursuits, including his continuing participation in the Newman Club and the Rio Grande Valley Club. But his primary nonacademic pursuit was the courtship of Bertha. The couple now saw each other during university holidays when Garza returned to Brownsville and during the Champions' visits to Austin to see Bertha's brother, Joe. In 1939 Garza spent spring break in Brownsville courting Bertha, who was now twenty years old. At the annual Brownsville Country Club Easter dance, they became engaged, but they did not set a wedding date. The couple decided to wait until Garza graduated from law school to announce their engagement to their families. After the university break, Garza returned to law school to finish the last month remaining in his law program and to prepare for his final round of exams. He studied diligently for one month while continuing to juggle a now-reduced work schedule. His final marks were not stellar but were sufficient to allow him to graduate.[50]

Garza received his diploma in June from the University of Texas Law School, as his entire family watched with pride and adulation. The Garzas had driven up from Brownsville to attend the graduation ceremonies, and, as Dean Hildebrand read Reynaldo G. Garza's name, they cheered enthusiastically. They were all there: mother Zoila, eldest brothers Ygnacio, Jr., and Leonel, eldest sisters Zoila, Lucila, and María Rosa, and youngest siblings Argentina and Osbaldo. But even as they celebrated Garza's accomplishment, they recognized the missing presence of family patriarch Ygnacio. Garza knew his father would have wept with joy if he had been alive to witness the culmination of this educational achievement. As Garza held his diploma, he nodded to his family and then smiled upward, inviting his father to join in the family happiness.[51] Soon, Garza would return to Brownsville, but for the next month he remained in Austin—now preparing for the Texas Bar examination.

Throughout the next three weeks Garza studied for the arduous examination. The exam lasted over three days and was composed of four two-hour tests covering sixteen different legal subjects. While preparing for bar exams, Garza continued working for the Department of Public Safety and Repp Cleaners to pay for his expenses in Austin. In late June, 1939, Garza took the bar examination, and a few days later, after the final test, he packed up his belongings to return to Brownsville.[52] He would not learn the results of the examination until the fall. If he passed, he could begin practicing law. If he failed, he would have to wait until the winter to retake the examination. He now busied himself with finding a job in Brownsville.

At the University of Texas, Garza had taken significant steps toward upward mobility in Anglo society. He had not only earned two degrees but had also developed friendships that would benefit him in achieving even greater accomplishment. Men like Lyndon B. Johnson and John Connally would lead the nation and the state of Texas in future years, and through Garza's friendship with these rising young Texans, he, too, would reach goals he had never imagined. For now, however, his years of preparation and effort were rewarded with what, to Garza, was the greatest prize—a law degree. And he was determined to hone the lessons he had learned at the university—not only the legal but also the social and cultural knowledge—to make his family and his community proud. Moreover, he resolved that he would never forego his Mexican heritage in his quest for success. For even in the predominantly Anglo university community of Austin, he easily moved back and forth through two cultures, never losing ground on either one.

CHAPTER 3

Peace and War

1939–45

In July, 1939, Garza returned to Brownsville, intent on forging his American legal career in his Mexican-oriented city. He could have established a practice in a more cosmopolitan area, such as Houston or San Antonio, where a larger income seemed assured by a wealthier client base and burgeoning middle-class Mexican American population. Yet, in choosing to begin his profession in his small city, Garza again fused his two distinct cultures, bringing the ultimate symbol of American society, a law degree, to his hometown. He knew it would be difficult to begin a legal practice in Brownsville, but he was determined.

He held grandiose aspirations. He would become one of a handful of Mexican American attorneys in the city and bring legal aid to citizens traditionally intimidated by what they viewed as an Anglo service. This would be his niche. It would allow him to make a living and stay in the town he so loved. But most of all, remaining in Brownsville would permit him to maintain his cherished family bonds, a familial tie that would aid in preserving his Mexican roots.[1]

Garza moved back into his childhood home on West Saint Charles

Street and was affectionately welcomed by his mother and younger sister, Argentina. Although his other brothers and sisters no longer lived at home, they still remained in Brownsville, with the exception of Osbaldo, who began his first year at the University of Texas at Austin. Ygnacio, Jr., and Leonel, now both married, were practicing accountants in Brownsville, and Garza's older sisters, Zoila, Lucila, and María Rosa, were all married and all living near their mother. With all this proximity, family gatherings were commonplace at the matriarch's home, and family members often joked that Zoila could become wealthy by installing parking meters on her front lawn.[2]

Garza's return to Brownsville also meant rejoining Immaculate Conception parish. His religious commitment deepened, and he began his lifetime practice of attending services every morning. On Sundays his family joined him for Mass, then congregated at Zoila's home for a traditional Mexican lunch.

While waiting for the results of the bar exam, Garza had more time for social life. He formally announced his engagement to Bertha and nervously asked Bertha's parents for their consent, assuring them that he wanted to wait until he was financially secure before he married their daughter. The Champions and Garzas were both overjoyed at the prospect of Bertha and Garza's union, and the families held a celebratory dinner in the Champion home.[3]

Increasingly, social discussions focused on the probability of the United States' military involvement in the war in Europe. Brownsville's location on the Gulf of Mexico and as a border town made its residents acutely susceptible to all the prewar anxiety existing in the country. Because most Americans characterized the Japanese and European Axis as irrational, Brownsville citizens, like most other Americans, did not rule out an attack on American soil by foreign aggressors.[4]

Reacting to threat of attack, the United States government requested that the state send Texas Rangers to reinforce federal border agents in Brownsville. But the Texas Rangers' presence and their racial intolerance towards Mexican Americans increased tensions already prevalent in the city. The common practice of citizens traveling to and from Brownsville and Matamoros decreased sharply as Texas Rangers began capriciously harassing people crossing the border. In one instance, a Texas Ranger detained Garza and his friends for more than an hour as they attempted to cross from Matamoros to Brownsville through the newly constructed Gateway Bridge. The Texas Ranger taunted the group and questioned their American citizenship. This incident was Garza's only memory of racial intolerance he faced in his hometown.[5]

By the fall of 1939, Garza's main concern was launching his legal career, made possible by the fact that in August he received notice that he had passed the bar. His accomplishment had been reported in the *Brownsville Herald,* as graduation from a law school and passing the bar exam were rare events in the city. The newspaper announced that Garza and Milton West, Jr., son of a United States congressman and Garza's elementary school peer, were the only two Brownsville citizens to earn law degrees and pass the Texas State Bar that year.[6]

The newspaper also carried the good news that Carlos Calderón, the Mexican consul stationed in Brownsville, had hired Garza as the consulate's attorney in the city. Once again, Garza forged a tie to his Mexican culture. The Mexican consulate's duties were to maintain amiable relations with the United States and to aid Mexican nationals requiring legal assistance. Since Mexico's civil law system, based on Roman and Spanish law, was markedly different from the common law tradition of the United States, Calderón required legal expertise to address the differences. Unfortunately, since the Mexican government did not provide Calderón sufficient funds to hire an attorney, the consulate decided to obtain legal assistance through the barter of office space in downtown Brownsville.[7]

Garza's rent-free office in the Calderóni Building was in a highly trafficked location across the hall from the Mexican consulate, which added to the prestige of Garza's newly opened practice. The day after signing a written agreement with the Mexican consulate, Garza placed a large wooden sign on the street entrance to the Calderóni Building. It read "Reynaldo G. Garza, Attorney-at-Law." On September 1, 1939, Reynaldo G. Garza, attorney-at-law, officially opened for business.[8]

Garza became a sole practitioner, a risky financial decision for a newly graduated attorney. Once again Garza consulted with his brother. Ygnacio, Jr., who had opened an accounting office in Brownsville two years earlier, helped his younger sibling financially plan for the legal practice and suggested that he postpone hiring any personnel until he could afford the expense. Without a staff, Garza became individually responsible for client development, administration of his law practice, clerical duties (including typing and sending correspondence), and a number of other legal matters.[9]

Garza's youth (only twenty-four), his lack of experience, and the area's limited economy would limit his initial efforts. But only a few weeks after the *Brownsville Herald* reported his passing the bar, he received his first case. He represented twenty-two Brownsville men, all of Mexican descent, who had been convicted of gambling, a crime then punishable by imprisonment, a fine, or both. Already convicted, the men awaited sentencing, and their families sought Garza's assistance. Garza met with the men and learned of their impoverished condition, a result, in large part, of the lingering effects of the Depression. For these men even one week without an income meant homelessness and hunger for their dependent families.[10]

In addressing the court Garza argued that the incarceration of the defendants would hurt so many Brownsville families that the judge should impose only a monetary fine as punishment. He further contended that as nonviolent criminal offenders, these men posed no danger to the safety of the Brownsville community and did not warrant incarceration. His arguments sufficiently persuaded the presiding judge, and each man received only a fine. Garza charged each client a meager two dollars as his fee for representation, making those forty-four dollars his first income as an attorney. Because his successful argument impacted so many people, word quickly spread among the small Brownsville community of his ability to achieve results in court.[11]

Garza now decided to become involved in community affairs. He found civic and charitable clubs eager to include him in their activities.[12] Community memberships also helped build up his budding law practice. He first joined the Knights of Columbus, a Catholic-based civic organization. The Knights of Columbus instituted a year-round program of religious and social functions that attracted Garza and reminded him of his Newman Club experiences at the University of Texas. Joining these organizations also helped him maintain his bicultural life-style.

Eager to join other community groups, Garza sought suggestions from Oscar Dancy, county judge in Brownsville. Almost twenty years older than Garza, Dancy was an established and popular figure in the city. He was also an active Democrat and campaigned for Democratic friends and acquaintances throughout South Texas. Dancy took an instant liking to Garza and became his mentor. The two shared a father-son relationship and occasionally spent time together hunting. The county judge gave Garza advice on building up his legal career and urged the young attorney to join the county's local bar association.[13]

Dancy also suggested Garza join the American Red Cross. Dancy knew there were few young Brownsville natives involved in local groups, and perhaps through Garza's membership others would be encouraged to become active. Dancy also explained that since the Red Cross was a highly reputed group in Brownsville, Garza's membership would increase his visibility in the city and, in turn, help him garner new clients. Garza took Dancy's advice and became active in the group.

So pleased was Dancy with Garza's active participation in the American Red Cross that he also encouraged him to join the newly formed Brownsville Development Committee designed to create a Girl Scout Council in the city. As a long-time Brownsville resident and the father of a baby girl, Dancy was concerned about the lack of organizations for the city's young women. He shared his concerns with Garza, suggesting to the younger man that Garza help lead the efforts to institute the Girl Scouts in Brownsville. As a former boy scout, Garza perceived scouting as an integral part of any person's childhood, so he was easily convinced to become involved in the venture. He became one of four men who organized monthly fund-raisers to help establish the organization. In the next few years, Garza assisted in efforts that eventually led to the first Girl Scout Council in his hometown.[14]

Membership in the Red Cross and the Development Committee only enhanced Garza's recognition in the city, and in the spring of 1940, officers in the League of United Latin American Citizens (LULAC) convinced him to join their organization. LULAC was well known as the first group to address the concerns of middle-class Mexican Americans in the nation. LULAC, a group of councils, originated in Corpus Christi, Texas, in 1929. In that year, twenty-five South Texans, representing leading Mexican American organizations in the state, agreed to consolidate their groups into LULAC. Following the Corpus Christi organizational meeting, the original twenty-five members initiated LULAC chapters in their cities, and LULAC councils spread throughout the Southwest. Since one of the initial representatives attending the Corpus Christi meeting was from Brownsville, the group established a firm base in that city. When Garza joined, the Brownsville LULAC group was already one of the oldest of the eighteen chapters in Texas.[15]

LULAC sought to gain equality for Mexican Americans "by integrating its people into the American social and economic mainstream." To achieve its goal the group's constitution defined its commitment "to develop within the members of our race, the best, purest, and more perfect type of true and loyal citizen of the United States of America." The constitution outlined a program designed to encourage Mexican Americans to become proficient in the English language, yet maintain ethnic pride through bilingualism; promote the training of Mexican American professionals; and advance active political participation. Most of all, LULAC sought to end discrimination. By channeling its efforts towards education, employment, and civil rights, LULAC hoped to up-lift Mexican Americans who for so long were denied civil liberties and full participation in American life. However, the group did not promote a restructuring of American political or economic life; instead LULAC worked to reform Mexican American attitudes in order to fit in with the Anglo majority. Reformation, rather than restructuring, became the group's strategy because the majority of members were middle-class Mexican Americans who, although concerned about discrimination, wanted to maintain the economic status quo.[16]

Garza's membership in LULAC was consistent with his life's phi-losophy. Like most LULAC members, Garza was strongly patriotic and embraced the United States, yet he opposed the racial intolerance found in his beloved country. He believed in the common LULAC theme that social mobility would combat racism. Accordingly, he recognized that once Mexican Americans were free to excel though their talent, hard work, and ability, specifically in educational accomplishments, social mobility would naturally follow. Inherent in this view was that each individual was responsibility for his upward mobility. "The effects of racism and poverty would emerge as relatively minor impediments to the success of a talented and determined individual," proclaimed the LULAC newspaper. LULAC's methods of achieving their goals in-cluded voter registration drives, public relation campaigns, and legal pressure—all politically conservative tactics that Garza's moderate out-look favored.[17]

Similarly, Garza believed and even patterned the bicultural life-style many LULAC members advocated. But he was uncharacteristic of oth-ers who compromised their Mexican culture for social mobility. He rejected "encourage[ing] the conglomeration and blending of races at the expense of distinction." In Brownsville Garza did not have to aban-don such aspects of his culture as the Spanish language, so he, like the more traditional LULACs, held firm to a Mexican cultural commitment. Additionally, Garza had lived with class-based, rather than ethnic-based, divisions in the city since his childhood, and, as a member of the middle class, he saw no need to change the economic status quo. Like most LULACs and members of his generation, class, and ethnic group, he was fully conscious of these class interests in his efforts to improve race relations and gain greater economic mobility for all Mexican Americans. As an upwardly mobile Mexican American eager to integrate his ethnic group into American society, Garza was naturally drawn to LULAC.[18]

During Garza's first few months as a member of the Brownsville LULACs, his chapter, like many other pre–World War II LULAC groups, channeled its efforts into educational achievement. Viewing education as a means toward upper mobility and professional employment, the Brownsville LULACs raised funds for a scholarship at the University of Texas. LULAC officers chose Garza, based on his status as a UT alumnus, as one of four judges who would designate the recipient each year.[19] With still so few Brownsville natives attending college, it was not difficult to choose one out of the handful of candidates seeking financial aid to attend the university.

The Brownsville LULAC chapter also recruited scoutmasters for the city's Boy Scout Council. Garza volunteered to become scoutmaster for Troop 56, the group he had joined less than twenty years earlier. Because of Garza's young age and youthful appearance, the eleven twelve-year-olds in Troop 56 viewed him more as an older brother than as a father figure. This became an advantage for Garza, for although the children respected and admired him, they also enjoyed this scoutmaster that not only taught them the Boy Scout code but also joined them in climbing trees or digging up imaginary hidden treasures. Garza grew to care about his troop. He constantly stressed to them the importance of education and his belief in their abilities to accomplish any goals. His spirited energy and determination that they succeed instilled a self-respect that many had never before known. In later years members of Troop 56 would grow up to become respected Brownsville professionals.[20] Like Garza, many of these scouts also learned to live within two cultures, adopting many of the beliefs and value systems of Anglos while maintaining pride in their Mexican roots.

Although integrating Mexican Americans into American institutions, such as the Boy Scouts, served LULAC's objective of equality in Brownsville, other Texas cities required aggressive forms of political activism, and at times the Brownsville LULACs joined forces with other chapters. In larger Texas cities, discrimination against Mexican Americans was pervasive. "In some places in Dallas, they wouldn't let Mexican Americans in the public pools," lamented Garza. "We would help LULAC groups demonstrate against discrimination. We never had the need for such protest in Brownsville, thank God." Brownsville LULACs aided Mexican Americans facing segregation by attending political rallies. Thus, through political activism, the group denounced racially intolerant laws and acts.[21]

Less than ten months after joining LULAC, Garza became president of the Brownsville organization. LULACs voted for Garza to lead their group because he exemplified LULAC's goals. He was a college-trained professional, active in American society, yet, he retained his ethnic origin through his Roman Catholic faith and his native Spanish language. The monthly LULAC state newspaper regularly addressed the characteristics vital to its middle-class leaders, and Garza embodied that composite picture. Like the ideal LULAC leader, Garza was American-born, had risen from a poor background to achieve education, and was a college-educated professional. He was also articulate, and his position as an attorney added credibility to the local organization. Garza met LULAC's criteria for political affiliation through his connections with state representative Augustín Celaya and U.S. Congressman Lyndon Johnson.[22]

As LULAC president, Garza continued Brownsville LULAC's political activism, its movement towards the advancement of Mexican Americans, and its activities designed to maintain cultural pluralism. He initiated a letter-writing campaign in which Brownsville residents wrote to their state and national congressmen urging them to join the fight for Mexican American equality. He also preserved the group's active involvement in recruiting scoutmasters for the Boy Scouts and in raising funds for an annual University of Texas scholarship.[23]

To encourage ethnic pride and thus maintain a bicultural existence, Garza involved the Brownsville LULACs in the city's annual Charro Days celebration. Organized in 1937 by a group of Brownsville businessmen, Charro Days consisted of parades and parties throughout Brownsville and Matamoros. The purpose of the celebration, held each February, was both to promote Brownsville tourism and strengthen ties with Matamoros. Throughout the four-day Charro Days celebration, citizens donned traditional Mexican costumes, with men wearing wide-brimmed, brightly decorated cowboy *sombreros* and multicolored *sarapes.* Women sewed flowered *charro* costumes complete with embroidered blouses of vivid reds, greens, and yellows and long, flowing skirts. Celebrants feasted, sang, and danced to Mexican music, while enjoying an array of entertaining activities including parades, rooster races, and jalapeño-eating contests. Garza volunteered the entire LULAC membership to help host the annual Charro Days parade down Brownsville's main street. For his part, he served as city spokesman, explaining the annual festivities' customs to Mexican dignitaries invited to the affair.[24]

Two weeks after Charro Days, Garza made his first entry into city politics. His political passage was a direct outgrowth of LULAC philosophies that viewed political participation by Mexican Americans as essential to producing respectability and, in turn, eliminating barriers to equal opportunities.[25]

Garza, twenty-five at the time, campaigned for a seat on the Brownsville Independent School Board. The school board, composed solely of Anglos, was an influential organization in the city. As in other small cities, a school board seat signified one's position as a major power broker in the community. Membership in the school board also represented an opportunity for Garza to advance LULAC's educational mission. He immediately crafted a campaign platform based on LULAC tenets. He laid claim to two issues: increasing half-day school sessions to full days in lower grades of the school system, and offering courses in conversational Spanish to elementary students.[26] His political platform demonstrated a dual cultural philosophy. Offering more hours in the school day would help advance the educational development of Mexican American students and, consequently, increase their chances for upward mobility. Garza's second platform issue addressed his desire to maintain Mexican cultural continuity. By allowing students to learn Spanish, the school would ensure that Mexican American youth would carry on their culture's native language.

During the campaign Garza's main opposition came from incumbent school board member James Pace, Jr. Pace commented to other city leaders that Garza was too inexperienced to run for a school board post and that Garza's knowledge about Brownsville's public school system was insufficient. Pace refused to give Garza his much-needed backing. Aware of Pace's opposition, Garza's mentor, Oscar Dancy, met with Pace and extolled Garza's qualifications. Dancy then suggested a meeting between Garza and Pace. When Garza met with the elder city leader and explained his ideas for improving the school system, Pace was impressed with his inventive plans and told Garza he would consider supporting him. A few days after meeting with Garza, Pace began publicly voicing his allegiance to the young attorney. Undoubtedly, Pace's conversation with Dancy, Garza's persuasive discussion, and newspaper polls predicting a large electoral victory for Garza influenced Pace, who astutely appreciated the reality of practical politics.[27]

With Pace's endorsement assured, Garza enthusiastically campaigned throughout the city. Few voters could resist his folksy appeal. He spoke at corner drugstores and in Market Square, and the *Brownsville Herald* regularly cited his views. He bought time on the local radio station and broadcast speeches in both English and Spanish. He attended most of the city's social events, from church picnics to garden club teas. At all these activities, he charmed prospective voters with his witty tales and gained their respect by his commitment to improve the local school district. His youthful dynamism was contagious, creating a flood of Garza supporters.[28]

On April 5, 1941, citizens of Brownsville overwhelmingly elected Garza to the school board. He received 1,756 votes, more than any other candidate. The election, termed by a Rio Grande Valley newspaper as the "heaviest vote ever polled in Brownsville schools," had a margin of victory so great that the Matamoros newspaper, *El Bravo,* ran an editorial suggesting that Garza's victory was due in part to Mexican American citizens who were rebelling against the all-Anglo Brownsville school board. The paper concluded that party stalwarts previously prevented Mexican Americans from election to the school board. The day after the election results, Garza bought advertising space in the *Brownsville Herald* to voice his appreciation "to my many friends who supported me" during the campaign. The gesture immediately endeared Garza to his supporters. With newfound political power, Garza's ability to balance two cultures would be made easier.[29]

The outcome of the school board election proved consequential for Mexican Americans. Garza became one of the few Mexican Americans to reach a leadership position in Brownsville. Most upper middle-class Mexican Americans in Brownsville did not face discrimination, yet only a selected few were city leaders in the 1940s. Following the pattern of many border cities, the Anglo business class, backed by its strong economic base, controlled most leadership positions. Although Mexican Americans still composed the majority population, the mayor, county attorney, and city council were Anglo. In 1941 Garza became the first and only Mexican American on the school board.[30]

During his term on the Brownsville Independent School Board, Garza forged many of his political opinions. His liberal stance emerged through his support of a teachers' pension plan in Texas. For Garza, the youngest school board member, this idea was a natural outgrowth of Roosevelt's New Deal policies. Other school board decisions also attested to his traditionalism. For example, the school board denied an appeal to a Jehovah's Witness family who demanded their child be excused from saluting the American flag in the classroom. Although in her appeal the mother of the child called the board's decision "the first step toward a dictatorship," the board unanimously decided, after a lengthy deliberation, in favor of a compulsory salute. In its public statement, the board confirmed that all public school children would be "gladly received into Brownsville schools" if they abided by district rules and regulations.[31]

The Jehovah's Witness decision was the clearest indication of Garza's first amendment views. As the primary supporter of the school board's call for a compulsory salute, Garza relied upon a Supreme Court decision rendered one year before. In 1940 Supreme Court Justice Felix Frankfurter wrote the majority Court opinion which upheld the constitutionality of a policy permitting the expulsion of students from public schools if they refused to salute the flag. Frankfurter stated, "Personal freedom is best maintained . . . when it is ingrained in a person's habits and not enforced against popular policy by the coercion of adjudicated law" (*Minersville School Board v. Gobitis*, 1940). Mirroring Frankfurter's actions, Garza spoke passionately about American allegiance and the role of public schools in instilling love of country. Motivated by his strong patriotism, Garza believed that Brownsville public schools' policy of saluting the flag superseded the Jehovah's Witnesses' free exercise of their religion. Although this strong patriotic rhetoric might appear to scholars as an example of complete cultural assimilation, it was simply a reflection of Garza's adaptation to many American values and beliefs.[32]

Garza now broadened his focus beyond Brownsville to state politics by joining Lyndon Johnson's United States Senate campaign. The June, 1941, election pitted Johnson against Texas Governor Pappy O'Daniel, the flamboyant politician inaugurated in 1939, during Garza's law school years. Texas Attorney General Gerald Mann and United States

Congressman Martin Dies were Johnson's major opponents. Although Johnson lagged behind, according to voting polls, President Franklin Roosevelt pledged his support to the young congressman. Consequently, many political pundits predicted a Johnson victory.[33]

Reminiscent of Johnson's congressional campaign in 1937, the majority of Johnson's campaign organizers were University of Texas law school graduates and acquaintances of Garza, such as John Connally, Jake Pickle, and Joe Kilgore. Kilgore was a recently graduated attorney practicing in the Rio Grande Valley city of McAllen. He would later represent Texas as a United States congressman. Johnson recruited the majority of his election workers from the ranks of these young college graduates. These young men became the driving force behind the campaign, enthusiastically encouraging voters throughout their region to vote for Johnson. In South Texas Garza and Kilgore helped lead a spirited campaign for the New Deal Democrat. They hosted luncheons and roused voters with lively speeches on behalf of the candidate.[34]

Johnson received support from South Texas not only through young community leaders such as Garza but also through the partisan coalitions prevalent in the area. Throughout the 1900s party stalwarts controlled a number of South Texas counties, from San Antonio to the Rio Grande Valley. These Democratic loyalists were traditionally Anglo civic officials, such as sheriffs or county judges, who delivered the vote of lower-class Mexican American laborers in their communities. Influenced by fears of bodily injury, the workers cast their ballots based on prior instructions. Garza strongly disapproved of the practice, as did the organization he represented, LULAC. The organization's newspaper spoke of the need to "cleanse" Mexican American politics by avoiding "machine politics." The alleged corrupt voting practices, however, were so ingrained in South Texas' political history that Garza could do nothing to stop it. Regardless of Garza's opinion on the matter, in the summer of 1941, the South Texas party stalwarts agreed to support Lyndon Johnson. Consequently, both Garza and the rural leaders favored the same candidate.[35]

In June, 1941, during the final vote count, Johnson's campaign manager, John Connally, felt confident his candidate would become the new United States senator from Texas. With the South Texas vote behind Johnson, along with Roosevelt's support and polls showing a first place lead, the Johnson camp sensed a clear victory. They were mistaken. After officials tallied the votes, O'Daniel won by more than one thousand votes. Johnson and Connally keenly suspected adroit manipulation of voters by the opposition, yet they did not contest the election. Although disappointed in the election outcome, Garza speculated that a long political career still lay ahead for his good friend, Lyndon.[36] Garza's participation in a campaign for an Anglo candidate affirmed his status in the Johnson circle, a place few Mexican Americans had reached in the 1940s.

After Johnson's loss, Garza absorbed himself in his legal work. During his first two years practicing law, he gradually gained a reputation as a capable, young attorney. He also sharpened his skills in the courtroom, trying both civil and criminal cases. He was especially adept at using facial and body expressions—a raised eyebrow, a point of a finger, a change in his booming voice—to make his case. "He had perfect timing in court," colleague Morris Atlas said. Brownsville attorney Emilio Crixel agreed: "He had an outstanding trial record, and many marveled at his ability to take a seemingly poor position and argue for successful client resolutions."[37]

Some Brownsville attorneys theorized it was Garza's air of confidence in the courtroom combined with his eye for detail that won him many cases. Others said the key to his success was his ability to persuade any juror with his colloquial and humble manner.[38] Based on diverse opinions of attorneys and jurors, it is evident that Garza controlled the courtroom, adjusting his demeanor in each case to become nearly unbeatable.

Garza's credible court reputation resulted not only in a steady stream of paying clients but in an influx of pro bono cases, which involved free legal representation. Occupied with his work for the Mexican consulate and his legal practice, he found time, mostly through the encouragement of his mother, to represent people in need. Zoila actively pursued pro bono cases for her son. "My mother was always for the underdog and the poor," said Garza. "She was the best runner in the world to get me pro bono cases."[39] Zoila's insistence that he take on pro bono cases reflected her liberal views, which helped shape Garza's own opinions on matters of social issues and human rights.

In the summer and fall of 1941, Garza worked on his most celebrated pro bono case involving a twenty-year-old Mexican American named Eleuterio Lerma Aguilar. The district attorney accused Aguilar of stabbing and killing an Anglo teenager named Maurice Waitman. The homicide occurred in August, 1941. Garza, along with attorney H. L.

Yates of Brownsville, defended Aguilar. According to newspaper accounts, Waitman and a group of friends taunted and threatened Aguilar
as he was wading in a *resaca*. After being incessantly harassed by Waitman,
Aguilar fought with and stabbed Waitman to death, then fled the scene.
Garza and Yates entered a plea of self-defense for Aguilar. The two attorneys produced volumes of evidence depicting the sequence of events
leading up to the stabbing, specifically demonstrating that Aguilar's actions constituted self-defense under the legal meaning of the term.
Regardless of Garza's and Yates's arguments, the civil court convicted
Aguilar of murder. He was sentenced to a five-year imprisonment, which
was later suspended. Garza and Yates, along with Aguilar, viewed the
suspended sentence as a victory.[40]

In December, 1941, Japanese air forces attacked Pearl Harbor, bringing the United States into World War II. As soon as Garza heard Roosevelt's war declaration, he was intent on enlisting in the service. Bertha's
and Garza's family feared for his safety and attempted to dissuade the
twenty-six-year-old attorney from joining the service. Zoila pleaded
with her son in an effort to change his mind. She told him that she still
grieved for the loss of Ygnacio, and she could not bear to lose Garza to
war. But as Garza watched friends and acquaintances enlist in the army,
his sense of duty heightened. Within a few weeks of the Pearl Harbor
attack, Garza, disregarding his family's appeals, enlisted at the
Brownsville United States Army recruiting office.[41]

Garza used the few days before he reported to combat training
to make the necessary arrangements for his extended absence. Along
with contacting his clients and the Mexican consulate, he placed his
personal finances in order and resigned from all of his civic posts,
including the LULAC presidency and his school board seat. Still concerned with the commitment he had made to the school board, Garza
encouraged his brother Leonel to run for his vacated position, which
he later won in a special election. With no idea of his wartime destination or whether he would return safely, Garza, his family, and fiancée
Bertha shared a tearful farewell. Four days after he enlisted, Garza left
for San Antonio to learn of his assignment.[42]

After spending a week in San Antonio, Garza was shipped to Arizona for basic military training. Fortunately for the new recruit, seven
months after arriving in Arizona, the army transferred him to the Rio
Grande Valley city of Harlingen, only twenty-six miles from Brownsville.
He spent five weeks in an intensive twelve- to sixteen-hour training

course at the Harlingen Gunnery Army School, graduated with honors, and was promoted to gunner sergeant, a position requiring a college degree. The day after his promotion Garza began training young recruits stationed at the gunnery school.

After one of his training sessions Garza received a letter from the War Bond Commission. The commission contracted Garza for a two-month period to serve as a spokesman in the United States Army Air Corps. As part of his duties, Garza was required to travel to nearby Rio Grande Valley cities, where he spoke at army-sponsored rallies, encouraging citizens to buy war bonds and support the war cause. At the rallies he presented moving patriotic speeches in both English and Spanish. In his own unique speaking style, Garza delivered short anecdotes and humorous one-liners that endeared him to his public. His friends praised his oratory skills and his ability to transfer English idioms to Spanish and vice versa, without losing their tone or meaning. On one occasion, a *Brownsville Herald* article, headlined "Spanish Speaking Soldier Cheered by Large Crowd," commended Garza's "eloquent and moving plea."[43] The assignment attested to the perception of Garza as a model American citizen who would be well received by the predominantly Mexican American region. Even in the American army Garza excelled through his bicultural life-style.

By April, 1943, Garza's public-speaking skills led him to a prestigious assignment in the United States Army Air Corps. Impressed by his bilingualism and public presentations, army administrators selected Garza to serve as translator in a meeting between United States President Franklin Roosevelt and Mexican President Miguel Avila Camacho. In calling the meeting, Roosevelt's goal was to promote his Good Neighbor Policy, which assured Mexico of the United States' position of non-intervention in Mexican affairs and encouraged greater Pan American interaction between Latin America and the United States. Avila Camacho refused to hold the meeting on American soil, preferring to speak to Roosevelt in Mexico. To comply with Avila Camacho's request, railroad officials moved a train a mere ten feet from its location in Brownsville to Matamoros where the meeting took place. At the April, 1943, meeting, Roosevelt became the first United States president to greet a Mexican leader on Mexican soil.[44]

For Garza, Roosevelt's visit was especially significant both because of its historic importance and, more notably, because he met the national leader he had voted for in his first presidential election. Although

Garza did not have an opportunity to speak with Roosevelt, his brief encounter with the president remained one of his most cherished war memories.[45]

The summer of 1943 marked another significant moment—Garza and Bertha's wedding. They had been unable to set a definite wedding date, as the war was at its height and Garza did not know when he would receive an extended leave. In the first days of June, 1943, the army granted Garza a ten-day pass. Because of the short notice and the time needed for a honeymoon, only six days were available to plan the entire ceremony. When Garza wired Bertha to tell her of his pass, she immediately visited a bridal boutique near her home. While Bertha bought her wedding day essentials, Bertha's mother arranged the religious service and reception, visiting first their priest and then Brownsville's finest bakery. She then walked to the nearby homes of her closest friends and family and invited them to the wedding.[46]

On June 9, 1943, the engagement that began four years earlier formally culminated in wedlock. At the afternoon ceremony, Garza wore his neatly pressed dress uniform. Bertha wore a long white satin gown with an elegant chapel-length headpiece. Nervously clutching a simple white orchid bouquet, twenty-four-year-old Bertha married her long-time sweetheart. Despite the time obstacles and war shortages limiting the wedding to a basic ceremony, guests recalled an idyllic celebration, which served as a much needed respite for everyone from war tensions.[47]

After their three-day honeymoon in nearby Corpus Christi, Garza immediately found a home for him and his new wife in Harlingen. They shared a rented, two-bedroom house near the base with another army couple. While Garza left for training duty in the mornings, Bertha occupied herself by joining various activities sponsored by the wives of army personnel.[48]

After one month of living in Harlingen, Bertha became pregnant. Seven and a half months into Bertha's pregnancy, her parents persuaded her to move back to Brownsville so that they could care for her. In March Bertha went into labor. She immediately called her husband, who obtained a pass and borrowed a fellow sergeant's car to drive the twenty-six mile trip south to Brownsville's Mercy Hospital. Garza's mother, Zoila, and two of his siblings greeted him at the hospital. A few hours later, on the evening of March 30, 1944, doctors delivered a healthy seven-pound baby boy. Bertha named the baby Reynaldo Jr., but most family members called him Rey. Bertha and Rey remained in Brownsville for another month, while Garza returned to active service. In early May Garza drove his new family back to Harlingen.[49]

Although Garza stayed home with Bertha and Rey nearly every night in Harlingen, the serenity of his home life still did not immunize him from the tensions of being a gunnery sergeant. Every few months, the army dispatched him to various sites throughout the world, including Brazil and North Africa, to spot-check crews. In late 1944 he came close to being directly involved in the entry of the atomic age. As a leading bomber instructor, the United States Army sent Garza to Yuma, Arizona, where he helped train the crew that flew the B-29 Enola Gay. Garza did not learn the mission's purpose until after the bombing. Although he believed that the dropping of the two atomic weapons saved many lives, as a devout Catholic, he opposed the indiscriminate killing caused by weapons of mass destruction.[50]

Garza spent his final period of active duty first in Florida, then Arizona, where the army transferred him months before the August, 1945, surrender. While he lived in these two states, Bertha and Rey stayed in Brownsville. Garza remained in Arizona until November 13, 1945, the date of his honorable discharge. He then traveled back to Brownsville to start a new life as a husband, father, and attorney.

For most of World War II, Garza had spent his army life in the Rio Grande Valley, not straying far from his family. Although the war was one of the most important events in the first half of the twentieth century, shaping events for decades to come, it did not radically change Garza's life. Instead, during the 1940s, he continued bridging the gap between his Anglo and Mexican cultures, becoming both a successful attorney and an influential civic leader. But as he ascended, he continued a close and effective association with both his ethnicity and the dominant American culture—a unique identification that propelled him on to grander avenues during the next two decades.

CHAPTER 4

The Professional, Family Man, and Politico
1945–59

The postwar years began the journey that would eventually elevate Garza to the federal judiciary. Along the path he reestablished a legal practice, enlarged his family, and distinguished himself as a community servant and politico. He moved smoothly through his life's course by drawing from the lessons of his bicultural heritage, including his family, community, and religious background. His life travels eventually brought him to the doorstep of the political elite in Texas with whom he established contacts that decisively affected his ascendancy to the federal bench.

In November, 1945, Garza returned to Brownsville to find a booming, yet still provincial, community which had benefited from growing prosperity. But Brownsville also remained below the national average in objective government census categories, such as employment, literacy, and family income. Although the number of jobs had increased, the majority of work remained categorized as unskilled, with hundreds of citizens working in the agricultural field. The city also experienced a 61 percent increase in population. Brownsville grew from 22,000 in 1940 to 36,000 in 1950.[1]

Once Garza arrived in his hometown, he began planning his reentry into both his legal practice and community life. To conserve funds, Garza, Bertha, and two-year-old Rey temporarily moved into their parents' home. They spent the first three weeks with Bertha's parents, the Champions. Thereafter, they moved to Zoila's larger house on West Saint Charles Street. While Bertha relaxed from the stresses of war and cared for her young son, Garza readjusted to civilian life. He organized his financial affairs and visited family and friends with whom he had not spent time since his enlistment in 1941.[2]

Family and friends recognized that army life had slightly changed thirty-year-old Garza. He was no longer the lanky, youthful fellow he was before the war. He had gained close to fifteen pounds during his four years of service, filling out his six-foot, two-inch frame. His charcoal black hair and mustache were graying now, and a few facial lines began to surface. His deep green eyes appeared a bit more sunken. For the first time in his life, he shed his boyish features and looked his age. But inwardly Garza maintained his keen wit. He honed his art for telling stories, as he shared his war experiences with high school chums. He began habitually punctuating each story with a whispery "hmm," as if to invite an opposing view from his listeners. Few dared to argue with the forceful speaker. Although, like his mother, Garza was a patient man, against those who exceeded his threshold of tolerance, Garza reacted swiftly and firmly. Although his appearance had altered, he still retained many of his personal attributes, including his deep religious commitment and love of family.[3]

Five weeks after returning to Brownsville, Garza plunged into his legal practice. He secured a single-room office adjacent to his brother Ygnacio's accounting practice. The two-story brick building on one of Brownsville's main downtown streets preserved the New Orleans French Quarter–style in architecture. It featured double French doors and a decorative cast-iron railing surrounding the second-floor balcony. Garza opened for business on January 2, 1946, and spent his first few weeks in the office contacting former clients. He soon restored his ties with the Mexican consulate, a position that had previously provided him high visibility in South Texas and helped him maintain ties to his Mexican roots.[4]

Garza also returned to civic affairs. He rejoined many of the social groups he participated in before the war, including his beloved Knights of Columbus. Garza's peers in the Knights of Columbus encouraged him to seek election, and he ran for office in the local organization. He was elected Grand Knight of the Brownsville council, an office equivalent to president. The position required that he attend meetings of the councils throughout Texas, planning and organizing future state civic projects. Accompanied by Bertha and Rey, Garza began to travel extensively for the organization, a practice that would continue throughout his life. Since the Knights of Columbus was a Catholic organization, many of its members were also Mexican Americans who, like Garza, represented the upper middle-class in their communities. Garza not only associated with Mexican Americans in Brownsville but also befriended members of his ethnic group throughout Texas, many of whom held a similar bicultural life-style.[5]

Although civic affairs consumed much of Garza's life, the majority of his time was devoted to his legal practice. A professional highlight of the late 1940s came, unfortunately, at the expense of human lives. On a balmy and clear June night in 1946, a group of thirteen young illegal aliens packed into a rusty, late-model pickup truck. As the teenagers crossed an unguarded railroad intersection in Brownsville, an oncoming train collided with the truck. The devastating impact demolished the vehicle and killed eleven of its passengers. The families of the victims, most of whom were Mexican residents, sought legal counsel in the United States. These families desired a Spanish-speaking attorney and, after learning of Garza, brought their case to him. The remaining victims' families whom Garza did not represent found legal counsel from the Brownsville law firm of Faulk, Sharpe, and Cunningham. The firm and Garza jointly filed suit in a district court against the owner of the train, the Saint Louis, Brownsville, and Mexico Railway and its trustee, Guy A. Thompson.

Budgetary constraints had precluded Garza from hiring a secretary or staff for the tragic case. Consequently, he dealt with not only the legalities of the lawsuit but also the paperwork. He took depositions, examined the accident scene, and prepared witnesses for trial. He also typed the correspondence related to the proceedings. The pretrial activities and trial itself lasted until the spring of 1947. During that time, he worked fervently night and day, missing many of his civic club meetings to master all aspects of the case. His tireless work on behalf of the distraught families culminated in early March, 1947, when the court awarded over $21,000 to the plaintiffs.[6]

A few weeks after the trial, railroad trustee Guy Thompson expressed interest in hiring Garza for future litigation in the Rio Grande Valley. Undoubtedly, the victorious attorney's legal cunning during the railroad accident case impressed Thompson, and the railroad official preferred to work with Garza as a legal ally instead of a courtroom opponent. Thompson invited Garza and Brownsville attorneys Paul Cunningham, Henry Faulk, and Gilbert Sharpe to a meeting held in a private railroad car office. He asked the four men to act as railroad attorneys for future litigation. After deliberating the proposal, the four agreed, beginning a long alliance among Garza, the railroad company, and the firm of Faulk, Cunningham, and Sharpe.[7]

The added economic benefits and social recognition attached to his railroad company alliance promoted Garza's integration with Anglo elites in South Texas. His achieving economic mobility meant that Anglos were more likely to accept Garza as an equal, thereby allowing him to easily maintain a dual cultural existence in the still predominantly racially intolerant South.

After the railroad meeting, the partners of Faulk, Cunningham, and Sharpe informally invited Garza to join their prestigious South Texas firm. Major Texas firms so highly regarded the attorneys of Faulk, Cunningham, and Sharpe that they frequently contracted the firm to handle litigation relating to incidents in the Rio Grande Valley. Clients of the firm included some of South Texas' most prominent professional and business leaders. To entice the thirty-two-year-old attorney, the men agreed to name Garza as a partner in the firm. Garza discussed the option with his wife and his two eldest brothers for the next few months. In early June he decided to join Faulk, Cunningham, and Sharpe. He set up a meeting with the partners, and the group agreed that Garza should formally begin his affiliation with the firm in January, 1949.[8]

During the one-and-a-half-year interim, Garza increased his involvement in local politics. By the start of city elections in September, 1947, Brownsville Mayor H. L. Stokely began persuading Garza to join his slate of candidates by running for city commissioner. In the election two years earlier, Garza, along with a small group of Mexican American professionals, opposed Stokely's mayoral candidacy. The group publicly voiced its opposition through the local newspaper, complaining that Stokely was not addressing the needs of Mexican Americans in the city. In the 1947 election, however, Stokely's first term successfully negated their initial opposition.[9]

By the late 1940s the city commissioner's race was one of many political arenas Mexican Americans in Brownsville entered. The city government consisted of one mayor and four commissioners. Of the other three commissioners on Stokely's ticket, all were incumbents and two were Mexican American. This was an unusual alignment, given that Brownsville and other cities in South Texas were one of the few areas in the country where Mexican Americans held local offices in 1947.[10]

Confident that the mayor's political agenda included Mexican American interests, Garza accepted Stokely's offer and entered the race. Garza's most effective campaign tool became his amiable personality. He possessed the politician's gift of making each person feel he was his close friend. He was unpretentious with a clever sense of humor which attracted both Anglo and Mexican American voters. He made the effort to speak to even the most humble citizens, asking them about their work, their family—a gesture rarely forgotten by prospective voters. He had long before established a close rapport with the *Brownsville Herald*'s city editor, Clarence La Roach. Consequently, weekly editorials routinely praised Garza. In November, 1947, Brownsville citizens voted for Stokely's slate of candidates by a more than 70-percent margin.[11] Voters swept Garza into office.

A few weeks after the election, Garza's future law partner, Henry Faulk, died of a heart attack. Faulk's death created chaos for his firm, and Garza and the remaining partners mutually agreed to postpone Garza's entry into the practice until January, 1950. The later date provided the firm time to address its finances. For the duration Garza continued his involvement with the railroad company, the Mexican consulate, individual clients, and community affairs. Most of all, he focused his energies on his position as city commissioner.

By the start of 1948, Garza's presence was leaving its mark on the city's administration. Garza initiated an important campaign to improve the distribution of water in Brownsville. Many of the city's pipes, laid out at the turn of the twentieth century, held an insufficient amount of water to sustain the growing Brownsville community. As a result, pipe stoppages occurred frequently in the city. Garza realized that Brownsville needed a water supply that could meet the demands of residential and commercial users. As the existing supply failed to meet these goals, Garza instituted the water reform program,[12] a plan that reflected his desire to bring his Mexican American community to a level equal to other Texas regions.

But as Garza was working to introduce new changes, he was also promoting a city hall restoration project. Completed in 1852, Brownsville's city hall had not been remodeled since 1912. To bring the deteriorating building up to modern-day standards, the city administration initiated renovation procedures. When the work was completed, city leaders held an official ceremony in which builders placed a stone plaque near city hall's front entrance. Brownsville craftsmen emblazoned the plaque with the names of the city administration, including Garza, the architect, and the contractor involved in the renovation work.[13] The marker remained on city hall throughout Garza's life.

Through his position as city commissioner Garza cultivated his passion for politics and soon became eager to participate in elections beyond his small town. His opportunity arose in 1948. In February of that year, United States Congressman Lyndon Johnson called on Garza to act as his campaign manager in the Rio Grande Valley. Johnson was running in the 1948 United States Senate race. The ambitious congressman needed support in the Rio Grande Valley, since he held no strong ties to anyone in that area except Garza. Since Johnson was a man who rarely forgot his allies or adversaries, he undoubtedly recalled Garza's ability to deliver the Mexican American vote in Austin during Johnson's congressional race in 1937. Garza, well aware of Johnson's desire to become a senator and having worked in Johnson's 1941 losing bid for the Senate, readily agreed to support the aspiring Texas officeholder.[14] Thus, Johnson became the first of many politicians seeking the South Texas contingency who courted Garza throughout the next decade. By 1941, Garza's abilities to encourage Mexican American voter participation had gained his acceptance in the larger Texas Anglo political establishment. His unique dual cultural perspective worked in his favor to bring him state political recognition.

Much like Garza's experiences with Johnson's 1937 congressional campaign and his 1941 Senate race, the 1948 election typified traditional Texas politics. In Texas, issues took a back seat to personalities. Although a member of the United States Congress, Johnson did not possess the name recognition of his opponents: former Texas governor and incumbent United States senator, Pappy O'Daniel, and the most popular governor up to that point in Texas history, Coke Stevenson. As widely recognized political officeholders, O'Daniel and Stevenson won their elections through statewide votes. As a congressman, Johnson garnered his political victory through a fractional number of voters in his district, not a majority from the state. An opinion survey taken before the height of election activity gave Stevenson 55 percent of the support, while O'Daniel and Johnson received 24 and 21 percent, respectively.[15]

With the magnified personalities of his opponents and Johnson's own popular disadvantage, the lanky Texan channeled his political genius toward the development of inventive campaign tactics. The astute campaigner's creative energy abounded, and Johnson brought forth a strategy that wowed voters throughout the state—the use of a helicopter. Johnson's unprecedented use of the tools of modern technology caused one author to note that Johnson launched "a whole new era in politics." Indeed, Johnson's campaign became associated with a spirit, thrill, and excitement that not only propelled Texas politics into a circus-like atmosphere, but immediately boosted the young congressman's name recognition.[16]

In traversing the state with his eye-catching helicopter, Johnson relied on local supporters to orchestrate the rallies. In Brownsville it was Garza who made the requisite plans. He persuaded city leaders to allow the landing and arranged for a helicopter site near Brownsville Junior College. He then requested that professors dismiss students a few minutes earlier than scheduled. Promptly at noon, students and Democratic political leaders in Brownsville rushed to the loud whirling sound of Johnson's helicopter. As the helicopter landed, the crowd could distinguish the large block letters distinctively announcing "U.S. Senator Lyndon Johnson." "There were hundreds of people there. We were all amazed, many of us had never seen a helicopter before," recounted Garza's nephew, Raul Besterio.[17]

Donning a large cowboy hat, which he flung dramatically as he spoke, Johnson delivered an address with the gusto of a Sunday preacher. He was a master orator when he spoke off-the-cuff as he did in Brownsville. A microphone attached to his neck and shoulders amplified the candidate's every word and enhanced its revivalist delivery. When he was finished, Johnson feverishly shook many of the hands of the large, mostly Mexican American, crowd and gave Garza a warm pat on the back. Garza responded enthusiastically by leading the crowd in a thunderous applause. Johnson then returned to his helicopter, ready to deliver his next campaign address at another small town destination.[18]

In March, 1948, although consumed with Johnson's Senate race,

Garza also took time to aid Rio Grande Valley resident, Lloyd Bentsen. A fellow graduate of the University of Texas at Austin, Bentsen was running for a United States Congress seat for the Fifteenth District of Texas. In the late 1940s the Fifteenth District included Brownsville and the other areas 350 miles along the Rio Grande Valley. Bentsen was a wealthy, young World War II veteran who was running against three other competitors, all well-known regional figures. While soliciting support for his congressional campaign, Bentsen traveled to Brownsville to ask Garza for his political backing. Bentsen knew that the Brownsville attorney's support could generate the votes needed for an election victory. The congressional candidate also was aware of Garza's strong allegiance to Lyndon Johnson, a man whose political views Bentsen rejected.[19]

Convinced that Garza would judge him on issues rather than political affiliation, Bentsen called on the Brownsville attorney. On a typical, sweltering afternoon in 1948, both men sat in the shade of the Garza family's porch discussing politics. While Garza puffed gently on his cigarette, Bentsen presented his political platform. Bentsen's knowledge of the complex problems plaguing the Fifteenth Congressional District and all the creative solutions the candidate offered impressed Garza. As the conversation progressed toward the dinner hour, both men agreed to continue the discussion. Bentsen remembers that at that point Garza jokingly called to his wife, "Bertha, put a little more water in the soup. Lloyd's staying for dinner." By the time dessert reached the table, Garza had pledged his support to Bentsen.[20]

At political rallies throughout the Rio Grande Valley, Garza would describe his experiences with the two politicians, explaining how each man's vision would improve the area. Fueled by the belief that Johnson and Bentsen cared about Brownsville's future, he arranged rallies and luncheons on behalf of the two office seekers. He also organized the printing and distribution of campaign flyers for the candidates. He then wired his friends throughout South Texas, who would in turn contact their friends, to ensure good attendance at rallies. Civic leaders whom he knew across the region through his intensive personal canvassing for the War Bond Commission during World War II were now called on as supporters. He easily persuaded them to campaign in their region for Johnson and Bentsen.[21]

During these Texas political campaigns, Garza experienced some positive personal changes. His growing client base provided the family the added income needed to rent a house and move out of Zoila's home. Bertha and Garza chose a temporary two-bedroom house on Hibiscus Street, just a few miles from his childhood neighborhood. A few weeks after moving, on August 15, 1948, Bertha gave birth to their second son. Given Garza's strong religious beliefs, they chose the classic biblical name David for their baby. Just like Rey, the second baby was both healthy and full of energy.[22]

Three months after David's birth, Garza celebrated Johnson's and Bentsen's political victories. Johnson won the November run-off primary, defeating Stevenson by eighty-seven votes. Although Johnson's opponent contested the election, the United States Senate Campaign Investigating Subcommittee granted Johnson his seat in December, 1948. Bentsen also was victorious in his congressional election, handily defeating his competitors. At a mere twenty-seven, Bentsen then became the youngest member of the House of Representatives.[23]

The new decade of 1950 brought to Garza a different career venue. After a two-and-a-half-year wait, Garza began his first day at his new firm. He smiled contentedly when he saw on the massive wooden doors of the downtown Brownsville firm the freshly stenciled firm name, Sharpe, Cunningham, and Garza. The firm was larger than most in Brownsville, with three partners, two junior partners, four associates, and three secretaries. Because of the firm's regional reputation, Sharpe, Cunningham, and Garza was part of virtually every large case in the Rio Grande Valley. "We represented so many insurance companies that the Brownsville court docket used to have Sharpe, Cunningham, and Garza week," Garza quipped. As sole practitioner, Garza had previously addressed all types of cases, but at the firm he focused on civil cases. He had already established a few corporate clients before he joined the firm, such as Southwestern Bell Telephone, Continental Trailways, Sears, Roebuck, and Company, and Missouri Pacific. Unlike the few Mexican American attorneys in the 1950s practicing what was termed poor people's law, including personal injury, Garza began dealing almost exclusively with high-level legal issues of corporate law.[24] Garza's legal focus can be attributed to his acceptance as a member of the higher economic and social strata in his region, marking him as one of the few Mexican American attorneys such corporate groups would allow to represent their interests.

The next several months saw Garza become enormously successful both financially and professionally. With partners Gilbert Sharpe and Paul Cunningham, he practiced almost exclusively in the insurance field, and his firm represented large corporations with needs in South Texas, including the Valley Transit Company.

During trials he was nearly unbeatable. He instinctively identified with jurors, putting his judicial adversaries at a disadvantage. Many of the jurors were working people to whom Garza was a familiar figure. His imposing courtroom presence was definitely an advantage in court. With his colloquial eloquence, which included Spanish idioms, his deep booming voice, and his gift of keen wit and spontaneity, Garza easily persuaded jurors to favor his clients. "His tremendous voice carried through the whole court," recalled Emilio Crixel, a Brownsville attorney who worked with Garza in the 1950s.[25] Through his courtroom style, Garza perceptively took advantage of his dual cultures, using aspects of his Mexican roots to persuade the mostly Mexican American jurors, while implementing his knowledge of legal precepts to succeed in the American judicial system. He had also reached the same financial plateau as many of Texas' most powerful litigators, the majority of whom were Anglo.

Garza once again moved back to state matters in March, 1950, when Governor Allan Shivers appointed him to the Texas Economy Commission. Garza had met Shivers through their common affiliation with the Democratic Party in Texas. As a corporate attorney, Garza had established great visibility with key Texas political figures, which undoubtedly led to the prestigious appointment.[26]

By the summer of 1950, the fear of a Communist challenge to the existing social order compelled the United States to respond aggressively, ultimately resulting in brother Osbaldo's call to active duty. On June 25, 1950, North Korean forces invaded South Korea, and President Truman reacted immediately by sending forces to Korea under the auspices of the United Nations. In 1951 the Army called reserve units, including Osbaldo's, into active duty. After a six-month tour of duty in Korea, Osbaldo returned to Brownsville safely.[27]

Osbaldo's involvement in the Korean War was one of a number of factors that shifted Garza's attention from city and state affairs toward the national scene. The 1952 presidential election year was unique for Garza, as he temporarily switched his alliance to a Republican candidate, Dwight D. Eisenhower. Although many Mexican Americans in Texas remained loyal to the Democratic party, Garza's position as a bicultural figure allowed him to move independently from the majority of Mexican Americans. Garza was confident that Eisenhower was best able to confront the challenges of the Cold War. Like many war veterans, Garza recognized Eisenhower's distinguished leadership during World War II. Worried about international issues and the possibility of unstable national conditions, he believed the next four years would be crucial to America's stability and that only Eisenhower could effectively curtail tragedy. Like most Americans, Garza also viewed Eisenhower as a nonpartisan figure, despite Eisenhower's position as the Republican presidential candidate.[28]

Garza's allegiance to Eisenhower was the norm for a majority of Texas Democrats who forced the party to split over the tidelands issue. The tidelands referred to the battle between the federal government and Texas over supposedly oil-rich offshore lands in the state. Eisenhower, the Republican nominee, favored state ownership of the tidelands while the Democratic nominee, Adlai Stevenson, would not accept outright state ownership of the area. The resulting split created two political factions: the Conservative Democrats and the Liberal Democrats. The Conservatives endorsed Eisenhower because of his stand on the tidelands issue. Although Garza's longtime political ally, Lyndon Johnson, supported Stevenson, Garza followed the Texas Conservative trend. Thus, Garza became a founding member of the Democrats for Eisenhower in the Rio Grande Valley. Just as with Johnson's Senate campaign in 1948, Garza now lobbied for Eisenhower within South Texas. On one occasion, he spoke to a Valley-wide audience in a radio address, urging Texas Democrats to vote for the "American war hero," Eisenhower.[29]

Garza's election activity was abruptly halted in the summer of 1952, after he learned the tragic news of his brother's death in Korea. The Army had activated Osbaldo for a second tour of duty in February, 1952. In July a Korean gunner shot at Osbaldo's B-29 aircraft while it was airborne. The shot hit the plane's gasoline tank. As the tank exploded, it engulfed the aircraft in an inferno. The plane crew lost control and spiraled to the ground, crashing in a thunderous blast. The eleven-member crew died on impact. The human remains were so severely burned that army officials could not specifically identify any of the servicemen. Consequently, all eleven crewmen, including Osbaldo, were buried in a combined grave at a military cemetery in Missouri. Osbaldo left behind a young wife, two young children, and a sorrowful family. The Garzas learned the painful news in late July. In early August, although still in shock over the tragedy, Garza accompanied Osbaldo's young wife Esther to Missouri where they attended the military burial for the entire crew.[30]

Osbaldo's death was devastating, especially for Zoila. Comforting his mother became Garza's therapy in coping with the loss of his younger brother. But he dealt with it by absorbing himself in his legal, civic, and political activities. Within a few weeks of returning from Osbaldo's funeral, he focused his energies on the election of Dwight D. Eisenhower.[31]

Garza approached the campaign with gusto. He continued to rally Rio Grande Valley residents' support of Eisenhower and solicited votes for the presidential candidate throughout the state. In November, 1952, through the Democrats for Eisenhower group, the Republican presidential candidate won 53 percent of Texas' votes. Eisenhower not only won Texas, but he won the presidency by handily defeating his Democratic opponent Adlai E. Stevenson.[32]

The day after Eisenhower's presidential victory, Garza and his political allies in the Rio Grande Valley celebrated at a Brownsville steakhouse. Dozens of guests crowded the restaurant as they chanted their allegiance to the Democrats for Eisenhower. The victory was especially gratifying for Garza, as Bertha used the occasion to inform her husband that they were expecting their third child. Although delighted at the prospect of a new baby, he worried about the safety of his children growing up in an unstable country. The thought of Eisenhower at the nation's helm, however, boosted his confidence in future stability.[33]

After his successful involvement in the 1952 national and state elections, Garza took a leadership position in Texas civic affairs. In 1953 the state council of the Knights of Columbus elected him state deputy, the highest office in the organization. In that position he oversaw 123 Texas councils and 23,000 members. He was the first Mexican American Texas leader of the Catholic club in a state still segregating Mexican Americans in schools, hotels, and other public facilities. Garza's ethnicity obviously never affected his gradual climb up the leadership ladder of the Knights of Columbus since he garnered more than 90 percent of the group's votes.[34]

On July 13, 1953, Bertha gave birth to a third son, named Ygnacio but called Nacho by family and friends. Garza and Bertha chose the name to honor the memory of his deceased father. The name fit perfectly, as the newborn's features mirrored that of his grandfather, with lightly tanned skin, large brown eyes, and a large frame. With the new family addition, Garza began to take a larger role in caring for the children, as the inexhaustible nature of the three young boys warranted the constant attention of both parents.[35]

Two days after Nacho's birth, Senator Lyndon Johnson wrote Garza asking him for his support. In the letter the senator wrote that "naturally, I would like to get as strong a vote as possible, and I would like to rely on you as one of my key friends to accomplish this in your county." The Brownsville attorney readily agreed to support Johnson and began planning Democratic gatherings throughout South Texas. Garza's position as state deputy also helped garner support for Johnson by the majority of Texas' Knights of Columbus members.[36] Throughout the 1950s Johnson and Garza continued to correspond, forming a mutually beneficial relationship for the future.

The summer of 1953 brought two more accolades. Garza served as an attorney for the diocese of Corpus Christi and built a close friendship with Catholic Bishop Mariano S. Garriega. Bishop Garriega held a deep respect for Garza and recommended the Brownsville attorney for the Medal Pro Ecclesia et Pontifice, an honor in the Catholic Church which Garza was later awarded. Individuals distinguished with the medal were granted a private audience with the pope in Rome.[37]

A few months later, through Garza's service to the Knights of Columbus, he received another prestigious honor for Catholic laymen, the Knighthood of Saint Gregory. Each year bishops throughout the world nominated Roman Catholics distinguished for personal character, reputation, and social accomplishments, then sent the nominees' names to the Secretariat of the State at the Vatican. After conferring with the Pope, the Secretariat selected individuals to receive the award. In late July, 1954, Pope Pius XII granted the knighthood to Garza. From his chancery office in Corpus Christi, Bishop Garriega immediately wrote Garza to congratulate him. The prelate enthusiastically explained to him that the diocese would help plan a regal ceremony in Garza's honor.[38]

Three weeks later, in an early evening weekend ceremony, Knights of Columbus members from throughout Texas, together with Garza's friends and family, congregated at Sacred Heart Catholic Church, where Bishop Garriega read the gold-sealed document sent by the pope, then ceremoniously placed a silver medallion emblazoned with the papal seal around Garza's neck. Garza's pastor, Reverend Daniel Lynch, ended the ceremony with a passionate speech extolling the honoree's virtues and encouraging other parishioners to follow Garza's example. As the honoree stood at the alter amid waves of applause, he looked at the medallion that hung elegantly around his neck, and tears of happiness overcame him. His life had been driven by the spiritual purpose to satisfy God's will, which he interpreted to mean serving humanity. Through the Knighthood of Saint Gregory, he firmly wedded his temporal secular sense of public duty to a spiritual gospel of service.[39] Garza's recognition by the Catholic church reflected his place as an esteemed representative of his Catholic faith.

Garza maintained his active campaigning for Lyndon Johnson and Governor Allan Shivers. In November, 1954, Johnson won a landslide victory against Dudley T. Dougherty, a relatively unknown state legislator from a small South Texas town. Johnson received more than 71 percent of the vote. Garza never doubted that Johnson would win reelection. The outcome delighted Garza, and he attended a boisterous victory party to celebrate his friend's achievement.[40]

A few months later Governor Shivers telephoned Garza to ask if he would consider accepting an appointment as a state judge. Garza considered the request but first discussed the prestigious offer with his law partners, his brothers, Bertha, and his mentor, Oscar Dancy. In discussing the possibility, a few concerns emerged. After all, as a partner in a successful firm, Garza was making a substantial living, but as a state judge, his salary would be greatly reduced. He worried whether he would still be able to afford to care for his family of four. Additionally, a Texas district judge was not a lifetime appointment as was a federal judge. Thus, Garza held no job security. There was also no guarantee that Shivers's successors would choose a Mexican American as a state judge, given the racial dynamics of the era.[41]

Based on his concerns, Garza decided that the only judgeship he would accept would be a federal one. A week after the Governor first called Garza to propose the appointment, Garza declined Shivers's offer. When Garza shared his rationale with the governor, he told Garza he understood his reasoning but would undoubtedly call on him again for future state appointments.[42]

As a city leader, Garza was heading such civic organizations as the Brownsville Planning and Zoning Commission and the Cameron County Child Welfare Board. But as his participation in community and state organizations increased, he still continued his relationship with Lyndon

Johnson, who in 1955 had become majority leader of the United States Senate. Garza worked as unofficial advisor to Johnson, providing counsel on such matters as political appointments in South Texas.[43]

In 1956 Garza faced a difficult decision when his longtime friends and political allies Lyndon Johnson and Allan Shivers squared off for control of the Texas Democratic party. The situation forced Garza to choose sides between what one national magazine declared a "war among Texas Democrats." The battle's roots lay in the 1952 Democratic national convention. After Shivers declined to support the Democratic party's nominee for president and, instead, campaigned for Eisenhower, many Texas Democrats felt betrayed. In response, a large group of Democrats, led by Lyndon Johnson, refused to allow Shivers to head the Texas delegation to the 1956 Democratic national convention. Roused by such men as Johnson and House Speaker Sam Rayburn, the Texas Democrats in effect dumped Shivers from the party.[44]

Shivers and Johnson waged a bitter, derisive battle to lead the Texas party loyalists, and both men asked Garza for his support. After much deliberation, Garza sided with Johnson. He favored Johnson's moderate political stance more than Shivers's increasingly Republican, ultraconservative views. Garza became a member of the moderate middle, the Rayburn-Johnson wing of the party, who opposed the liberal Democrats led by Ralph Yarborough. Garza called Shivers to tell him of his decision. Although upset, Shivers told Garza he understood his choice and would continue to consider him a friend. As Garza would learn in later years, Shivers's assertion was not a hollow political statement. In May, 1956, Johnson won control of the state party convention.[45]

On January 4, 1957, grief again struck Garza's life when his seventy-three-year-old mother died. Garza's two nieces and his eldest sister were enjoying their daily lunch with Zoila when the subject of Osbaldo arose. Zoila, still deeply distraught over his death, was known to weep uncontrollably at the mere mention of his name, so when her lunch guests complimented her on the entrée she prepared, Zoila began crying. Between her sobs, she mentioned that Osbaldo often wrote to her from Korea telling her how he longed for her cooking. The three women attempted to console Zoila, who then put her head down. When she would not raise her head, Garza's sister, Lucila, called Zoila's doctor, who rushed to her side. The doctor moved Zoila to her bedroom, sadly nodded his head, and pronounced her dead. As with Osbaldo's death, Garza was grief-stricken by his mother's passing.[46]

For the remainder of 1957, to cope with his mother's death, Garza immersed himself in family activities, his legal practice, and his civic and religious organizations. In April Bertha learned that she was pregnant for the fourth time. Bertha's pregnancy encouraged the couple to contemplate moving to a larger home. The Garzas had been living in a two-bedroom home, where the three young boys shared a room. Once the baby, due in December, was born, they could keep the child in their room for a while, but soon their expansive family would need more space. Garza began assessing the family finances in preparation for the future moving and house expenses.[47]

In May Garza again received a call from Governor Shivers, who now persuaded him to accept an appointment to the Texas Good Neighbor Commission (GNC). The position was reminiscent of Garza's role as interpreter between President Roosevelt and Mexican President Avila Camacho during World War II. The commission had originally been charged in 1943 with enforcing Texas' public policy of guaranteeing equality to all Mexican Americans, but by the 1950s the GNC's functions had greatly weakened. Shivers had subtly subverted the liberal policies of the GNC, mainly because he was embarrassed by a 1947 GNC report about his corrupt labor practice in the Rio Grande Valley. Shivers successfully weakened the GNC by redirecting its goals to foster improved relations between the United States and Latin America. The commission also acted to enhance relations between Anglos and Mexican Americans in Texas.[48] For Garza, the position signified his stature as a conservative figure among Anglo leaders such as Shivers. Indeed, Garza was no radical. Although concerned about Mexican Americans' social and economic status, he continued to believe that conditions would improve through socially sanctioned means.

While involved in the GNC, Garza also took an active interest in the state judicial campaign of his law school friend, Joe Greenhill. Texas Governor Price Daniel, Allan Shivers's successor, had recently appointed Greenhill to the Texas Supreme Court, a position appointees maintained by running for election. In September, with little funds and challenged by the popular district judge Sarah T. Hughes, Greenhill began traversing the state of Texas to gain votes. He eventually found he needed Garza and the South Texas vote. Aware of Greenhill's political needs in South Texas, Garza immediately called and volunteered to act as his campaign manager in the area. "I couldn't have looked around and found a better or more persuasive campaign manager," said Greenhill.

A few days later, Greenhill traveled to Brownsville, where Garza introduced the Central Texas judicial candidate to prominent South Texas figures, many of whom were attorneys trying cases in Brownsville's federal court. A few months later, Greenhill won the judicial seat. After his victory, Greenhill thanked Garza and told supporters, "It's quite possible that Reynaldo's participation was the difference between being elected and not winning." Once again, Garza aided a rising Texan towards political victory.[49]

Two weeks after Greenhill's victory, Governor Daniel appointed Garza to the Texas Education Standards Committee, initiating Garza's statewide commitment to scholastic improvement. The committee worked on Texas' high school curriculum. It designated which courses should be mandatory for Texas students.[50] Similar to Garza's membership in the Texas Economy Commission, the Texas Education Standards Committee not only was a prestigious appointment but also acquainted Garza with additional members of Texas' political elite, the majority of whom were Anglos.

Once again Garza's family increased. On December 31, 1957, Bertha gave birth to their first daughter, named Bertha but nicknamed Bertita by the family. The newborn was enamored by Garza and Bertha as well as by her three older brothers who were unaccustomed to the delicate and more subdued nature of a baby girl. The Garza parents kept Bertita in their bedroom and again began contemplating moving into a larger home to accommodate their growing family. Yet, Garza's active civic and professional calendar, in addition to the constant attention required in raising one teenage son, two young boys, and a baby girl, postponed their plans.[51]

By the late 1950s, Garza had become one of a handful of Mexican Americans allowed to join the Texas party machinery, largely through his support of Senate Majority Leader Lyndon Johnson and Texas Governors Allan Shivers and Price Daniel. He had become an influential political figure in South Texas, a supporter of what he termed the "big boys" in Texas politics, and an appointee to influential state committees. As he entered the new decade, his success in Texas' political world would eventually launch him toward national acclaim.

CHAPTER 5

Approaching the Bench
1959–61

In September, 1959, Garza learned that Federal Judge James V. Allred had died while holding court in Corpus Christi. Garza was deeply saddened over Allred's death, as he had greatly admired the judge during their two-decades-long association. Beginning with Garza's undergraduate years at the University of Texas, when then-governor Allred had invited Garza and other university students to the governor's mansion, then later during Allred's monthly judicial visits to Brownsville, the two had cemented their relationship. Allred had also served as the only federal judge in South Texas when Garza argued many cases in Brownsville's federal court. The two also visited socially at bar association functions. Garza considered Allred's death not only a loss to the community but also to the judiciary and was optimistic that legislators would recommend a worthy replacement. He never anticipated, of course, that his bicultural status would help single him out among those considered for the prestigious position.[1]

Pursuant to the United States Constitution (art. 2, sec. 2), the president is responsible for nominating a federal judge "by and with the advice and consent of the Senate." Traditionally, United States senators sponsor judicial nominees and can block any appointments they find unacceptable. The individual appointed to fill Allred's judicial seat would require the acceptance of not only senators but also the United States attorney general. Once senators recommend a candidate, the attorney general addresses all preliminaries in the appointment process, including instituting an FBI investigation. Since 1958 the attorney general has authorized the American Bar Association (ABA) to conduct a preliminary inquiry into all federal judiciary candidates, with the exception of Supreme Court nominees. After the inquiry, the ABA issues a final report on its findings. Typically, if the ABA report is favorable, the attorney general recommends the individual to the president, who then officially nominates the prospective federal judge. The nominee then undergoes a brief interview conducted by the Senate Judiciary Committee and is voted on by the entire Senate.[2]

Given a senator's seemingly sovereign power in the nomination process, an established practice developed in which individuals who endeared themselves to the United States senator representing their state would be considered for federal judicial nominations. The most common method of endearment was political participation or personal friendship with a politician. Thus, a common joke among attorneys was that one needed to have the foresight to choose a future United States senator as a law school roommate or as a first law partner.[3]

Garza, however, not only possessed the requisite political associations, through his friendship with Senator Lyndon Johnson, but also held an impressive track record of courtroom trial experience and a host of responsible positions of leadership throughout the community and South Texas. As a result, the Brownsville attorney became a logical and highly competitive potential candidate to fill the vacancy— at least in the eyes of fellow Rio Grande Valley citizens. These citizens recognized Garza as a qualified successor to Allred. He embodied the qualities typically sought by those involved in the judicial selection process: he possessed prominent stature as an attorney, was an active civic participant, and resided in the district the new federal judge would serve.[4]

Garza, however, was a Democrat, and although he campaigned for the Republican president's election, he was not affiliated with President Dwight D. Eisenhower's party. Eisenhower, like many of his predecessors and successors to the presidency, appointed only long-standing members of his party to the federal bench. It was unusual for any president to sway from this practice. By the time the vacancy arose in the United States District Court, Eisenhower have given approximately 94 percent of his appointments to Republicans. Additionally, no president had ever appointed a Mexican American to the federal judiciary.[5]

Fueled by a desire to fill the district court vacancy with a Republican, Eisenhower selected Houston attorney and Republican party loyalist, Everton Kennerly, as a candidate. Kennerly had come to Eisenhower's attentions through his valuable work for the Republican party in Texas. Coincidentally, Kennerly was the son-in-law of Garza's mentor, Cameron County Judge Oscar Dancy. Despite his association with Dancy, Garza was unaware of Kennerly's consideration to Allred's judicial post. Encouraged by other attorneys in South Texas, Garza began considering potential candidates to fill the vacant federal judicial seat in his region.[6]

While Garza contemplated a worthy replacement for Allred, members of the American G. I. Forum, a Mexican American political organization comprised of war veterans, began a concerted effort to have the president appoint a Mexican American to the position. As the group was not established in Brownsville, Garza was not a member of the G. I. Forum. The group selected Texas State Judge E. D. Salinas of Laredo as their appointee. Aware that judicial selections occurred along partisan lines and that Salinas, too, was a Democrat, the G. I. Forum hoped that their nominee would be among the small minority of nonpartisan appointments by President Eisenhower. In an effort to encourage President Eisenhower to appoint Salinas, Dr. Héctor García, founder of the G. I. Forum, wrote the White House. He discussed Salinas's qualifications and the importance of having a Mexican American representative in the judiciary.[7]

Unaware of the G. I. Forum's actions or of Kennerly's proposed nomination, Garza dispatched a letter to Senator Lyndon Johnson in January, 1960, suggesting that he consider Garza's law partner, Gilbert Sharpe, to succeed Allred. Johnson responded that he would carefully consider Sharpe. A few weeks later, because of growing differences between Sharpe and law partner Paul Cunningham, Sharpe left the firm. After thanking Garza for the letter sent on his behalf, Sharpe told Garza he no longer desired the vacant judicial post.[8]

As the 1960 presidential election neared, Everton Kennerly's opportunity to be confirmed for the vacant judgeship weakened, but, unknown to Garza, his own chances strengthened. The Eisenhower administration's efforts were focused on achieving a presidential victory for the Republican vice president, Richard Nixon. Therefore, the administration would not concern itself with any judicial appointments and decided to wait until after the election to nominate Kennerly to fill the judicial vacancy.[9]

With election activity reaching its pinnacle in the fall of 1960, Garza also turned his efforts toward the campaign. Naturally, he pledged his support to his longtime friend, Lyndon Johnson, who was now Senator John F. Kennedy's running mate in the Democratic party. From San Antonio to El Paso, Garza crisscrossed the state to gain votes for the Democratic candidates. He planned rallies in cities throughout Texas and spoke in both English and Spanish to mostly Mexican American crowds. He also traveled to Albuquerque, New Mexico, by request of Johnson. Garza, however, was not a member of the Viva Kennedy campaign, a Hispanic political group backing John F. Kennedy, as the organization was not active in Brownsville. During Garza's travels he enlisted fellow members of civic organizations, such as the Knights of Columbus, to campaign throughout their home regions. He represented Mexican Americans throughout the Southwest, and he inspired this populace to vote for a presidential candidate who seemed to care about them.[10]

Spirited by the support Garza helped garner for the Kennedy-Johnson ticket, Johnson decided to make a campaign stop in the Rio Grande Valley. He first telephoned Garza, who volunteered to host a political rally for Johnson in nearby Harlingen. In October, 1960, Garza served as master of ceremonies for the rally and introduced Johnson to an enthusiastic audience, as a Mexican mariachi band played in the background. While Garza was introducing Johnson, the vice presidential candidate spoke to Congressman Joe Kilgore. They discussed possible candidates to fill Judge Allred's judicial vacancy, and Garza's name quickly surfaced. But before the two politicians could further contemplate Garza as Allred's replacement, the crowd roared loudly beckoning Johnson to take the stage. The discussion stalled for the moment. As he walked toward the podium, Johnson hugged Garza affectionately, in an expression of devotion and gratitude. Johnson then launched into a brief but typically fiery speech. Immediately after the address, secret service agents escorted Johnson to his private airplane. Garza then took Johnson's place on the podium, delivering stirring remarks on the Democratic ticket's behalf. Garza ended the rally by leading the crowd in a roaring cadence of "Lyndon, Lyndon."[11]

When the polls closed in November, 1960, Garza nervously watched the election returns at his home. Tensions peaked in the Garza household as news reports showed a virtual tie between the two candidates. Garza's telephone rang constantly as equally anxious Kennedy-Johnson supporters in Brownsville looked to the local Democratic leader for reassurance of their party's victory. Garza attempted to fall asleep once the midnight hour approached and no election news was forthcoming, but, instead, he stayed up most of the night replaying both losing and winning election scenarios in his mind. The next day he stayed at home, working on legal papers in an effort to block out his concerns about the race. Not until lunchtime did Garza hear a radio report announcing that Nixon conceded defeat. In one of the narrowest margins of victory in the nation's history, Kennedy's electoral vote stood at 300, while Nixon's total was 185. In popular vote, however, the two candidates ran virtually even. Once again Garza's phone rang continuously. Only his complete exhaustion kept him from speaking to the dozens of Democratic supporters eager to discuss the festive victory parties that would monopolize Garza's weekend.[12]

After the Democratic victory, filling the judicial vacancy became a priority for party loyalists in South Texas. One of the first individuals to encourage quick action by the new administration was Cameron County Judge Oscar Dancy. Three and a half weeks after the election, Dancy sent identical letters to Vice President–Elect Johnson and Senator Ralph W. Yarborough, asking them to nominate Garza to fill Allred's federal judicial seat. Dancy wrote that he had heard rumors "that the administration will appoint a Latin to the job." Although he expressed regrets that President Eisenhower did not nominate his son-in-law, Kennerly, to the position, he added, "I do not personally know Judge Salinas of Laredo, but if a Latin is to be appointed, I do not merely recommend but urge that it be the Honorable Reynaldo Garza of this city." Dancy believed that Garza's legal prowess combined with his civic leadership made the Brownsville attorney the most qualified candidate to fill the federal judicial position. The county judge also wrote of the biculturalism of Brownsville and praised Garza as the best example of this unique society where "harmony" existed between Anglos and Mexican Americans.[13]

Dancy's recommendation of Garza was reinforced by the endorsement of another Texas figure, former United States Congressman Lloyd

Bentsen. Garza had aided Bentsen's congressional campaign in 1948, and the two often saw each other during the former congressman's frequent visits to the Rio Grande Valley. Bentsen knew of Garza's outstanding legal reputation in South Texas. Although no longer a congressman in 1960, Bentsen still maintained a powerful political voice, backed by his multimillion-dollar financial services holding company in Houston. Bentsen had also established a lasting relationship with Yarborough and, like Dancy, urged the Senator to support Garza's nomination.[14]

Yarborough, however, was being influenced by the G. I. Forum, which continued to lobby for a Mexican American to fill Allred's vacated judicial post and encouraged the senator to support the appointment of their candidate, E. D. Salinas. As leader of the state's liberal movement through most of the 1950s and 1960s, Yarborough possessed a powerful voice in Congress and was well aware of the influence of Mexican American votes in the political process. Ostensibly, then, he lent his support to Salinas, giving G. I. Forum members confidence that Salinas would become the new federal judge in South Texas.[15]

By January, 1960, in part through the organizational efforts of the G. I. Forum, the new administration resolved to appoint a Mexican American to the federal bench. The decision also undoubtedly stemmed from President Kennedy's desire to support the civil rights movement by rewarding Viva Kennedy clubs in the Southwest with appointments of qualified Hispanics to government posts. Kennedy began promoting civil rights cautiously, however, fearing any rapid acceleration in anti-discrimination measures against minorities would eliminate his critical mass of Democratic voters. President Kennedy worked to balance his large minority electoral base and his Anglo Southern constituency. The latter group strongly opposed civil rights. Remaining politically pragmatic, President Kennedy, nonetheless, promised he would conquer racial discrimination through his executive power.[16]

Executive power granted the president the authority to make federal appointments. But influence also played a part, and no one had stronger influence over Kennedy than his brother Robert, the newly appointed attorney general. RFK began actively recruiting qualified minorities for federal positions in the administration's New Frontier. With the judicial vacancy in the United States District Court, RFK saw an opportunity to further civil rights by appointing the first Mexican American to the judiciary. Working with Assistant Attorney General Ramsey

Clark, RFK searched through the *Martindale-Hubbell* directory, which listed and rated attorneys in the nation, to find qualified attorneys with Spanish surnames.[17]

While RFK and Clark pursued a worthy Spanish-surnamed candidate, Vice President Johnson began unofficial lobbying efforts on Garza's behalf. Johnson had recalled his discussion with Congressman Joe Kilgore during the campaign rally in Harlingen, where the two spoke of Garza's potential appointment to the federal bench. Kilgore, who represented part of the area the new federal judicial appointee would serve, encouraged Johnson's efforts to garner a federal judicial seat for Garza. Kilgore knew of the high respect Garza evoked from his legal peers and was confident that Garza was the most qualified candidate to fill the federal vacancy. Furthermore, the congressman believed legislators involved in the judicial selection would come to the same conclusion once they learned of Garza's outstanding legal reputation.[18]

Johnson was not as convinced as Kilgore that Garza's prominent legal standing alone would influence legislators. Johnson's main concern was Senator Yarborough. In efforts to determine Yarborough's position on Garza, Johnson met with the senator. He found that Yarborough was "not thoroughly pleased" about Garza filling the vacancy. The Senator was torn between two belief systems: he loved the idea of a Mexican American on the federal bench, as it captured the liberal philosophy he embodied, yet, he hated the idea of supporting someone who backed his major nemesis, Allan Shivers. Yarborough was well aware of Garza's past political support of the Texas governor. As Assistant Attorney General Clark explained: "It wasn't personal. Yarborough thought he stood for something and Shivers stood for something quite different. Yarborough naturally assumed that the vast majority of Mexican Americans would support his liberal vision of the future. Here was Garza, who supported Shivers, and it was very hard for Yarborough to reconcile," said Clark. With Johnson's urging, however, Yarborough began contemplating Garza's nomination, yet refused to give the vice president–elect a definitive answer.[19]

By February, 1961, Garza became one of a handful of candidates on RFK's short list to be considered for the federal judicial vacancy. As a fellow Texan, Assistant Attorney General Ramsey Clark learned through his contacts in the state of Garza's outstanding civic and legal reputation. Once Clark informed RFK of Garza's distinguished legal status, the attorney general ordered the FBI to begin a routine background investigation of Garza. During the FBI probe Congressman Kilgore began suspecting that Yarborough was supplying the FBI with misleading information about Garza. In mid-January Kilgore received a call from Vice President Johnson, who told Kilgore that the FBI had sent him transcripts of two political speeches Garza made: one on behalf of President Eisenhower and one on behalf of Allan Shivers, Yarborough's opponent. Kilgore immediately called Garza, first, to inform him that he was being considered to fill Allred's judicial seat and, second, to share the FBI information on him. "If they have two transcripts, then I made both speeches," Garza firmly told Kilgore. "It is a great honor to be thought of, but if I am not chosen because of my past alliances with Eisenhower and Shivers, then God did not want it to be," Garza asserted.[20]

After receiving a favorable report from the FBI, RFK began to contemplate suggesting Garza's name to the president. At first, RFK was hesitant about appointing Garza. He believed that the appointment would strengthen Johnson's position in Texas more than it would aid the president's cause because of Garza's support of Shivers. To the Kennedys, Shivers was seen as a threat to the national Democratic party because of his increasingly Republican stance. Yet, after learning of Garza's decision to support Johnson instead of Shivers in the 1956 battle for control of the Texas party convention, RFK began to favor Garza's appointment. Other factors, such as Garza's high standing with the ABA, finally convinced RFK to back Garza.[21]

A few weeks after Garza spoke to Kilgore, Ramsey Clark telephoned the Brownsville attorney to offer him the nomination to the district court. Clark knew that Garza, like most attorneys in South Texas, held a high regard for deceased Judge James Allred. Clark advised Garza that as Allred's replacement he would have to "fill the shoes of the highly beloved man." Clark then congratulated Garza and explained to the prospective nominee that various Texas leaders had praised Garza as an outstanding attorney and the best legal mind to replace Allred. Garza thanked Clark for his praises and the recommendation of others. He then shared with Clark his need to discuss the matter with his family and law partners and told him he would telephone back within the week.[22]

Many thoughts raced through Garza's mind as he contemplated Clark's proposal. Attaining an appointment on the federal bench crossed most attorneys' minds at least once. Garza was no different and had even turned down a state judgeship to hold out hope for a position on the federal judiciary. Becoming a federal judge, however, meant many personal changes. Garza thought about possibly moving to a city with a larger court docket. He knew that neither he nor Bertha would find it easy to leave their bicultural hometown. Then he considered financial matters. As a father of four, his salary sufficiently supported his family, but the salary of a federal judge in 1961, at $22,500, was considerably less. He would have to sell most of his small land holdings and drive a less expensive automobile so as to afford his children's college tuition. He first shared his thoughts with Bertha. She enthusiastically congratulated him on the great honor and encouraged him to follow his long-standing goal of becoming a federal judge. She assured him the family would learn to manage on the lower income. Heartened by his conversation with Bertha, the deeply religious man conferred with his pastor, Reverend Frank Walker. Garza outlined his options, and Walker told him he would support any decision he made. Garza then discussed his nomination with his brothers and law partners, who encouraged him to accept the nomination.[23]

While deliberating the decision, Garza also received a call from Robert Kennedy. Like Lyndon Johnson, Kennedy was intent on having Garza fill the judicial position. Although Johnson and Kennedy disagreed on most matters, appointing Garza to the United States District Court was one matter in which they found harmony.[24] Their concurrence undoubtedly played a major factor in influencing President Kennedy to consider Garza.

During their conversation, RFK asked Garza if he had made a decision about the appointment. Sensing Garza's uncertainty, the attorney general urged him to accept the nomination. Acknowledging Garza's efforts on behalf of other Texans for the position, RFK told Garza, "The man doesn't seek the job, the job seeks the man." With such encouragement, Garza immediately replied that he would accept. Extremely pleased, RFK invited Garza to Washington, D.C., to meet with President Kennedy. The two then confirmed an upcoming date for Garza's visit.[25]

A few weeks later the American Bar Association reviewed Garza's qualifications and submitted their report to RFK. "The ABA was strong for Garza," recalled Clark. After the American Bar Association's review, RFK issued a formal letter to President Kennedy in which he briefly described Garza's life and accomplishments and voiced his recommendation of the candidate. President Kennedy decided he would officially nominate Garza after meeting with him at the White House.[26]

On March 23, 1961, three weeks after speaking to Robert Kennedy, Garza arrived in Washington, D.C. As threatening rain clouds loomed overhead, Garza hailed a taxi to transport him to his hotel. Vice President Johnson's secretary had made reservations for Garza at the historic Hay-Adams Hotel, located directly in front of the White House. While the cab weaved through the downtown streets toward the hotel, Garza admired the monuments, memorials, and architecture that characterized the nation's capitol. It was Garza's first time in Washington, D.C., and he soaked in the historic surroundings.[27]

After settling into his hotel room, Garza first called Bertha to inform her of his safe arrival. He then telephoned the vice president to finalize his plans. Johnson was extremely busy with a foreign affairs matter, so he suggested that Garza first speak to Assistant Attorney General Clark. Clark invited the prospective nominee to dinner. Garza was instantly charmed with Clark, a low-key, candid man with an unassuming nature. They were similar in many ways. Both believed in devotion to American institutions and blended their idealism with a love of country. "I found out he was a beautiful man, with dignity," recalled Clark. "Everyone agreed he was a good lawyer. And if you're not a good lawyer, you can't be a good judge." The two spent most of the evening discussing their native state of Texas.[28]

The next day Garza was to be escorted to the White House by a vice presidential driver. As Garza stood by the hotel entrance, he noticed the hustle of Washington politicians moving at a frantic pace. For years the Hay-Adams Hotel had been the gathering place for the nation's congressmen and senators. Lobbyists and congressional aides also flocked to the hotel, creating a burst of nervous energy that gripped all that stood around, including Garza. Taking a moment in the lobby allowed Garza time to reflect on his situation. He was about to meet the president of the United States. He began to pace nervously and puff briskly on a cigarette until he caught sight of a large black limousine. Garza walked toward the limousine, introduced himself to the driver, then settled into the black leather seat for the short ride to the White House.[29]

Once Garza arrived at the White House, Johnson's secretary escorted him to the vice presidential office. As he walked past the massive pillars, Garza glanced at the distinctive paintings that adorned the walls and the crystal chandeliers hanging from the ceilings. Before entering Johnson's office, Garza quickly disposed of his cigarette. The vice president waved hello to Garza as he spoke on the telephone to a foreign leader. Within a few minutes, Johnson hung up the telephone and asked Garza whether he liked his accommodations. In dealing with others, Johnson used what friends came to call "the treatment." His imposing physical stature overpowered people, and he leaned into them as dozens of sentences spewed from his mouth. Garza experienced "the treatment" in Johnson's office that day, as the White House photographer captured the scene. Sensing Garza's nervousness at meeting the president, Johnson kidded Garza about the Brownsville politico's past association with the Democrats for Eisenhower. "You must not mention your association [with Eisenhower] to the Kennedys," Johnson sternly warned, then flashed one of his Texas-sized smiles and told Garza it was time to meet the president.[30]

At 3:30 P.M. Johnson and two Secret Service agents escorted Garza to meet President Kennedy and Robert Kennedy. The president's secretary showed the four men to Kennedy's office. When they arrived, Kennedy and RFK rose simultaneously. Johnson introduced Garza to the two men, then President Kennedy requested everyone but RFK, Johnson, and Garza to leave his office. The group spoke for about half an hour, until Kennedy's secretary knocked on the door to remind the president of an afternoon meeting. As President Kennedy shook Garza's hand, he told Garza that he thought the appointment, his first as president, would help promote other Mexican Americans in the country. Garza smiled at the president, hoping to assure Kennedy he would not let him down. The president then called in his press secretary, Pierre Salinger, who photographed Garza and Kennedy in the Oval Office. A few hours later, the president officially nominated Garza to fill the United States District Court judicial seat.[31]

After leaving the Oval Office, Johnson and Garza made plans to meet later that evening. In the interim, Garza had planned on spending time in Congressman Joe Kilgore's office. As he walked outside of the White House with a Johnson aide, however, the two men saw FBI Director J. Edgar Hoover approaching. The aide introduced Garza to Hoover, who was about to deliver the federal judicial nominee's report to President Kennedy. Hoover told Garza that FBI agents had not found a single piece of negative information about him and then allowed Garza to glimpse at his record. Garza smiled as he read the glowing tributes by fellow attorneys, judges, and past university professors. After thanking Hoover, Garza, beaming with pride and happiness, left the White House to meet with Kilgore.[32]

Kilgore's office was in the Old House Office Building, which housed congressional offices; it was later renamed the Cannon House Office Building. Kilgore's administrative assistant, Celia Hare Martin, greeted Garza enthusiastically as he entered. Martin and Garza had known each other more than ten years, ever since Martin had worked as assistant for Kilgore's predecessor, Lloyd Bentsen. Martin immediately buzzed Kilgore's office, and the congressman rose to greet Garza at the door. Garza had established a close relationship with every United States congressman from his district since his college years, and Kilgore was no exception. The two men had maintained their friendship largely based on their mutual admiration for their common alma mater, the University of Texas at Austin, and its Longhorn football team. Kilgore escorted Garza back to his office, where Garza recounted his meeting with the president.[33]

After Kilgore and Garza had conversed for a few hours, Johnson telephoned from the White House to say that his driver would pick up Garza later that evening. Just before leaving his office to meet with Garza, Johnson also placed a call to Assistant Attorney General Ramsey Clark's White House office, where Robert Kennedy and Clark were meeting. Johnson told the men that he wanted to chat and that he would pick them up on his way to his office in the Capitol. "I think what he wanted us to do was to go by and pay our respects," stated Clark.[34]

As the Washington, D.C., skies opened up to a heavy downpour, Johnson, RFK, and Clark rode to Kilgore's office where Garza joined them. The men returned to Johnson's spacious office, often termed the Taj Mahal because of its grand size and regal, almost gaudy, style. Known as the "exclusive lair of the powerful," the Taj Mahal had been Johnson's office as majority leader and remained his suite even after his departure from the Senate. Out of respect for Johnson, the new majority leader and Johnson's protégé, Mike Mansfield, graciously allowed Johnson to keep the office.[35]

RFK, Clark, and Garza walked into the plush, royal green and gold office and took their seats on Johnson's elegant gold-trimmed couch to begin an entertaining evening. Earlier that day, Johnson had arranged for food for his guests, and a small feast was now set on one of the office's grand tables. Poised at his desk and illuminated like a religious figure by two overhead spot lamps, Johnson began telling humorous anecdotes about his relationship with Garza. Garza, with his keen wit, shared his own memories of bygone days. As Johnson and Kennedy did not get along well, the attorney general soon excused himself from the office.[36]

But the vice president was in an especially effusive mood that evening, and he soon began to monopolize the conversation, espousing his hopes for Garza on the bench. Johnson spoke of the need for Garza to become an exalted federal judge explaining, "Reynaldo, I want you to be such a great judge that when you walk down the streets of Brownsville, all the Mexican American boys will think you're the second coming of the Lord." Clark noticed that Garza's eyes became teary and knew that the Brownsville native now felt the impact of his trailblazing appointment to the federal judiciary. "When Johnson came on strong it was awesome, and he came on strong that night as if he could touch your soul in a way that was indelible," stated Clark.[37]

After nearly five hours, the group decided to close their discussions. Johnson's driver took Clark back to the White House and then dropped Garza at the hotel. Garza slept only a few hours, as the excitement of the day's events kept him awake. The next morning, as he was about to hail a cab to the airport, he saw Johnson's limousine coming towards him. Johnson was returning to the White House from an early morning meeting and, after seeing Garza leave the hotel, decided to give his old friend a ride to the airport. During the short ride Johnson told Garza he looked forward to visiting with him when Garza returned for his confirmation hearings. As the car reached the airport, Garza expressed his gratitude to Johnson and wished him well. Half an hour later, after riding in the vice presidential limousine in Washington, D.C., Garza was on his way back to Texas.[38]

By the time Garza arrived in Brownsville, news of his prospective appointment to the federal bench had already reached fellow citizens. As he stepped in his front door, congratulatory flowers and wires inundated him. The telephone rang constantly with well-wishers throughout the state. News reporters converged on the Garza family, seeking more information on President Kennedy's nominee. Photographers snapped dozens of pictures of the Garzas. Mementos of Garza's World War II days and his service to the Brownsville community were found by reporters, who were aided by Bertha's meticulously organized scrapbook.[39]

Congratulatory letters not only filled the forty-five-year-old judicial nominee's home but also deluged the White House. Many Texans voiced their approval of Kennedy's nominee by sending letters to the president. One Texas businessman writing to President Kennedy stated that by appointing Garza "you will obtain a magnanimous ally who will dignify himself in the scales of justice and gain for your administration our [Mexican Americans'] wholehearted support." Other letters echoed similar sentiments, reflecting heartfelt pride felt by Mexican Americans because of Garza's selection.[40] For many members of his ethnic group who knew or were familiar with the federal judicial nominee, Garza became an example of the inroads Mexican Americans could make in Anglo society.

Even Mexican Americans in the Rio Grande Valley who were unaccustomed to discrimination viewed Garza's appointment to the federal bench as a groundbreaking opportunity for their minority group. Lino Pérez, a postmaster in the Rio Grande Valley, exclaimed when he learned of Garza's selection, "Finally, we have justice." By 1961 Anglos still continued their positions as power brokers in Mexican American communities; they were the judges, sheriffs, and mayors.[41] Given this climate, it was understandable that Mexican Americans saw Garza as their hope for equality as well as for status and recognition.

The loudest accolades occurred in Brownsville, a city greatly influenced by the status of its native son. Garza was the first federal judicial nominee to have an official residence in Brownsville. A keen reporter observed, "It was almost if the president was appointing a part of Brownsville itself."[42] As a small town, Brownsville rarely gained recognition, except during tragic events such as natural disasters. By becoming one of four other federal judges in the Southern District of Texas, Garza gave his hometown a national spotlight.

Ironically, the only opposition to Garza's nomination came from members of the G. I. Forum. After Kennedy selected Garza as his nominee and ignored G. I. Forum candidate E. D. Salinas, activist Mexican Americans felt betrayed. Because Garza had supported Eisenhower's presidential bid, this largely Democratic organization presumed Garza held no allegiance to their party. The group believed that Kennedy had ignored their advice and had based his decision largely on the Anglo stereotype—all Mexicans are alike. These individuals undoubtedly viewed Garza as an assimilated Mexican American, who possessed no loyalty to his Mexican roots. Founding G. I. Forum member Dr. García, however, broke with his ranks and defended Garza's nomination.[43] He undoubtedly sensed Salinas's chances to be appointed were over and realized the importance of backing Garza.

Garza returned to Washington, D.C., on April 11, 1961, one day before he was to appear before the Senate judiciary committee. He arrived in the late afternoon, checked into his hotel room, then met with Congressman Kilgore. After chatting for a few hours with Kilgore, Garza returned to his hotel room, neatly set out his suit for the senate hearing and retired to bed. At 9 A.M. on April 12, Garza met one last time with Johnson, who visited the judicial candidate in his hotel while Garza nervously ate a small breakfast. The vice president delivered a moving oratory much like the one he gave a month before during Garza's first visit to Washington, D.C.[44]

By the morning of the inquiry, Senator Yarborough had still abstained from openly pledging his support for Garza. Traditionally, during confirmation hearings, a United States senator from the nominee's home state walks ceremonially beside the judicial candidate into the Senate judiciary committee meeting room. Since the junior senator from Texas, William Blakely, was presiding over the hearing, he could not escort Garza. Since the other senator, Yarborough, still refused to voice his approval of Garza's nomination, the nominee asked Kilgore to accompany him. As Garza and Kilgore approached the committee meeting room, Yarborough suddenly came running up behind them. The senator abruptly took Garza by the arm, while a stunned Kilgore followed behind.[45] Yarborough had waited until the last possible moment to change his mind regarding his support for Garza.

At 10:35 A.M. Senator Blakely began the hearing with two taps of his gavel. The two other committee members, Senators James Eastland and Kenneth Keating, sat beside Blakely. After eloquently praising Garza, Blakely officially introduced Senator Yarborough to the committee. Yarborough gave an equally laudatory statement, giving credit to Cameron County Judge Oscar Dancy for his decision to support Garza. "Judge Oscar Dancy . . . gave one of the highest accolades I have ever heard an attorney receive," Yarborough stated. He also added that Garza's nomination was unique because not a single person attempted to block it. In closing, Yarborough stated that Judge Allred's family was "highly pleased" with Garza's nomination. Praises also followed from United States representatives from Texas, Kilgore and John Young. Once Young completed his statement, the three committee senators, Blakely,

Eastland, and Keating, began querying Garza. Most of the questions focused on Garza's legal career and political activities. At 10:50 A.M. Senator Blakely adjourned the hearing, and Garza returned to his hotel.[46]

As Garza nervously awaited the results of the committee hearing, he contemplated returning to Brownsville. Since deliberations usually lasted a few days, Garza wanted to be with his family, instead of in a hotel room, when he heard the decision. As he was about to inquire about travel reservations to Brownsville, Johnson telephoned Garza. "They've decided," Johnson said and cheerfully informed him that the Senate had confirmed his nomination. Garza immediately called Bertha to tell her the good news. She was jubilant. As he hung up, Garza received a call from Deputy Attorney General Byron White, who a year later would become a Supreme Court justice. White congratulated Garza and told him that he was preparing Garza's official commission to the judiciary. Garza asked White to send the document to Brownsville, then the new federal judge took an afternoon flight back home to Texas. He received the commission three days later, officially marking his position as the first Mexican American federal judge in the nation.[47]

The next few weeks were a time of great preparation and celebration for Garza. After receiving his commission, Garza followed the required judicial obligations which required that he not practice law while serving as a justice or judge. He conferred with his law partners, and together they reached an amiable and equitable dissolution of the partnership. He also composed a letter to his former clients, informing them of their need to decide if they wished to remain clients of the firm, and he further informed both his partners and his clients that ethical guidelines required that he recuse himself from any cases related to them for at least the next three years.[48]

For Garza the letter to his clients signaled the final chapter of his practice. He thought about the first time he contemplated a legal career as a young boy. He smiled, remembering his childhood. He would never forget the more than twenty years spent as an attorney. He felt great pleasure in finding intricate legal details that led him to a winning case and delighted in making a compelling closing statement that would motivate juries to find for his client. As Garza finished signing the letters to his clients, he paused, reflected, and then in humility, he bowed his head and prayed.[49]

Garza now began calling friends and associates in search of recommendations for a court staff. The Southern District of Texas court faced a heavy backlog after Judge Allred's death. With only four judges assigned to the vast area the court represented and with Allred's seat vacated for close to two years, three judges had been juggling the massive docket. Aware of the strain on the court, Garza planned to begin working a few days after his installation. In mid-April, Garza hired his former law firm secretary, Josephine Sizelan, as his office assistant. Sizelan, steadfastly loyal to Garza, had been a motherly figure in the firm's office. Brownsville attorneys affectionately called her Mama Sizelan. Garza then hired Pete Bouis as his bailiff. Bouis, a man in his sixties at the time, would manage many aspects of the daily court procedures. Garza filled the four remaining positions with Allred's former court personnel.[50]

The Constitution also allotted Garza one law clerk, whose responsibilities included preparatory research and decision drafting. Federal judges usually selected law clerks from the recent crop of newly graduated law students at or near the top of their class; they typically served a one- or two-year term. Garza followed this established practice and hired Graham McCullough, a Rio Grande Valley native and recent law school graduate of Garza's alma mater.[51]

While Garza readied himself for the federal bench, the Cameron County Bar Association arranged Garza's installation and luncheon. The events took place on April 29, 1961, at the Fort Brown Auditorium, just two blocks from Garza's birth home. More than five hundred people attended the opening installation ceremonies. Major Texas newspapers covered the event, reporting it was the largest turnout ever accorded a federal judge in Texas. State judges, members of the Cameron County Bar, and various civic and political leaders from Texas and Mexico were also present. United States Representative Joe Kilgore and Senator William Blakely flew in from Washington, D.C., for the occasion. The three other judges from the Southern District also attended. Each one had been appointed by three different presidents: Chief Judge Allan B. Hannay, an appointee of President Franklin D. Roosevelt; Judge Ben C. Connally, an appointee of President Harry S. Truman; and Judge Joe Ingraham, an appointee of President Dwight D. Eisenhower.[52]

Although President Kennedy, Vice President Johnson, and Attorney General Robert F. Kennedy could not attend the ceremony because of the Cuban crisis, which had erupted just one week before the installation, and the war in Laos, they sent congratulatory wires to Garza. The powerful Speaker of the House Sam Rayburn of Texas and Governor Price Daniel also wired their congratulations.[53]

At the installation distinguished jurists throughout Texas praised Garza. Attorney Leon Jaworski of Houston, then a member of the federal judiciary committee of the American Bar Association, had led the investigation of Garza's career. Jaworski stated: "We found that his conduct has been above reproach, that he had held more than one position of trust and honor in his community. . . . His character was marked by integrity and industry." After numerous other speeches Chief Judge Hannay performed the swearing-in ceremony.[54]

After the oath of office, Garza introduced his wife Bertha, his brothers and sisters, their families, and his young children to the cheering crowd. "It was a thrilling and exhilarating occasion that I will never forget. The entire family sat in the front row, and he recognized us all," said Garza's nephew, Raul Besteiro, who later became superintendent of public schools in Brownsville. Garza delivered a brief but emotional speech, outlining his goals and thanking his many supporters. He also singled out Judge Dancy and Brownsville pastor Frank Walker as longtime friends who had contributed to his position. Throughout his moving address, Garza repeatedly thanked God for his appointment to the federal judiciary. As he concluded his remarks, the entire audience rose to applaud the newly installed federal judge.[55]

In the spring of 1961 the concerted efforts of Mexican American political organizations, such as the G. I. Forum, opened the doors to Mexican American involvement in government affairs. Garza's ascendance to the federal judiciary made him the first to pass through an opening previously blocked to Mexican Americans. He was the right Mexican American appointee for these times, and the future of other Mexican American federal appointments would now depend on Garza's actions on the United States District Court.

CHAPTER 6

Early Years on the Bench
1961–63

By 1961, at the age of forty-five, Garza had reached a level occupied by few Americans and no other Mexican American. Individuals and groups perceived a Mexican American federal judge as an interloper, scrutinized Garza's actions, and sought fodder to justify their discriminatory beliefs.[1] This sense of heightened scrutiny concerned, but did not consume, Garza. The new appointee felt that by becoming an effective jurist he would not only pacify detractors but also encourage the appointment of other qualified Mexican Americans to the federal bench.

Garza's rise to prominence in the 1960s occurred when many Mexican Americans found themselves stigmatized as second-class citizens throughout some parts of the United States. Despite a few regions, such as New Mexico, where Mexican American participation in the sociopolitical process had occurred for decades, the Anglo majority continued to create legal and social barriers for Mexican Americans, excluding them from active participation in society. Although President Kennedy emphasized the "equality of treatment" for all Americans, his statement reflected a goal, not the reality.[2]

The racial bias found throughout the United States, especially in the South, generally evaded Brownsville, El Paso, and Laredo. In those three border cities, class rather than ethnicity continued to dictate relations. Even in these largely Mexican American populated areas, however, Anglos retained dominion over most facets of economic, social, and political life. In Brownsville, for example, Anglos constituted the majority of members in elite social activities, such as the Debutante Ball, and political associations, such as the Brownsville Independent School District Board. With a total population of 48,000, of which approximately 44,000 were Mexican Americans, the majority of citizens in Brownsville still found themselves subject to Anglo control.[3]

Garza's life, however, was in contrast to the average Brownsville native, and even before he presided over his first case, his judicial position inspired others. "It is much easier to imagine the future if you have seen someone who has already been there and done that. I think the pioneering that he did not only opened doors but also opened dreams, and possibilities, and options," claimed Juliet García, a Brownsville public school junior high student in 1961, who went on to become the first Mexican American woman president of a university. Garza not only motivated Brownsville's youth but also a few professional attorneys in the city. "He was on the cutting edge and served as a role model for many who would some day aspire to become federal judges," remarked Federico Peña, who was schooled in Brownsville, clerked in the city in the 1960s, and who later became United States transportation secretary. "They saw the trail that he blazed, and it provided them with inspiration," Peña added.[4]

For each federal district court, the United States Congress had designated certain regions where district judges heard cases. In the Southern District of Texas, these regions included Brownsville, Corpus Christi, Galveston, Houston, Laredo, and Victoria. Like his predecessor, James Allred, Garza principally was in charge of the Brownsville and Corpus Christi docket but would also hear cases in Laredo and Victoria. Occasionally, Chief District Judge Allan Hannay could assign Garza to district courts in Houston and El Paso. With regard to El Paso, located in the Western District of Texas, Garza could sit by designation to help alleviate the West Texas docket. Federal district courts often exchanged judges with other district courts when heavy dockets necessitated additional personnel.[5]

In April, 1961, under the watchful eyes of many observers, Garza embarked on his new career. His first official duty as a federal judge occurred in Victoria, Texas, a small town 125 miles north of Brownsville. Victoria citizens had invited him to inaugurate the new federal courthouse. From Brownsville, Garza drove to Houston to keep an important meeting with fellow district court judge, Joe Ingraham. Because United States federal judges often plunged into their duties with little official training to explain their tasks, Ingraham had suggested that the newly appointed judge confer with him regarding the responsibilities of the federal district bench. They met in Ingraham's chambers. After outlining a typical judicial schedule, Ingraham gave the new appointee a few pointers and stressed most of all the importance of quickly establishing authority in the courtroom.[6]

Every new federal judge, regardless of background, went through a period of adjustment. Garza was no exception. Most new appointees were well versed with such common law issues as torts and contracts. Yet, new federal judges were not as familiar with more esoteric federal fields, such as patent and admiralty law. Only experience could teach a new judge methods of calmly presiding over a lawsuit and mediating in the occasionally caustic legal battles between attorneys.[7]

Garza's experience came immediately as a result of the heavy court docket in South Texas. Because of the backlogged district caseload, Chief Judge Hannay assigned Garza cases to hear in Corpus Christi only two days after the new judge had met with Ingraham. Corpus Christi, a port town north of Brownsville, contained a substantial Mexican American population. As such, its regional culture was similar to that of Garza's hometown. Unlike Brownsville, however, Corpus Christi maintained remnants of institutionalized discrimination against Mexican Americans. A mid-1960s study demonstrated that rigid segregation practices against Mexican Americans prevailed in nine Texas cities. Among those cities, Corpus Christi ranked ahead, in descending order of magnitude, of all other major Texas cities.[8]

Garza drove into the ethnically hostile climate of Corpus Christi; he was principally focused on clearing the area's docket. He felt a tinge of nervous energy, keenly aware that his first impression would set the tone for this and future judicial proceedings in the city. Two years prior to Garza's trip, the federal district court had ceased hearing cases in Corpus Christi. After Garza's predecessor, James Allred, died while holding court in the city in 1959, none of the three other district judges could spare time to travel to the region. Naturally, local attorneys were eager both to begin trying cases and to meet the new judge. Tensions peaked when Garza and his law clerk, Graham McCullough, arrived at the courthouse an hour late, delayed by an unexpected Gulf Coast storm.[9]

As Garza walked up the courthouse steps and approached the crowd gathered by the courtroom, he cordially introduced himself to the Corpus Christi attorneys. After escorting the group into the court-room, he addressed them briefly, then announced that he expected them to know the law and the facts of a case. He emphasized his de-sire for attorneys to abstain from making frivolous motions and to seek to settle outside the court before pursuing a trial. Determined to ad-judicate the growing court backlog, he scheduled the first trial to begin two days later. Garza then inspected his chambers and the courthouse facilities. For the remainder of the afternoon and the following day, Garza and McCullough studied the records and briefs for each case in preparation for Garza's first trial.[10]

Forty-eight hours after Garza arrived in Corpus Christi, the local bailiff opened the new judge's first session on the bench with a re-sounding "Oyez, oyez." Garza appeared confident as he walked from his chambers toward the bench. For most of the day and the rest of the week, Garza sat back quietly, taking in attorneys' arguments. By his second week in Corpus Christi, he had gained an even higher degree of confidence and began engaging himself in the courtroom discussions. While the attorneys argued their cases, Garza occasionally interrupted to ask pointed questions. He soon realized that the booming voice that he so skillfully used as an attorney was again working in his favor to control the courtroom. Two weeks into Garza's first trial, Corpus Christi attorneys were praising the new judge's courtroom skills.[11]

Most of the praises were aimed at Garza's ability to issue immedi-ate rulings from the bench. When presiding over a trial, judges must often quickly issue rulings that grant or deny motions, determine ad-missibility of evidence, and, in general, keep the proceedings running smoothly. Rather than being deterred by the pressure to issue on-the-spot rulings, Garza was encouraged, and Corpus Christi attorneys re-peatedly voiced their admiration of his skill.[12]

After two weeks in Corpus Christi, Garza was anxious to spend the weekend with his wife and children; he was not yet accustomed to the long separation. Despite being exhausted from the strain of his first time on the bench and his arduous road travels, Garza and the entire family drove to nearby Harlingen that weekend to attend a track meet for eldest son, Rey. The eighteen-year-old was one of the top athletes at his private Catholic high school, Saint Joseph's Academy. Garza and Bertha spent many weekends driving their children—thirteen-year-old David, eight-year-old Nacho, and three-year-old Bertita—throughout the Rio Grande Valley and Texas to attend Rey's out-of-town varsity athletic events. Garza treasured these family moments and vowed to continue spending time with his family throughout his tenure on the federal bench.[13]

Just as he had with his family, Garza also developed a close relationship with his judicial staff. After his first few months as federal judge, Garza had come to know most of the courthouse members personally. He knew the names of each staff member's spouse and children and often invited them to Garza family gatherings. He built an especially close and affectionate relationship with his law clerk, Graham McCullough. Both McCullough and his wife regularly visited the Garza household for cocktails or dinner, so when the news was announced that McCullough's wife was expecting a baby, both families celebrated.[14]

Garza's interest in his staff was returned in personal loyalty. Aware that each of their actions reflected on Garza, every member was motivated by personal pride and respect to excel. The staff's relationship with Garza took on a paternalistic tone. At times, when the staff made mistakes, Garza reprimanded those at fault. But if he pointed out specific deficiencies, he also helped them seek solutions. His warm, yet stern, management style produced positive results in his courtroom.[15]

Garza's staff was not the only group who revered the new federal judge. South Texans, especially area attorneys, showered Garza with adulation. Griffin Bell, a United States Court of Appeals judge in 1961 and later attorney general under President Jimmy Carter, described Garza's position in South Texas as that of a "country baron." Bell attributed Garza's status to the small number of federal judges in South Texas: "Being the only federal judge in the area was a huge thing; you were adored. There were only a few judges like that, and he [Garza] was one."[16] With the sole power to adjudicate federal laws throughout South Texas, Garza quickly became a renowned regional figure.

Garza's recognition soon achieved for him another milestone; he became the first Mexican American selected by the Texas State Bar Association to the Latin American law committee.[17] Although bar association members chartered the committee to promote communications between legal entities in Latin America and the United States, the group had remained composed solely of Anglos. Garza's stature as a federal judge had undoubtedly provided him with sufficient visibility to warrant this selection, a position typically unavailable to Mexican Americans involved in the legal field.

But such visibility had its price. During Garza's many discussions with the vice president, Johnson often warned him that as a Mexican American on the federal bench, some individuals would anticipate judicial errors. Legal observers had, in fact, questioned whether Garza would follow Constitutional or religious precedents when administering justice. Also drawing scrutiny was the large number of illegal immigration cases in Garza's docket, and critics worried that Garza might grant Mexican nationals preferential treatment in court. And just as with President Kennedy, some even speculated whether Garza's Catholicism meant the pope would direct his decisions. Aware of these concerns, Attorney General Robert F. Kennedy followed Garza's career during the new federal judge's first few months on the bench.[18]

Garza was concerned, however, with what he considered a more immediate problem—the deteriorating condition of the Brownsville courthouse. To him, the existing court facilities seemed inadequate for efficient office operations, and they progressively began to interfere with his ability to adjudicate. Brownsville's existing courthouse, built in 1933, served as a way station for judges visiting the city, but no law library existed, and the judge's chambers, clerk's quarters, and secretary's office could not support a full case docket.[19]

Garza felt the judicial way station must be transformed into a full-scale outpost. Accordingly, he sought and was granted approval to establish a functional law library and expand the existing chambers. Expansion costs remained relatively inexpensive because the actual court and the judge's chambers occupied only one-half of the second floor of the four-story federal building. The post office and the General Services Administration border station took up the remaining area. By taking office space from the other government groups in the building and constructing a legal library, the Brownsville facility became as efficient as other courts in the district.[20]

With the improvement of the courthouse facilities, Garza now turned his focus toward a larger dilemma, district court operations. After his first six months as judge, Garza had discovered that the district's operational infrastructure was not efficient. The district's problems stemmed primarily from numbers: too many cases, too vast a geo-graphic area, and too few judges. Thousands of civil and criminal cases filled the court's docket.[21] The district covered a rapidly growing area, which exacerbated the crowded conditions. Comprising the district was the entire Texas Gulf Coast, except for Jefferson County, but including Houston and Galveston, and the region southeast of Austin and west of Laredo, on the Rio Grande. The paucity of judges further compounded the court's problems, since by the 1960s the United States Congress had established only four permanent judges for the district. Although visiting judges occasionally assisted in reducing docket delay, the four permanent judges remained overburdened.

Aware that he could do little to lessen the number of court cases, reduce the district's territory, or increase the number of judges, Garza sought to resolve one of the docket's major difficulties—illegal immi-gration. Illegal immigration continued at a feverish pace in the 1950s and 1960s. Although agricultural labor shortages in Texas had created new opportunity for unskilled laborers, most of whom arrived illegally from Mexico, it also caused a flood of Mexican nationals into Texas border cities in search of work. To thwart the problems caused by the overflow, United States Border Patrol officers arrested and jailed hun-dreds of illegal aliens, who then remained prisoners for prolonged periods of time because of the federal district court backlog.[22]

As illegal aliens filled the jails, crowded, cramped conditions arose, requiring frequent and immediate court action in South Texas. In an earlier congressional hearing focusing on the issue, Garza's longtime friend and former congressman, Lloyd Bentsen, described Rio Grande Valley jails: "I have seen many of our small cells, say ten by twelve feet, with as many as ten or twelve men housed in them." In addition to humanitarian concerns, the issue drew considerable attention because of the high expense related to housing prisoners. The area's limited financial resources could not meet these costs.[23]

Motivated by the numerous ill effects of jailing illegal aliens, Garza focused his efforts on an effective adjudication program termed "jail delivery days." Once a month, Garza requested that federal marshals deliver all jailed illegal aliens in Brownsville to the federal courthouse. The illegal aliens were tried en masse, instead of individually, as was the traditional practice. Ninety percent of the aliens pleaded guilty, served light sentences, and then were deported. In this manner, Garza effi-ciently relieved one of the major strains on the district's judicial docket and lessened the negative humanitarian and economic impact of pro-longed imprisonment. Garza's jail delivery days became so successful that he established a reputation for his speedy resolution to the illegal immigrant problem. Ramsey Clark and Robert Kennedy delighted in hearing stories of Garza's skillful treatment of the illegal aliens. Both knew that the alien issue hindered the Southern District of Texas court and were pleased at Garza's innovative approach to the problem.[24]

In October, 1961, the United States Congress lessened Garza's heavy docket pressures by creating a fifth judgeship in the Southern District. Historically, the creation of more judgeships was the remedy for crowded dockets. With Garza's appointment to the court, President Kennedy swayed from the established practice of nominating residents of Houston to the Southern District of Texas Court. But in September, 1961, Kennedy followed the old pattern and nominated a Houstonian, James L. Noel, Jr., who was approved by the Senate.[25]

With Noel's appointment, the court could divide the caseload five ways, easing Garza's work and allowing him more time from incessant judicial pressures. Since he had first stepped onto the federal bench six months before, Garza had traveled to hear cases almost every two weeks. Noel's appointment would slightly decrease Garza's travel. The timing was perfect for Garza, since soon after he attended Noel's investiture ceremony, Bertha learned she was pregnant with their fifth child. Less time spent traveling would afford Garza more time to spend with his still growing family.[26]

The free time also allowed Garza to return to one of his favorite sports, hunting. An avid hunter since his early teens, Garza began week-end hunting excursions with his sons and a few of his friends, including fellow judge, Ben Connally. Garza's favorite hunting spot was the massive King Ranch, located one hundred and thirty miles north of Brownsville. For Garza, this mammoth area allowed him to escape daily pressures and find solace in the outdoors. But because of Garza's absorbing judicial schedule, hunting trips could only last a single day, Saturday. Garza and his hunting partners would spend the daylight hours hunting and return home by early evening. Back in Brownsville, the Garza family would dine together on venison, along with many of Garza's favorite accompaniments, such as tamales and Mexican rice. After dinner Garza frequently returned to his chambers for a few hours of preparation for his upcoming Monday docket.[27]

On other free weekends and evenings, the Garzas socialized. Prior to his appointment, Garza and his wife had maintained a brisk social life in Brownsville. But now, after Garza's investiture, his social calendar swelled with new activities throughout the Rio Grande Valley. Bertha accompanied her husband to the majority of his engagements, complementing his charismatic personality with her gregarious disposition. The couple seldom tired of their entertainment duties and thoroughly enjoyed their public life.[28]

On May 7, 1962, Bertha gave birth to their last child, a daughter named Monica. The time had come for Garza and Bertha to find a larger home. Not finding a suitable replacement in the still developing Brownsville area, Garza took out a mortgage in a new subdivision, Rio Viejo. Located off one of the city's main streets, Palm Boulevard, Rio Viejo was only a ten-minute car ride from Garza's chambers at the Brownsville Federal Courthouse.[29] Garza worked with the subdivision's primary builder on a set of plans that Garza and Bertha agreed upon. Their two-story house took six months to build.

As soon as the major construction was completed, the Garzas moved into their new home. Bertha took on the task of decorating the residence and filled it with many family heirlooms. Given the family's strong religious beliefs, Bertha decorated the walls with crucifixes and paintings of Jesus and the Virgin Mary as well as family pictures and many of Garza's framed awards. Over the fireplace, Garza mounted his prize buck captured at the King Ranch. Since the subdivision was newly developed, there were only two homes within sight of the Garza home. Developers planned to build the new campus of St. Joseph's Academy, a private Catholic junior high and high school directly behind the Garza house. Before construction began on the academy, however, out of respect for the city's most prominent citizen, developers asked Garza for his permission to build the facility. Long a supporter of the school that two of his sons were attending, Garza readily agreed to the construction.[30]

As Garza approached his third year as federal judge, he began receiving several tributes. In February, 1963, Garza traveled to Laredo for the city's annual George Washington celebration, where city leaders designated Garza as Mr. South Texas, a title conferred each year by Laredo residents on a notable Texan. Much like Brownsville's Charro Days, the Laredo celebration included both Mexican- and American-themed events, such as parades, costume balls, and dinners. For the Garza children, the highlight of the revelry was riding a brightly adorned

Texas-sized float as more than 100,000 spectators lined the streets. The George Washington Celebration became an annual tradition for the Garza family, and for many years to come they returned as honored guests.[31]

One month after Laredo city leaders distinguished Garza as Mr. South Texas, Governor John Connally appointed him to the Committee of Twenty-Five on Education beyond High School. Connally, Garza's college friend and past political ally, knew of Garza's service in the Texas Education Standards Committee in the late 1950s and of his long-standing commitment to educational goals. Impressed by Garza's background, Connally appointed Garza, along with other members of Texas' elite, including chairmen of Texas Instruments, General Telephone, and Shamrock Oil and Gas. As a self-proclaimed education governor, Connally designated the committee as one of his top priorities in the state government. One of the major benefits Garza viewed in the appointment was the opportunity to allocate educational funds to South Texas. Although Garza did not succeed in this goal because the majority of monies were channeled to larger, established universities, his efforts on behalf of his region endeared him further to the South Texas community.[32]

In April Garza made his first appearance in El Paso. For two weeks he aided District Judge R. E. Thomason, who conducted one of the busiest and most backlogged federal courts in the nation. Garza soon became a popular figure there because of his reputation as an efficient jurist. On his last day there, city leaders honored him with a small banquet and asked him to participate in the city's Law Day celebration. As part of the celebration, Garza administered the oath of allegiance to more than two hundred aliens, the majority of whom were Mexican.[33] Garza was truly an appropriate role model of biculturalism for these newly sworn citizens.

Garza was also honored by the city of Kingsville. Mayor James H. McCrocklin informed Garza by letter that the city was naming a day in Garza's honor. Since Garza's docket handled the majority of cases from Kingsville, attorneys and court workers from the city had grown to know Garza well. Garza had also been friendly with a few leading Kingsville residents because of his membership in the Knights of Columbus and his many hunting trips to the city's famed King Ranch. To commemorate Garza's success as a Mexican American federal jurist and to honor his charitable work for the Knights of Columbus, the mayor proclaimed June 16, 1963, as Judge Reynaldo G. Garza Day. On that day the town held a small parade, attended by Garza and his family, and awarded him a key to the city. He was also presented with a formal proclamation listing his achievements. Garza celebrated the event with a day of hunting with his sons at the King Ranch.[34]

Whether they were colorful parades or solemn memorial services, Garza was often the only Mexican American included in the activities. One of the events was the funeral of United States Senator Tom Connally in October, 1963. Connally, eighty-six at the time of his death, served in the Senate for thirty-five years and was a close friend of Lyndon Johnson. Garza, too, had met the distinguished senator shortly after 1961 through Garza's frequent hunting partner, Judge Ben Connally, who was Tom Connally's son. At the funeral Garza found himself in the company of Vice President Johnson, Texas Governor Connally, and Attorney General Robert Kennedy. Garza took the opportunity to reacquaint himself with Kennedy and also to speak to Johnson at length about prospective Mexican American appointments in Texas.[35] Ironically, Garza was socializing with Kennedy and Johnson at the very time Mexican American groups were seeking attention from these and other powerful leaders.

A few days after the funeral, Johnson called Garza at home to invite him and Bertha to a November reception at the LBJ Ranch.[36] Johnson boasted to Garza that workers would transform the ranch into a splendid gathering place to honor President Kennedy during his scheduled November visit to Texas. Greatly enthused about the prospect of attending the lavish affair and visiting with President Kennedy again, Garza cheerfully told Johnson he and Bertha would attend the event. A few days later the Garzas received an official invitation to the barbecue.

Three weeks before the barbecue, Garza's old college friend, Governor Connally, came to Brownsville for an official visit. Garza and Bertha graciously opened their home to the governor and his wife Nellie, who stayed in the Garzas' guest room for two days. During the visit the couples reminisced about their college years and discussed the upcoming LBJ Ranch affair. Since Connally was responsible for much of the president's itinerary while in Texas, Garza learned the details of Kennedy's proposed trip. The Secret Service planned a two-day, five-stop visit for the president to San Antonio, Houston, and Fort Worth on the first day, and Dallas and Austin on the second. The last day's events in Austin would be capped by the barbecue at the nearby ranch.[37]

Connally knew of his old friend's deep admiration for President Kennedy and arranged for the president and the first lady to be seated next to the Garzas at the event.

After the Connally's departure from Brownsville, Garza and Bertha planned their schedules for the barbecue. Garza would be holding court in Corpus Christi during the president's trip, so Bertha would make the three-hour drive to pick up her husband, then the two would drive on to Austin. The children would stay with Bertha's family for two days while the Garzas were out of town. Although the Garzas regularly attended large celebrations, the LBJ event became especially significant. To the Garzas, as to many Brownsville citizens, the Kennedys were beloved figures.[38]

Unfortunately, on November 22 tragic events in Dallas forced a change in the Garzas' plans. News of the assassination quickly spread through the stunned nation. In Brownsville, border officials closed access to the Gateway Bridge linking Brownsville with Matamoros for fear anyone involved in the Kennedy assassination would attempt to leave the country. In Corpus Christi, Garza and Bertha had just finished lunch at a restaurant. The two passed a television in the hotel lobby and saw CBS anchorman Walter Cronkite delivering the news of the president's death. Stunned by the announcement, Garza summoned his law clerk to the courthouse, where Garza sorrowfully addressed the attorneys and told them that all the day's cases would be tenured until his next visit to Corpus Christi. A grief-stricken Garza and Bertha then drove back to Brownsville to await more information on the assassination. In Dallas, an hour and a half after the assassination, Federal Judge Sarah T. Hughes swore in Vice President Johnson as the thirty-sixth president of the United States.[39]

For the next twenty-four hours after Kennedy's assassination, the nation remained paralyzed by grief, shock, and fear. By sunrise, Dallas police had charged twenty-four-year-old Lee Harvey Oswald with Kennedy's murder. Soon after, the Brownsville border crossing reopened, but the local streets remained silent, for fear still prevailed that the assassination could trigger war. Garza acted in numbed disbelief as he attended a midnight Mass on the night of the assassination. The next day he returned to church for several other services held in Kennedy's memory. Instead of pleasant socializing with Kennedy and the first lady at the LBJ ranch, Garza mourned sorrowfully for the slain president.[40]

As the nation grieved, Garza participated in helping his community heal. At church services throughout the city, Garza tried to comfort members of his strongly pious community through remembrances praising the country's first Roman Catholic president. Garza's position as the highest-ranking Mexican American in the federal government, along with his deeply religious reputation, gave his words added significance. His personal knowledge of Kennedy provided the element of sincerity and empathy required in this emotionally draining situation.[41]

Kennedy's death deeply affected Garza. After all, Garza had benefited from Kennedy's actions on his behalf. Although Lyndon Johnson was the driving force behind Garza's nomination to the federal bench, Kennedy alone appointed Garza. And he never forgot Kennedy's words of support during their meeting at the White House. Garza also long remembered the moving statement of Sir Winston Churchill after the assassination: "Those who come after Mr. Kennedy must strive the more to achieve the ideals of world peace and human happiness and dignity to which his presidency was dedicated." Clinging to these words, Garza pledged to continue administering justice, this time under the leadership of the new president, his good friend, Lyndon Johnson.[42]

Members of the Garza family in front of their West Saint Charles Street home, Brownsville, circa 1918

Garza, left, with an unidentified person at his first Communion, 1923

The Garza family in 1925. Standing, left to right: *Reynaldo, Leonel, Ygnacio, Zoila, Lucila, and Maria Rosa;* seated: *Osbaldo, Zoila, Ygnacio, and Argentina*

The Garza Hardware Store in 1928

Garza at the University of Texas at Austin campus, 1937

Garza and Bertha dressed in costume at the 1940 Charro Days celebration, an annual Brownsville event

President John F. Kennedy, Vice President Lyndon B. Johnson, and Garza in the Oval Office, prior to Garza's Senate confirmation vote in 1961

Newly elected president Johnson introduces Mexican film star Cantinflas (Mario Moreno) to Garza during a barbecue at the LBJ Ranch in 1964.

First Lady Rosalynn Carter welcomes Garza and Bertha to a 1979 White House reception, a few weeks after the Senate approved Garza's nomination to the United States Court of Appeals.

The Garzas welcome Texas governor Ann Richards, center, to their home for dinner in 1993.

CHAPTER 7

The Turbulent Sixties

1963–69

Urging continuity and unity, President Lyndon Johnson consoled the nation in his 1963 televised Thanksgiving address: "A great leader is dead; a great nation must move on." To help heal the grief-stricken country, Johnson said: "I am resolved that we shall win the tomorrows before us. So I ask you to join me in that resolve, determined that from this midnight of tragedy, we shall move toward a new American greatness." As Johnson addressed the nation, Garza listened attentively from the comfort of his den. He remained one of Johnson's most ardent admirers. With his old friend at the nation's helm, Garza was confident that a great future lay ahead for the country and, especially, the state of Texas.[1]

While Johnson adjusted to the presidency, Garza focused on his own career. By late 1963 Garza had established the work routine he would follow throughout his more than three decades on the federal bench. When in Brownsville Garza would arrive at the federal courthouse between 8:00 and 8:30 A.M. As soon as he dashed through the doors of his chambers, the day quickly progressed as he read briefs, ruled on legal motions, wrote opinions, held trials, met with litigants, and dictated correspondence. He would return home at about 7 P.M., dine and socialize with his family for a few hours, and then work on his docket until he retired to bed.[2]

During out-of-town court appearances, the schedule was similar, but the pace was faster and longer. Garza was constantly faced with the pressures of having only one to two weeks to clear a city's docket before he returned home. To meet the judicial demands, Garza and his clerk worked ten- and twelve-hour days, attempting to move the voluminous workload. The two often dined together in nearby restaurants, reflecting on the day's cases.[3]

With more than two years of judicial experience behind him by late 1963, Garza had honed his skills in the courtroom, keeping cases moving in an orderly manner. He had become adept at ruling decisively on the admissibility of evidence. Garza proved to be a very active participant in the court, peppering attorneys with questions. He maintained little patience for unprepared attorneys and sternly reprimanded those who did not meet his expectations in court. "I was the recipient of his vociferous reprimands on more than one occasion," said Filemón Vela, an attorney in Brownsville in the 1960s and later a federal judge.[4]

His most difficult task was sentencing. For all judges, sentencing decisions rely not only on legislative recommendations and prosecution requests but also life experiences and personal philosophies. Garza focused on the impersonal legalities of each individual case, but his deep religious convictions also made him concerned about the personal consequences. Frequently during criminal sentencing, the victim's and the accused's families would file into court to plead their side to Garza. "You could see how it stirred the judge to see the gathering of young children and weeping mothers asking for clemency," recalled his former law clerk, William Mallet.[5]

For minor crimes he usually gave first offenders a second chance, but he was never so generous with second offenders. He often lectured second offenders, espousing fatherly advice from the bench and hoping that a few nights in jail might jolt them into realizing the consequences of breaking the law. The soft lines on his browned face hid his agony at having to deliver these jail sentences. "It's a terrible feeling when you know you have a man's life in your hands. You can either let him continue to be a free man or cage him like an animal," Garza solemnly lamented to a reporter. His deep religious views and his belief in man's ability to repent made the task especially difficult for the judge.

Consequently, he began the practice of kneeling down and praying in the privacy of his chambers before each sentencing hearing.[6]

A more formally religious man would have been hard to find. Garza not only attended Mass daily, but when faced with a difficult sentence, he would find solace in prayer. He befriended many South Texas priests, who became his confidantes and spiritual advisors. When he delivered an especially severe sentence, he found comfort in religious doctrine. Theology interested Garza immensely, and he had known the Bible well since childhood. He often used religious references when discussing cases with his clerks, but he never forgot that his task on the bench was to follow Constitutional, rather than biblical, precepts. He prayed daily for divine guidance and was well aware of his responsibility to balance the scales of justice, striving for fair sentencing as dictated by law. He often arranged religious retreats for attorneys in South Texas in an effort to remain involved in religious affairs.[7] In this manner he maintained the strong faith of his Mexican roots while following the precepts of the American judicial system.

Garza's attention constantly centered on the backlog of cases in the district docket. Because of the 1960s population growth in Texas and ever-increasing litigious feelings in the nation, an onslaught of lawsuits burdened the already strained district court. Between 1950 and 1960 Texas' population had increased by almost two million, approaching close to ten million by 1960. The growth in citizenry created more disputes, which in turn, resulted in more litigation. Relief for the heavy burden, in the form of additional judges, was often bandied around among federal lawmakers; however, Congress declined to add additional judgeships to address the problem. For Garza, the growing workload continued to make demands on his schedule.[8]

Regardless of the time constraints imposed by his judicial duties, Garza kept his children on course. Much like his own father, Garza, too, preached the message of advancement through education. So he was delighted when eldest son Rey followed his educational path and was accepted to the University of Texas School of Law. Second son, David, a sophomore in high school, excelled both academically and socially. He ranked number one in his class and maintained an active extracurricular schedule as class president and a member of the football, track, and basketball teams. The three youngest children consumed both Garza's and Bertha's activities: Nacho was a rambunctious fifth-grader at Sacred Heart School; Bertita was a kindergartner at the private Mrs. Wideners' School; and Monica was an energetic toddler.[9]

Garza also made time for a few events he found significant. In February, 1964, he again attended the George Washington celebration in Laredo, the very event that had named him Mr. South Texas a year before. The festive occasion gave Garza an opportunity to visit with his friend, Texas Governor John Connally, the new Mr. South Texas honoree. When they arrived in Laredo, the Garzas immediately met with the Connallys at a local restaurant, where conversation focused on the upcoming presidential election. Connally remained one of President Johnson's closest political strategists, and the Texas governor was heavily involved in politicking efforts. Judicial ethics precluded Garza from participating in the 1964 presidential election, but he enjoyed listening to Connally's discussions about many upcoming political rallies. Garza's interest stemmed from the excitement involved in planning political events and his recollections of past electoral victories. Garza and Connally reminisced about Johnson's first run for Congress, when Garza was a young law student urging Mexican Americans to vote for Lyndon. The 1964 election would mark the first time Garza would not campaign for Johnson, and although the federal judge longed to help his old friend, he was contented learning about Connally's strategy for the campaign.[10]

Just as Garza supported Johnson, so did the electorate. By the fall of 1964, polls showed strong support of Johnson, influenced significantly by the president's response in Vietnam. Following the Gulf of Tonkin resolution in November, 1964, a nationwide television audience witnessed Johnson garner the largest popular vote that any presidential candidate had received to date. Watching from their Brownsville home, Garza and his family celebrated Johnson's overwhelming 61 percent majority vote. Garza delighted in the popular mandate the American people bestowed upon his good friend and found great satisfaction in the Democratic win. Most of all, he knew the victory's importance to Johnson as a means to break from the shadow of the still beloved President Kennedy.[11]

Johnson's landslide victory also mitigated Garza's frustration at being precluded by federal judicial ethics from participating in the election. Garza missed his role as a political leader—planning rallies, strategizing, making speeches. He began to reminisce about Johnson's past political campaigns. He enthusiastically told his family how he first met Johnson in 1937 and about the president's political career.

Garza spoke of the many speeches he gave on Johnson's behalf and the energetic response of the crowd. He enjoyed telling his family about Johnson's campaign rallies where the candidate arrived in a whirling helicopter. He punctuated each story with his habitual "hmmm," daring anyone to question his recollections. Garza would imitate the sound of the helicopter as his younger children screamed in delight. The memories continued to be among Garza's favorite, and they would be told for decades to come.[12]

Soon after Johnson's landslide victory, the president invited Garza to a gathering at the LBJ ranch. Johnson's wife, Lady Bird, had planned a barbecue to honor the president-elect of Mexico, Gustavo Díaz Ordaz. In the persuasive Johnson speaking style, filled with boasts of the barbecue's inevitable magnificence, the president urged Garza to bring Bertha with him to the event. Garza was excited to see his old friend once again and told Johnson that Bertha would arrange for her family to care for their younger children so that the two could both attend.[13]

Garza and Bertha eagerly anticipated the visit to the ranch, knowing that some of the most powerful and influential Texans and Mexicans would be present. The November date soon arrived, and the barbecue met the Garzas' expectations. Johnson sent a limousine to the Austin airport to drive Bertha and Garza the one-and-a-half-hour trip to Stonewall, Texas, the site of the ranch. Riding through the winding roads of the Austin hill country, Garza looked forward to visiting with many old friends.[14]

Once he arrived at the ranch, Garza scanned the crowd of close to one hundred and fifty people gathered at the affair. He sighted many Texas politicians, most of whom he had worked with during prior political campaigns. Chatting under one of the massive oaks adorning the ranch were the Kazen brothers, Abraham and Philip. Abraham Kazen knew Garza from law school as they had both graduated from the same 1939 University of Texas class. The two had often visited during Garza's many trips to Laredo where Garza had met the rest of the family, all influential Democratic leaders in South Texas. The Kazens were conversing with two of Garza's longtime friends, Congressmen Henry B. González of San Antonio, another college chum, and Eligio (Kika) de la Garza, an attorney from the Rio Grande Valley who a year later would represent Garza's district in the U.S. Congress. As Garza joined the group, Bertha was escorted to another area by Nellie Connally, the Texas governor's wife.[15]

For Garza the barbecue became a chance to meet interesting people and reacquaint himself with old friends. One of the guests was Mexican comedian Mario Moreno, known as Cantinflas. Brownsville citizens idolized Cantinflas, especially after his appearance in the American film, *Around the World in Eighty Days*. In fact, the adoration of the Mexican film star was so great that Garza's hometown had honored Cantinflas with the title of Mr. Amigo 1965 as part of the city's annual Charro Days. Custom dictated that prominent leaders in Brownsville host receptions for Mr. Amigo, and in February, 1965, city leaders asked Garza to welcome Cantinflas with a speech. At the barbecue Garza and Cantinflas conversed in Spanish about the upcoming festivities. For Johnson, the meeting of Garza and Cantinflas made an excellent photo opportunity. The president summoned the White House photographer to snap a shot of himself with the two men.[16]

Another interesting LBJ invitee was the guest of honor, Mexican President Díaz Ordaz, whom Cantinflas introduced to Garza. The three spoke for close to an hour. When Díaz Ordaz learned Garza was from Brownsville, he began discussing a future proposal intended to connect the economies of the American and Mexican border regions. President Díaz Ordaz officially announced the project, known as the Border Industrial Program, two months after the LBJ barbecue. Under the program, incentives such as Mexican government loans and tax concessions would entice American industries to establish manufacturing plants known as *maquiladoras* in Mexican towns bordering the United States. Eighty percent of the products created by the plants were sold outside of Mexico. Garza, who learned about the *maquiladoras* a few months before most Americans, contemplated the advantages and disadvantages of the system. He concluded that *maquiladoras* would greatly benefit the economic future of his hometown. It gladdened him to see Brownsville progress, and he continued to endorse the *maquiladora* program throughout the next three decades.[17]

As Brownsville's economic conditions seemed to be on the verge of improving via the *maquiladora* system, President Johnson also sought to improve the conditions of Brownsville's native son. On a balmy Friday morning in March, 1965, while Garza sat immersed in a stack of law books, he received a telephone call from the president. Johnson told Garza he needed to fill the vacancy created by United States Court of Appeals Judge Joseph C. Hutcheson, Jr.'s retirement on the Fifth Circuit. In the hierarchy of the federal court system, ten courts of appeal rested below the United States Supreme Court. The Fifth Circuit listened to appeals from the federal district courts in Alabama, Florida, Georgia, Louisiana, Mississippi, Texas, and the Panama Canal Zone. In 1965 there were only thirteen judges overseeing federal law in the immense area, and, as such, it was an extremely prestigious honor to be on the appeals court. Johnson told Garza that his first choice for the position was district court judge, Homer Thornberry. Since Thornberry was still uncertain about accepting the appointment, however, the president asked Garza if he would consider the position.[18]

Caught off guard by the offer, Garza told Johnson he was sure Thornberry would accept the vacancy. Johnson had appointed Thornberry to the United States District Court in 1963, and Garza knew of Thornberry's prominent legal reputation in Texas. Although Johnson said Thornberry's position was still speculative, he urged Garza to give the proposal some thought. Confident that Thornberry would readily accept the nomination, Garza ended his conversation with Johnson with an enthusiastic promise that he would call him back within a week.[19]

A whirlwind of thoughts now filled Garza. Indeed, the position would bring prestige to an appointed judge, but, in 1965 an appointee to the Fifth Circuit would face exhausting challenges. Mirroring the United States District Court for the Southern District of Texas, the Fifth Circuit faced identical problems: overcrowded dockets, too vast a geographic area, and too few judges. By the summer of 1964 new filings in the Fifth Circuit exceeded one thousand, the largest number of any court of appeals. Although the 1964 Judicial Conference of the United States recommended splitting the Fifth Circuit to alleviate the pressure on the judges, it would take more than fifteen years of political bickering before Congress divided the court.[20] With no alleviation in sight, the thirteen Fifth Circuit judges were overburdened. Garza battled the same problems in the district court.

Aware of the troubles in the Fifth Circuit, Garza knew that the position could be advantageous, especially to Mexican Americans. Garza's decisions could leave a distinguishing mark on a court that embodied "the institutional equivalent of the civil rights movement itself." In their efforts to champion civil rights, the Fifth Circuit judges dealt with uncharted legal waters. Although there was one Supreme Court Justice assigned to the Fifth Circuit, the judges experienced little intervention from the Supreme Court, which granted the Fifth Circuit sole power to enforce civil rights. This responsibility meant that a Fifth Circuit decision could become a definitive constitutional decision.[21] Accordingly, with Garza on the court in the mid-1960s, the Fifth Circuit could shape much of the civil rights legislation and, thereby, benefit Mexican Americans.

Garza deliberated the offer only one day before he learned through close Washington friends that Thornberry had decided to take the position. Thornberry had been reluctant at first to become a circuit court appointee because he was unsure of his judicial expertise. "He [Thornberry] hadn't really been deeply involved in law," explained Assistant Attorney General Ramsey Clark. "He turned out to be a very good judge, but you wouldn't think of him as a person intellectually keen on the law, whereas you'd think of Garza as sharp in the law." Before Johnson officially nominated Thornberry, he first telephoned Garza's office. Garza told the president he knew of Thornberry's decision to accept the position and voiced his approval of the candidate. During his conversation with Johnson, Garza told Johnson he was still unsure whether he would have taken the position. Years later, however, Garza came to believe that being elevated to the Fifth Circuit in 1965 would have been among his wisest career moves.[22]

By the summer of 1965 Garza was distraught over Johnson's rapidly declining popular support, primarily because of the Vietnam conflict. But as the specter of increasing war causalities and the resulting downswing in Johnson's popularity lurked in the background, Garza's life received a slight boost. In July, 1966, the United States Senate approved the addition of two judges, which helped reduce Garza's taxing workload. The new additions, Woodrow B. Seals and John V. Singleton, were both Houstonians Garza had met several times in federal court. Seven judges would make the district court docket easier to manage. For Garza, the additions meant a reduction of traveling venues and a greater amount of time in Brownsville.[23]

Back home more regularly, Garza was able to focus even greater attention on his family. In spring of 1966, David received notice of his acceptance to Notre Dame University. He had applied to the prestigious college in hopes of receiving a scholarship; yet, university officials informed David that his family's assets disqualified him from consideration. With three younger children left to raise, Garza was forced to tell David that he could not afford the costly private university. It was a decision that disappointed Garza much more so than David, who as the valedictorian of his high school, was accepted to various universities. David urged his father not to dwell on the situation. He comforted Garza by explaining that his goal was to attend the University of Texas law school, and as long as he excelled at any undergraduate school, he was convinced he would be granted admission to Garza's alma mater.[24]

As David prepared to begin college, Garza received upsetting news about Rey. Distraught and shaken, Bertha called Garza one day, while he was holding court in Corpus Christi, to tell him Rey had enlisted in the army. Without consulting either of his parents, Rey withdrew from the university a week before the fall, 1966, semester began, then drove home to prepare for active duty. Rey said hypocrisy was his rationale. He could no longer stand by watching others his age fighting for their country while he attended school on a deferment. Rey was twenty-two years old. A long future stood before him, he told his mother, and joining the army would become another step in enriching his life. He believed his actions were both patriotic and sensible. Yet, Rey conceded that part of his decision centered on the monotony he found in law school and the excitement he foresaw in Vietnam.[25]

For Bertha his actions took her memory back twenty-five years to Garza's path during World War II. Like Rey, Garza had ignored his family's pleas and dropped his promising legal career to enlist in the service. Feelings of fear, anger, and distress swelled in Bertha's mind as she envisioned her eldest child in a country thousands of miles away, slumped in a muddy swamp, dodging bullets and bombs. Rey did not know the meaning of war, Bertha tried to explain to him. During World War II Bertha witnessed war's repercussions. She knew the weeping widows and the pain of waiting weeks and months to hear from loved ones. During the Korean War she felt the anguish, along with her husband, after a Korean gunner turned Garza's youngest brother's aircraft into a fiery coffin. Bertha could not bear the thought that her son would be among the body bags she saw on television daily. "He broke our hearts," Bertha lamented. She tried in vain to persuade Rey to return to school.[26]

Rey's decision also troubled Garza. He knew that war caused not only physical but mental devastation. Uncertainty over Rey's ability to handle the pressures of war with maturity worried Garza. Rey's decision to quit law school also unsettled him. These feelings collided with Garza's pride in his son's decision to enlist. Garza remembered his own obstinate behavior when he enlisted during World War II, and he knew his son would be resolute in his decision. After returning from Corpus Christi, Garza spent the entire weekend with Rey. On Monday morning Rey left Brownsville to report for active duty. A few months later, Rey began serving as a radio traffic intelligence analyst in Okinawa.[27]

As news reports about the war grew graver each day, the Garza family's concern over Rey increased. Rey sought to ease the family's apprehensions by writing a letter every week or two. Yet, letters could not quell Bertha's uneasy feelings. Garza attempted to comfort her but hid his incessant fears. In the courthouse, however, Garza's office staff witnessed his pain. They saw him flinch when the radio reported the names of injured and dead soldiers from the Rio Grande Valley. A few months after Rey left home, the family received the distressing news that one of Bertha's young nephews was missing in action. But as the months progressed, Garza learned to manage his anxiety, focusing on work and family.[28]

In the wake of Vietnam, President Johnson began receiving fan mail for Garza. The majority of the letters came from South Texas professionals who knew Garza through the Knights of Columbus or through his stature as a federal judge. The correspondents wrote letters praising Garza's skill in the courtroom and his legal expertise. They encouraged Johnson and members of his administration to continue Garza's elevation in the federal government based on his extensive knowledge and fair actions in the court. Most of all, the letters spoke of the tremendous impact of Garza's federal position on Mexican American struggles for equality.[29]

One of the letters was from Tony Bonilla, a Texan actively involved in Chicano civil rights issues. Bonilla wrote to Ramsey Clark recommending that Garza fill a Supreme Court vacancy. During Garza's appointment to the judiciary in 1961, Bonilla had encouraged the selection of the liberal state judge, E. D. Salinas of Laredo. As Assistant Attorney General Clark recalled, "If you had gone back to 1961 and asked someone like Tony Bonilla whether Salinas or Garza would be the right pick, almost surely he would have said Salinas." Activist Mexican Americans had voiced their concerns over Garza's support of Republican President Dwight D. Eisenhower as the majority of Mexican American organizations were affiliated with the Democratic party. Bonilla's letter, urging Clark to promote Judge Garza to the Supreme Court, exemplified the change in attitude regarding Garza. Mexican American leaders such as

Bonilla now viewed Garza as a role model. They continually praised his distinguished career on the bench and voiced their belief that his stature would serve to elevate their ethnic group.[30]

In 1967 Johnson continued to turn to Garza for counsel. Aware of Garza's numerous contacts in the legal community, Johnson sought nominees from Texas to fill federal positions. The president often wrote to Garza soliciting his opinions on upcoming appointments. In one letter Johnson thanked Garza for his advice, writing, "Your counsel is important to me, and I am always grateful for your helpfulness and friendship."[31] Throughout the Johnson presidency Garza continued advising his old friend, with the counsel gradually turning from advice on appointments to suggestions on Johnson's career moves.

As polls showed Johnson losing ground politically, Garza increasingly speculated that little chance existed for a Johnson victory in the 1968 election, especially with Gallup polls reporting that only 50 percent of Americans approved of Johnson's actions—a drastic shift from the number of Americans approving of Johnson during his electoral landslide in 1964. Polls taken a year before the 1968 presidential election had indicated that Johnson's primary Republican challenger, former Vice President Richard Nixon, led Johnson in the popular vote. Garza witnessed Johnson's image wither, largely damaged by Vietnam.[32] Ever optimistic, Garza suggested to Johnson that he needed a positive public relations campaign to resuscitate the ravaged image.

To save a tattered reputation Johnson looked to reviving his dying Great Society and its civil rights agenda. The Great Society had withered by 1967 because of antiwar protests and massive financial war costs, and many of the president's Great Society proposals became sidetracked in Congress. To combat the Great Society's deterioration, Johnson used his presidential power of appointment. In August, 1967, Johnson appointed the first black associate justice to the Supreme Court, Thurgood Marshall. Marshall filled the vacancy created by Johnson's good friend, fellow Texan Tom C. Clark, who had resigned to avoid a conflict of interest with his son, recently appointed Attorney General Ramsey Clark.[33]

For Garza the appointment seemed to signal Johnson's continued good intentions in the area of civil rights. Garza viewed the struggle to advance equality for minorities much as he had during his years as LULAC president in the 1940s. He preferred no minority representation at all unless the individual was of superior qualifications and performance. Thus, he abhorred tokenism. Garza explained his beliefs regarding his own appointment to a reporter: "I've always said I hope I got the appointment because I was qualified, not because I was Mexican American." He added, "But I knew I had to do a good job or else my actions would reflect not only my ability but that of other Mexican Americans."[34]

Accordingly, Marshall's appointment seemed a progressive move to Garza. The district judge was well aware of the new Supreme Court justice's distinguished legal record, including his successful litigation in *Sweatt v. Painter.* In that case, Marshall had defended an African American attempting to gain admittance to Garza's alma mater. The case especially touched Garza because it opened access to his beloved university to all qualified individuals regardless of race.

In addition to concern about the African American community, the president's interest in the Mexican American population remained unwavering. As a symbol of his concern for the minority group, Johnson sent Garza a freshly minted medallion marking the Chamizal Agreement. With the medallion, Johnson enclosed a brief note to his good friend, which read: "Because I share the deep hopes of the Mexican American community for a better future, I thought you might like to have from me a little remembrance . . . [of] the Chamizal Agreement." The agreement concerned the final resolution of a century-old boundary dispute between Mexico and the United States. Through President Kennedy's efforts the two countries reached a final resolution in 1963. Kennedy's assassination occurred before he could sign official documents, so Johnson formalized the arrangement in Kennedy's place. Although the medallion was produced a few years after the agreement's final resolution, the gift touched Garza. The federal judge felt honored to own the goodwill symbol of his two countries.[35] The gift of the medallion reflected Johnson's view of Garza as a representative of the Mexican American people. Through Garza's persistent bicultural lifestyle, he was deservedly perceived by Anglo leaders as a representative of both societies.

Johnson's diplomatic victories in Latin America were in counterdistinction to his defeats in Southeast Asia. By the late 1960s the Vietnam War dominated American life to the apparent extinction of Johnson's Great Society, or, as historian David Halberstam referred to it, "Lyndon Johnson's Great Whateveritwas."[36] But there were still a few bursts of life left in Johnson's dream society in the arena of civil rights.

By 1967 the nation moved toward a civil rights revolution in the form of racial integration. In the middle of the revolution lay the United States District Court for the Southern District of Texas and the start of a new brand of cases for its federal judges.

Civil rights legislation flooding federal courts gave judges the authority to integrate schools, businesses, and other organizations. Personally, Garza was not totally comfortable with his extended judicial powers. He explained, "Traditionally, the judicial branch neither desires nor was designed to perform daily operational supervision over any other governmental entity but itself." He added, "But the opinions of the Supreme Court have mandated that we get involved. The idea being that every American, no matter where he lives in this country, will enjoy the same rights as any other." Garza believed federal courts were ill prepared to handle the massive administrative duties brought on by Supreme Court mandated powers. Burdened with overflowing dockets, it would be difficult for the judicial branch to take over daily supervision of public entities such as schools or jails. Garza knew that conditions were so unique, however, that the Supreme Court faced little other choice than to require such action, and he steadfastly followed the law.[37]

With civil rights and the Vietnam escalation as a backdrop, illegal substance cases also began to fill Garza's docket. "Kids objecting to the war started taking uppers and downers," stated Garza, "and it was the precursor. They went to marijuana, cocaine, and heroine." The district court's location in border towns such as Brownsville made drug cases predominate in the docket because drug smuggling from Mexico into the United States was a simple and frequent phenomenon.[38]

The outgrowth of the tumultuous 1960s for Garza's court, drug and integration cases, almost doubled the workload, and Garza and the other federal judges took steps to remedy the problem. Garza learned of a bill proposed in Congress to replace the former United States commissioners with United States magistrates. Magistrates would have a larger scope and authority in the federal judicial system than did commissioners. They could try, with the consent of the accused, minor federal offenses and preside over preliminary hearings and trials, thus giving district judges the time to deal with other matters. In 1967 Congress circulated the draft of the bill to Garza, who readily lobbied for its approval within judicial circles. In 1968 Congress approved the bill, and Garza immediately volunteered to become part of the pilot program planned for his district. Since the 1968 bill gave federal judges the power to appoint full-time magistrates, Garza called William Mallet, whose tenure as Garza's law clerk had ended in 1966. Garza easily persuaded Mallet to become his magistrate. But Garza would have to wait two more years before the implementation of the magistrate system. With relief in sight, however, Garza's focus began to turn once again to his old friend Lyndon Johnson.[39]

Although Johnson was steadfastly losing popularity, Garza knew there was nothing he could do to aid him. Politically, a majority of the country lost confidence in Johnson both because of racial backlash and the president's mishandling of the Vietnam war. Two major events, however, sealed Johnson's presidential fate. First, Senator Eugene McCarthy from Minnesota came close to winning the New Hampshire primary through an antiwar challenge. Second, Robert Kennedy announced his decision to seek the presidency.[40]

By the spring of 1968, Johnson began to turn inward, and Garza maintained little contact with the president. Garza sensed a substantial change was on the horizon. Along with many other longtime Johnson supporters, he eagerly anticipated the president's upcoming televised address. In March, 1968, the entire Garza family, excluding Rey but including Garza's eldest brothers Ygnacio, Jr., and Leonel, sat in the family den awaiting the address. The noisy room turned silent as Johnson's image appeared on the black-and-white television. Garza, flanked by his two brothers, suddenly sat tensely upright on the family couch as Johnson made two historic announcements. He first promised to de-escalate the Vietnam war. Johnson then explained to the American people, "I do not believe that I should devote an hour or a day of my time to any personal partisan causes or to any duties other than the awesome duties of this office." He concluded, "Accordingly, I shall not seek, and will not accept, the nomination of my party for another term as your president." Garza slumped back on the couch as tears swelled in his eyes. The entire room was silent, in shock by the solemn announcement that Johnson would not seek another term as president.[41]

Although distraught by Johnson's announcement, Garza felt relief for the president. Garza knew that the political climate would not allow Johnson another presidential victory, and a defeat might ultimately destroy Johnson. Garza saw the effects of the growing popular discontent; it had aged and depressed the president. He thought a respite from politics might be in Johnson's best long-term health interests.[42]

While Johnson attended to his immense responsibilities during his last months as president, he did not forget his good friends. In the early spring of 1968, Garza received an eight-inch, ceramic bust of Johnson and a note attached, thanking Garza for his decades of support. Garza placed the bust on a pedestal against his chamber wall. The bust became a reminder of his long association with the United States president. Garza long remembered his cherished moments with Johnson as the bust remained in his chambers close to thirty years later.

Garza remained optimistic that Johnson's successor to the presidency would continue the president's liberal dream. He fully expected the American people to vote for a Democratic president in the 1968 election. The rising social upheaval, however, thwarted these expectations. In April, 1968, an assassin murdered civil rights leader Martin Luther King, Jr. Several American cities erupted in flames. In Brownsville, with an African American population still under 1 percent, King's death became just another example of the growing violence in the country. Two months later, another assassin shot Robert Kennedy as he celebrated his victory over Eugene McCarthy in the California primary. The incident shocked the nation while simultaneously depriving antiwar Democrats of the only dissenter with a chance to gain the party's presidential nomination.[43]

Robert Kennedy's assassination deeply saddened Garza. His personal ties to Kennedy had begun in 1961 when RFK, then attorney general, had urged Garza to accept the federal judicial appointment. They continued to visit periodically throughout the years at judicial conferences, and RFK reveled in the fact that Garza was the first Mexican American on the federal judiciary. Through Garza's successes on the bench their initially formal relationship had turned to one of informality and great mutual respect. Despite Garza's attachment to Johnson and RFK's intense dislike of Johnson, both Garza and Kennedy had found an abundance of common ground, including their Catholic faith. When conversations turned to Garza's name, Kennedy often spoke with admiration about him. The former attorney general even recited courtroom anecdotes told to him by many Garza admirers. With the wound to Garza's heart after President Kennedy's death barely healed, the pain reemerged with RFK's assassination.[44]

Johnson departed the White House in January, 1969. Rushed and dejected, Johnson felt his liberal dream had deteriorated. It remained up to historians to comment on his years as commander-in-chief. For Garza and the Rio Grande Valley Johnson's legacy was one of civil rights advancement and a genuine concern over the plight of South Texas.[45]

As Johnson flew back to Texas and his ranch, Garza settled down to the new conservative climate under Nixon. The presidential focus was now on Republican-appointed judges, and, thus, any hopes of Garza's elevation to a higher court were put on hold. With the Nixon presidency Garza ceased having the close relations with the White House he had cultivated during the last seven years. During the Nixon years Garza forged forward, continuing to adjudicate in the district court while simultaneously tending to his family and his hometown of Brownsville.

CHAPTER 8

The Chief
1969–76

Garza's family and the United States District Court remained the centers of his life throughout the Nixon-Ford years. The two evolved through an exciting period in American history, characterized by a vicious war, a triumph in space, a rebellious counterculture movement, civil rights abuses, and a controversial decision concerning human reproduction. Throughout the era, Garza maintained a steady path, directing his many followers both in his family and on the court. Personally, there were happy times for Garza, laden with his children's weddings and graduations. Professionally, he was no longer the neophyte judge acclimating to the federal bench. By 1969 Garza was a seasoned federal jurist and soon ascended to the position of chief judge.

After eight years on the bench, Garza's esteem had grown within his legal community. "Reynaldo had an inherent sense about what the law was and overwhelmingly, he was right," recalled famed Fifth Circuit Judge John Minor Wisdom. Former law clerk William Mallet concurred: "He would rule right from the bench. He wasn't like other judges that waited on weeks of research while a case lingered forever." Garza's near photographic memory facilitated his quick and precise rulings.

"He remembered defendants that had committed the same crime many years prior. It was incredible," said Mallet. Undoubtedly, Garza's ability to recall details of legal precepts impressed attorneys and law clerks, who saw it as a clear advantage to his skill at adjudication.[1]

Garza held little patience for unnecessary delays and often scolded attorneys who hampered speedy trials. "He didn't like wasting time, and he didn't like foolishness in the courtroom. He had the reputation of making lawyers scurry for cover when they tried his patience," stated law clerk P. T. Moore. "He also needed to let off a little steam once in a while. This was not necessarily bad, as it kept everyone on their toes." With his dominating presence in the courtroom, Garza methodically cleaned out the backlog of cases in his docket.[2]

Despite his stern judicial image, Garza was also sympathetic at times. His treatment of one of Brownsville's oldest attorneys, Polk Hornaday, illustrated his compassionate demeanor. Hornaday was in his nineties and still practicing law, yet he was showing the effects of his age; he tired easily. Once, towards the end of a tedious legal argument, it was Hornaday's turn to address a witness. Instead, he slumped in his chair, turned to Garza, and said, "I'm sorry, Your Honor. I'm getting tired." From his elevated bench, Garza looked down at the elder attorney sympathetically and replied, "That's all right, Mr. Hornaday. I'm tired too." The federal judge then adjourned the trial.[3]

Because of Garza's efficient legal reputation, former Supreme Court Justice Tom Clark, a board member of the newly established Federal Judicial Center, asked the federal judge from Brownsville to teach a judicial orientation seminar. For close to a decade, Garza would continue teaching the one-week seminar in Washington, D.C. During those trips Bertha often accompanied Garza to the nation's capital, where she enjoyed an active social calendar filled with White House teas and dinners for Supreme Court justices. The couple was often the only member of a minority group present at events hosted by members of Washington society.[4] Their inclusion in activities normally reserved for Anglo elites further shielded Garza from the discrimination still prevalent in American society.

Court work kept Garza perpetually busy, yet his family remained important. In February, 1969, the Garza family found a brief reprieve from the tensions accompanying Rey's enlistment. The young soldier received a two-week leave. He boarded the first available transport from his station in Okinawa, Japan, and telephoned the family to tell them he would be spending that time in Brownsville. Garza, excited about his son's return, announced to his court staff that he would take the rest of the week off to be with his eldest child. The delighted family greeted the thinner, yet spirited, Rey at the airport waving American flags.[5] This public display of patriotism was typical of many families of Garza's generation who took great pride both in their Mexican heritage and their deep allegiance to the United States.

The year 1969 proved to be a tumultuous time for Garza, his family, and many other Americans with servicemen in Vietnam. All feared that the increasingly unpopular war would continue indefinitely. After Rey returned to Okinawa in late February, Garza, like the rest of the nation, continued to keep abreast of the war. In June, 1969, President Richard Nixon announced the withdrawal of 25,000 United States troops from Vietnam. For the federal judge, the promise of the war's de-escalation seemed a progressive move toward ending the quagmire.[6]

In the summer of 1969, Garza and the entire nation received a much-needed burst of public spirit with the news that America had conquered the moon. Garza and his family delighted in witnessing astronaut Neil Armstrong's walk on the moon. The feat was especially moving for Garza both because of his personal acquaintance with President Kennedy and his strong patriotic feelings. Ever since meeting Kennedy in 1961, Garza had long cherished the promise Kennedy brought the country. Through Kennedy, Garza had become an integral part of a government that had accomplished this monumental task. The belief in the United States' superiority seemed undeniable to Garza after the moon landing. The federal judge who was the son of immigrants swelled with pride in his country.[7]

Several months later, Garza spoke of his family's immigrant experience when he presided over a large naturalization ceremony. The passionate speech he delivered detailed the significance of the victory in space and the honor his parents had felt for their countries, Mexico and the United States. Possibility in America was boundless, he told the audience. He urged the new citizens to work hard and gain an education so they could accomplish their goals. Most of all, he told them, they should take pride in becoming United States citizens during one of the country's most glorious moments. To the citizens in attendance, Garza exemplified their version of the American dream, and many, moved by his words, rushed to shake his hand after the ceremonies.[8]

Garza's years on the bench gave him a mastery of the court's processes, which, in turn, allowed him more time with his friends and family. Garza and Bertha began entertaining regularly with small dinner parties, socializing with Brownsville's elite families, such as the Longorias, Gavitos, and Yzaguirres. The Garzas and their friends often dined or just spent relaxing evenings together playing bridge or poker. In the summers the family vacationed in a small beach house at South Padre Island that Bertha had won in a raffle. The beach house was only twenty-five miles from the federal courthouse.[9] The Garzas were friends to both Anglo and Mexican American middle- to upper-class families, thus, maintaining the class-, rather than race-based, social system still evident in the late 1960s.

Garza continued to forge a strong relationship with his children. There were the usual sporting events to attend, but one memorable moment occurred in December, 1969, when David graduated from an accelerated college program. The entire family, except for Rey, who was still in Okinawa, drove to Austin to attend the ceremonies. Garza desired few things more than to have his children attend college, so he was delighted when, soon after David's winter graduation, the University of Texas law school accepted the gifted student. Courthouse personnel recalled that the federal judge was especially jubilant for weeks after David's acceptance.[10] Garza's happiness undoubtedly stemmed from his belief that a law degree, or any other form of advanced education, would guarantee his son's future achievement, much as it had determined Garza's own success. Garza had truly espoused the LULAC ideological vision of education as the pathway to success.

A month after David's graduation, the army transferred Rey to Virginia, where he continued his military intelligence activities. Soon after his arrival there, Rey married a twenty-one-year-old girl he had first dated in college. The Garzas were overjoyed at the union and extremely relieved that Rey was now safe in the United States.[11]

With his family relatively stable, Garza's attention focused back on the court. In the summer of 1970, Garza presided over a case the *Houston Post* termed the "biggest civil rights trial of his career." In *Equal Employment Opportunity Commission v. International Longshoremen's Association*, the district court ruled on whether racially segregated longshore unions provided equal working opportunities to minority employees. At issue was whether the International Longshoremen's Association (ILA), the

South Atlantic and Gulf Coast district of the ILA, and thirty-seven Texas deep-sea locals that were racially segregated should be merged. A ruling in favor of the Equal Employment Opportunity Commission could end the historically all–African American, all–Mexican American, and all-Anglo longshoreman locals in Texas and set a precedent for similar government suits throughout the South.[12]

Oral testimony began in July in Houston, with attorneys for the ILA contending that a majority of the locals in Texas opposed merger and practiced voluntary segregation. The Justice Department, which filed the suit acting under the Civil Rights Act of 1964, fervently believed otherwise and presented its case accordingly.

In mid-July, with no hopes of closing the deliberations, Garza recessed the trial until September to return to Brownsville to hear other cases on his docket. In the interim Garza contracted special masters to review the case. A master is a private attorney, retired judge, or a law professor whom judges appoint on an ad hoc, case-by-case basis. The master generates facts in cases that involve complicated situations, such as the ILA matter. Courts use masters only on rare occasions. Garza contacted law professors at the University of Houston law school to serve as masters.

In August, 1970, before resuming the ILA case, Garza assumed another legal matter. He heard the first of what would become a series of school regulation cases in the district courts. During the 1970 school year, a Rio Grande Valley school district suspended a high school student for distributing antiwar leaflets. Appalled at the school's flagrant disregard for the student's First Amendment rights, Garza ordered the school district to remove any record of the student's suspension. In the ruling Garza stated that the actions of the school district were unconstitutional. Although the conservative judge preferred that federal courts divorce themselves from school issues, he refused to let institutions trample on students' civil rights.[13]

In mid-September, 1970, the ILA case resumed, amid a caustic clash between Garza and a union official. During oral arguments by ILA attorneys, Garza became concerned at what he saw as a union member's attempt to "play footsie." After the official had stated that there were no obstacles preventing African Americans from working out of Anglo locals, Garza tersely reprimanded the official for the blatant lie. This was Garza's courtroom style in action. He was blunt, firmly stating his opinion. A few days later, attorneys ended oral testimony, and Garza gave them until December to file final briefs. But it would be another year before attorneys closed the case.[14]

Although Garza later ruled that the system of separate locals violated the Civil Rights Act of 1964, he did not order the segregated locals to merge. Garza found that the law was sketchy on the issue and urged an immediate appeal. In asking for an appeal Garza hoped that the ruling of the higher court would help "advance the ultimate termination of this litigation."[15]

Garza rarely openly critiqued race-based stratification, which was at issue in the ILA case. Yet, his lack of criticism did not entirely stem from his belief in maintaining the status quo. In the ILA case his reasoning was based on the economic realities of the segregated local system. After examining the analysis of the masters, he concluded that a merger would not solve the problem of economic inequalities that was at the heart of the longshore union suit. Instead, he wrote that inequities would continue to exist regardless of a merger because of the discrepancies among the various locals regarding such issues as seniority systems. These discrepancies, he wrote, must first be addressed before the higher court could consider a merger. Upon appeal, the Fifth Circuit did order a merger.[16]

As civil rights cases lay in the background, domestic repercussions of the Vietnam war continued in the foreground for Garza. In the fall of 1970, the army granted Rey an honorable discharge. He and his wife, now pregnant, moved to Austin so that he could finish law school. That year David began his first semester at the University of Texas law school.[17]

As the 1970 United States senatorial campaign reached its height, Garza avidly followed the race, especially since his longtime friend Lloyd Bentsen was running for a Senate seat. Garza was pleased when Bentsen won the race in November. But, although Garza did not participate in election activities, he dealt with a controversial campaign issue that came before his court.

A few weeks after the election, the United States attorney indicted twenty-two Starr County residents for vote fraud, alleged to have occurred during Bentsen's May primary. At the state trial, the jury acquitted nine and freed four of the defendants of all charges, as a result of a mistrial. Prosecutors charged the remaining nine with conspiring to "dilute" the vote in the May primary by improperly handling ballots.

Garza had known many of the men involved because of his past political activities in South Texas, so when the case came before federal court, he repeatedly told attorneys he was willing to disqualify himself. Attorneys on both sides, however, declined to have Garza disqualified. In his ruling, with overwhelming evidence pointing to a ballot conspiracy, Garza found eight of the defendants guilty. They immediately appealed. The Fifth Circuit reversed two of the eight convictions but affirmed the other six indictments.[18]

With the Starr County vote fraud ruling, Garza and the Fifth Circuit plunged a dagger into the heart of the partisan coalitions that had come to dominate South Texas. For years federal law had seemed to evade the area, allowing a corruption of the political process. Ballot tampering and other forms of vote fraud had became routine aspects of politics, giving party stalwarts hegemony over South Texas.[19] With the indictments Garza sent a clear message: South Texas would no longer be an outpost for federal law violations.

In December, 1970, the prestigious Delta Theta Phi legal fraternity at the University of Texas Law School initiated Garza into their membership as an honorary member. Garza would join famous past recipients, such as former President Lyndon Johnson and United States Senator John Tower. Garza and Bertha had driven to Austin for the ceremony, and, while they were there, they received an unexpected announcement when their daughter-in-law went into labor. In the late hours of December 5, 1970, Garza's first grandchild, Jessica, was born. Throughout the night Garza hovered over the baby, glowing with the same intense happiness and pride he had felt when his own children were born. The next day he attended the Delta Theta Phi ceremony in his honor. That night, the entire family, excluding the new addition and her hospitalized mother, celebrated both events at a casual dinner in Rey's small apartment. But at the crack of dawn, Garza arose and went to Our Lady of Guadalupe Catholic Church, the same church he had frequented in college. There he prayed for the health and happiness of his new grandchild.[20] As he bowed his head in church, Garza was probably unaware of the significance of the previous events. Indeed he was grateful for the honor that this traditionally Anglo institution had bestowed on him, yet he chose to express his thanks in a church named after the patron saint of Mexico, the land of his parents.

Back in Brownsville a week later, Garza learned that many city figures were discussing President Richard Nixon's appointment of

John B. Connally as U.S. Treasury secretary. Garza's reactions to the appointment ranged from skepticism to outright pleasure. But after speaking to Connally at a University of Texas event, Garza leaned toward a more optimistic view of Connally's position in the Republican cabinet. Although Garza remained apolitical, privately he believed, as did Connally, in conservative fiscal measures and liberal social actions. Like many Mexican Americans of his generation who were formally aligned with LULAC, however, Garza did not favor such liberal policies as expanded public assistance programs. He believed in individual self-reliance and saw these programs as promoting a loss of independence and initiative. Yet, he also was well aware of the poverty-ridden conditions in his region and believed these programs could be helpful on a solely temporary basis.[21]

In January, 1971, William Mallet began working as one of the first federal magistrates in the nation. Congress had finally initiated the Federal Magistrates Act of 1968, which Garza strongly lobbied for years earlier. With Mallet expediting appellate procedure, Garza could focus his attentions on the larger federal matters in his court.[22]

Although unencumbered of some duties through the magistrate system, Garza found the growing drug problem in the nation reinflated his docket. As the country's appetite for illegal narcotics swelled, so did smuggling in border towns such as Brownsville. In early 1971 a presidential task force concluded that the "ready availability" of Mexican marijuana "significantly affected the increase in drug abuse" in the nation. To combat the problem, President Nixon launched a campaign to cut back drug trafficking. For Garza, the campaign succeeded in filling his docket with evidentiary, constitutional, and due process issues. The most common cases dealt with illegal search and seizures as border agents, eager to apprehend drug smugglers, occasionally crossed legal bounds.[23]

Despite additional pressures from the heavy criminal docket, Garza continued his community activities. He became involved in a newly formed committee seeking to establish bachelor-level education in Brownsville. More than thirty years after Garza had earned his undergraduate and law degrees, the educational situation in his hometown had remained substandard. According to the first Catholic census of the Diocese of Brownsville, 22 percent of all Anglos, but only 5 percent of all Spanish-surnamed citizens, had completed high school in the Rio Grande Valley by the 1970s. Similarly, 7 percent of all Anglos and less than 1 percent of Spanish-surnamed Rio Grande Valley citizens had completed college.[24]

Community leaders, including Garza, decided to end the grim statistics. For many middle-class Mexican Americans raised in the 1930s, education was the panacea for much of what ailed the Mexican American community. Garza, too, advocated the message that through education individuals could uplift themselves and advance in society. He readily endorsed the planning committee's decision to invite Pan American University, an institution north of Brownsville, to the Rio Grande Valley city of Edinburg, to establish an upper division college and graduate center in the city. For the next few years Garza would speak at rallies and dinners to urge university regents to bring Pan American University to the Valley.[25]

The early 1970s for Garza followed the pattern of the decade before. He was actively serving his community, with his involvement in such organizations as the Knights of Columbus. Through his continued civic interest, Garza was firmly situated in the elite sphere of his society, as were his siblings and eventually his children. Civic service remained the family pantheon, with eldest brothers Ygnacio, Jr., and Leonel also active leaders in dozens of Brownsville organizations. They, like many middle class, college-trained Mexican Americans of their generation, made great inroads into Anglo society.

Through his brothers' activities, Garza was able to learn of the steady progress occurring in his hometown. The *maquiladora* system, arising in Brownsville six years earlier, began to enhance the city's economic stability. Tourism also brought a financial upswing to the poverty-ridden area. In 1971 the Sams Foundation, which Garza's brother, Leonel, served as principal accountant, opened the Gladys Porter Zoo. The thirty-one-acre zoo attracted nationwide visitors and, in turn, brought tourist funds to the community.[26] Garza took great pride in his hometown and cheered at each progressive step forward.

By 1972 Garza's rulings increased in impact. In June of that year, Garza ruled in *Medrano v. Allee* as part of a three-judge panel consisting of fellow federal judges John Brown and Woodrow Seals. In the Medrano case the United Farm Workers Organizing Committee of the AFL-CIO sued Texas Rangers, state officers, and county officials for using oppressive measures to break up a 1967 melon strike in Starr County. At issue was whether five Texas laws regarding organizational protests were unconstitutional and whether Texas Rangers stepped over the line of neutral law enforcement during their attempts to break the strike. After a few months of deliberations, the three judges held that not only were the five Texas laws unconstitutional but also that "the police authorities were openly hostile to the strike and individual strikers and used their law enforcement powers to suppress the farm workers strike."[27]

The Medrano case served as another example of the judicial presence firmly establishing the federal law in South Texas. In immigrant communities with uneven levels of bargaining power, strikes had been one of the few ways to effect change. In South Texas, however, strikes were not a plausible solution because of fears of strikebreakers, in the form of imported Mexican labor, and accostment by law enforcement officials. With the Medrano ruling, farm workers secured their only recourse in combating deplorable working conditions. The impact of the ruling rippled from the Southwest to the West Coast, prompting even major labor organizer César Chávez to celebrate the decision. Chávez followed the case from its inception in 1967, as the breaking of the strike catalyzed the Chicano civil rights movement, according to some historians. The strike "ignited a broad resentment among all classes of the Mexican American community," and, thus, awakened a movement bent on destroying social inequities. Chávez voiced his pleasure regarding the federal court ruling through the press.[28]

Garza took pride in the impact of the Medrano case. Since his law school years, when he had addressed the Mexican Chamber of Commerce and Texas legislators, Garza had voiced his concerns for the plight of Mexican Americans. The Medrano case allowed his rhetoric to turn into what he perceived as the best possible action, a legal mandate for change. Thus, Garza and many members of his generation believed that the conditions of Mexican Americans could improve not only through educational advancements but through legal victories. Ironically, this conservative ideology was in stark contrast to the liberal teachings of organized labor from which the Medrano case evolved.[29]

Garza's concern for the plight of his ethnic group did not interrupt his relationship with Anglo elites. By censuring the Texas Rangers for their abusive actions, Garza and the two other federal judges denounced the Texas governor, John Connally, who ordered state law enforcement to break the strike. Although he and Garza had been intellectual allies regarding most social issues of the day, this was one point on which they disagreed. But Garza never addressed the strike with the former

Texas governor. The federal judge from Brownsville won a victory over a repressive social order he personally never endured, and he believed there was no need to deliberate a moot issue, especially with a friend of more than thirty years.[30]

A few months after ruling on the Starr County case, Garza spoke at a University of Texas reception in Austin, attended by Lyndon B. Johnson. As the former president walked into the crowded room, Garza paused briefly in his speech, alarmed at how the political veteran had changed in appearance. The robust Texan Garza had remembered had disappeared into the shell of a haggard, white-haired, elderly man. Unaccustomed to seeing Johnson in such a disheveled state, Garza quickly concluded his address and made his way toward the feeble figure. Sitting next to Johnson, the federal judge uncomfortably witnessed Johnson's intense chest pains, brought on by angina. Between long pauses in his speech, Johnson would take a small nitroglycerin pill from his pocket and placed it under his tongue to relieve the discomfort. Uncharacteristically, Johnson spoke very little, and when he did he spoke only of far-off days and of early campaigns. The former president also reminisced about his first meeting with Garza on the University of Texas campus more than thirty years earlier.[31]

Garza tried to lift his old friend's spirits by congratulating him on the developing plans for an LBJ library and the proposed School of Public Affairs at the University of Texas. He could now become an elder statesman, Garza told him, sharing his vast political knowledge with devoted university students. But Garza's attempts to cheer his old friend were unsuccessful. Johnson solemnly acknowledged that this would be the last time the two men would meet. He thanked Garza for their long friendship and noted the irony of the journey taken by each man: meeting in Austin, both rising to national heights, and, finally, the return to the capitol city to bid each other farewell. Johnson was reflective and deathly tranquil as he spoke. Garza left the reception shaken and mournful.[32]

On January 23, 1973, Lyndon B. Johnson died of a heart attack at the LBJ ranch. Maurice Pipkin, former state representative living in Austin and Garza's high school mentor, called the federal judge to tell him the sad news. Although he had been expecting the call for close to four months, Garza was unnerved by Johnson's death. He was optimistic that Johnson would find some type of cause and be spirited back to his old self, taking charge, ordering those around him, leading the people. Instead, Johnson died at the age of sixty-four, alone and shattered. When he heard the news, Garza wept. He then headed to his church to pray for his departed friend. After an afternoon of spiritual healing, he wired Lady Bird his and Bertha's deepest sympathies and assured Johnson's widow he would always treasure the memories of her husband.[33]

Ironically, the former president, who had escalated the Vietnam war that ended his political future, died on the eve of the Vietnam peace negotiations. For Garza, the peace announcement thirteen hours after Johnson's death seemed a worthy tribute to a man he felt tried unsuccessfully to end the tragic war. Johnson would have relished peace negotiations if he were alive, Garza believed. President Nixon echoed Garza's sentiment when he stated, "No man would have welcomed this peace more than he." In Johnson's death, Garza would celebrate the moment on behalf of his old friend.[34]

In newspapers throughout the nation, headlines reporting Johnson's death shared front pages with stories on the Supreme Court's ruling allowing early-stage abortions. The landmark decision in *Roe v. Wade* upheld a woman's constitutional right to an abortion. For the devoutly Catholic Garza, the decision depressed him almost as much as Johnson's death. In his position as federal judge, Garza would have to reconcile the law of the state with the law of God, which in the United States were two separate entities. According to the nation's law, the church did not have the authority to enforce morals. Regardless of the legal rationale for the Supreme Court decision, Garza, like others in the conservative movement, regarded abortion as murder. As a pious Catholic, he viewed abortion as a morally incomprehensible alternative. Fortunately for Garza, the abortion dilemma would not face his district court, and, thus, his cultural and religious philosophies would remain relatively unruffled.

By the summer of 1973, Garza's influence on Rey's and David's career seemed evident. In May, 1973, David graduated from law school and accepted a position on the Texas Constitutional Revision Commission. The commission's purpose was to prepare recommendations calling for a new, shorter, and more general state constitution. David agreed to take the prestigious position for a two-year period. Garza's eldest son, Rey, was establishing himself as an able attorney in a small Brownsville firm, while Nacho was completing his second year in college.[35]

Garza remained a strong influence in his children's lives. Just as he had when eldest sons Rey and David were in college, Garza now sent Nacho a letter every Friday, on which he paper-clipped a ten-dollar bill to be used as Nacho's spending money for the week. In the letter Garza always ended with the same closing, "Be good, study hard, love, daddy." The small gesture was one his children long remembered, and it reinforced their feelings that they were Garza's top priorities.[36]

For Garza the workload of hearing motions and presiding over trials made for steady pressure. He continued to search for capable clerks to aid in his work. By August, 1973, the district court allowed Garza two clerks, and he hired as his second clerk Charlie Lewis, a recent graduate of the University of Texas. With two clerks Garza began a few new work rules. The senior clerk would take Garza to and from work every day and remain in the courtroom when the judge was also present. The newer clerk would drive the judge to his out-of-town venues. For Garza, Lewis proved to be an ideal driving companion. Because they shared a Catholic faith, the two entertained each other singing Latin spiritual hymns during their drives to Houston, Victoria, or Corpus Christi. The clerks also drove Garza to engagements across the state, including one in early 1974 when the Mexican American Bar Association honored the federal judge in Dallas.[37]

In May, 1974, Garza presided over his most arduous case, *Turner v. The American Bar Association.* Supreme Court Chief Justice Warren Burger and Fifth Circuit Chief Judge John Brown designated Garza to sit in ten cases filed in the federal district courts in the states of Alabama, Indiana, Minnesota, Pennsylvania, and Wisconsin. In the Turner case the main plaintiff, Jerome Daly, charged that his group possessed a constitutional right to have an unlicensed lay attorney assist in court proceedings. Daly represented a group who was under indictment for tax evasion. The group's suits claimed that the United States' judicial entity represented an organized conspiracy against individual rights. The group believed that federal judges were the "self-anointed High Priests" and the licensed attorneys were the "ministers," whose goal was to overthrow the Constitution and establish an "oligarchic dictatorship with orchestrated nobility." To combat this perceived injustice, the plaintiffs refused to pay taxes. Once indicted for tax evasion, the group named the entire federal judiciary, with the exception of Garza, as defendants.[38]

In excluding Garza from the complaint list, the federal judge noted that "the plaintiffs obviously engaged in a vigorous form of forum shopping." The group was aware that no federal court could try them if they named judges in that court in a lawsuit. The plaintiffs undoubtedly believed Garza would be sympathetic to their case and excluded his name to ensure he would preside over their dispute. The plaintiffs' forum shopping was futile. Garza denied their claims asking for an unlicensed lay attorney to assist them in their court proceedings. Through an intense historical analysis of the First, Sixth, and Fourteenth Amendments, he ruled that the state and federal courts were not obstructing the plaintiffs' rights. Finding no constitutional precedent that allowed an unlicensed attorney, Garza emphasized that the "plaintiffs lack standing to bring this antitrust action against any of the defendants" and denied all requests for relief. Garza's ruling proved crucial to the federal judicial establishment. Representation by an unlicensed attorney would have resulted in an entire overhaul of the legal system.[39]

Garza now experienced one of the significant events of his career. In July, 1974, after thirteen years as a circuit judge, fifty-nine-year-old Garza became the presiding officer of his court. The judicial leader ascended to the chief judgeship, not as a reward for outstanding work. The sitting judge with seniority of service automatically inherited the esteemed position. Garza now assumed the place of his old friend and hunting partner, Ben Connally, who had retired as chief judge of the court. With this designation, Garza became the first Mexican American chief judge of a federal judicial district. He was also the only chief judge in the history of the district to live in Brownsville.[40]

The job was more than an honor. It required Garza to take on many administrative duties, all potentially burdensome. A few months before Garza had become chief judge, the United States Congress created additional judgeships on the United States District Court for the Southern District of Texas, bringing the number up to eight judges. One of Garza's most challenging tasks was dealing with the responsibility of administering to seven different individuals, each with varying personalities and egos. Through Garza's decisive action, however, in both minute and substantial matters, the court was able to maintain a collegial atmosphere. Along with assigning cases and designating judges to sit by designation, Garza oversaw all administrative matters in the district, including personnel decisions regarding the court's staff. With all of his additional duties, however, his $40,000 salary remained the same.[41]

To honor Garza's appointment to the chief judgeship of the district court, the Cameron and Hidalgo County Bar Associations held a celebratory dinner at the Harlingen Country Club. Garza's longtime friend, United States Senator Lloyd Bentsen, praised Garza at the event attended by approximately 350 attorneys and other guests. Bentsen spoke of the historic importance of Garza's appointment and added, "Judge Garza is scoring another first as he becomes the first judge of Mexican American ancestry to achieve the status of chief judge." Bentsen pointed to Garza's long history of public service, especially in the area of education that for Garza was "the gateway to opportunity and service." Bentsen concluded the laudatory remarks by stating, "Judge Garza's dedication to the law and to the constant pursuit of excellence in everything he undertook has brought to reality what others might have looked upon as a dream."[42]

Garza recognized that his new administrative tasks would take up a significant amount of time. During his first few months as chief judge, he spent 60 percent of his time on formal administrative duties. He sought to become a superb administrator and attended to administrative chores punctiliously, not allowing them to govern his life or his work as a judge. His most successful time management accomplishment was in multiple jury selection. Before Garza's ascension to the chief judgeship, jury selection had been a time-consuming process. In a two- to three-day period, the court would select only one jury for each case.[43]

Jury selection was a two-step process governed by legal statutes. First, the clerk's office assembled the group of citizens, known as veniremen, from which they would select a jury panel of twelve or less. Second, the attorneys or the judge questioned the prospective jurors determining their qualifications and suitability to serve on the panel. The Constitution terms the questioning process voir dire. Garza initiated a new process in which the court selected twenty to twenty-five juries at one time instead. In this manner, Garza's two clerks would call hundreds of potential jurors into court twice a month. The law clerks, along with the deputy clerks, and deputy marshals were responsible for lining up the jurors correctly and bringing them into the court room at the appropriate time. Garza, his clerks, and attorneys would then spend the entire two to three days in the voir dire process, choosing jurors months in advance for future cases. The new program quickly became adopted throughout the district.[44]

Cleared of a large percentage of his jury duties through the creation of multiple jury selection, Garza could now enjoy one of his most satisfying tasks, naturalization ceremonies. A few weeks after being appointed to his new position on the district court, he presided over his first naturalization ceremony as chief judge. Garza, the courthouse personnel, and the new citizens and their families were all in exuberant moods during the legal function. Unlike the other district judges, Garza did not view naturalizing citizens as a typical administrative duty. Instead, he took steps to make the ceremonies memorable. He insisted that each of his clerks deliver a speech regarding immigrant experiences. The chief judge would then recite a poignant address, filled with messages of patriotism and the struggle for the American dream. For the Mexican American federal judge, the son of immigrants, naturalization duties became personally significant.[45]

By the fall of 1974, in the wake of Nixon's resignation and Vice President Gerald Ford's subsequent presidency, the chief judge continued administering his arduous legal schedule. In October he presided over one of his best known cases, *Partida v. Castañeda*. In this case the court addressed an equal protection challenge brought by a Mexican American against Texas' county grand jury selection system. The defendant petitioned for a federal writ of habeas corpus, claiming discrimination in the selection of grand jurors. A writ of habeas corpus means that an individual can come before a judge or court based on a constitutional challenge. The writ's purpose is to release the individual from unlawful imprisonment.[46]

Garza studied the evidence carefully and ruled that although the defendant had established a prima facie (legally sufficient) case of discrimination against Mexican Americans in the grand jury selection process, such prima facie cases were rebutted by evidence produced by the state. Accordingly, Garza denied the writ and dismissed the case. Although Garza was concerned about discrimination, in this case, he balanced his allegiance to his Mexican roots with his loyalty to American law, with the latter winning out.[47]

With Garza as chief judge, his clerk selection often became one of his most important decisions. Law clerks were indispensable to him now that he dealt with additional administrative tasks. In the spring of 1975 Garza began looking through dozens of résumés to find the ideal clerk. For the chief judge ideal meant a top law student from a national university who could easily adjust to life in the Mexican-oriented Brownsville. During interviews Garza went out of his way to put nervous young applicants at ease. He preferred to telephone prospective clerks himself rather than have his secretary schedule interviews. The telephone call often overwhelmed law clerks, who were unprepared to receive a personal message from a federal judge. Marc Knisely, the law clerk Garza selected in 1975, remembered the unexpected telephone call. "The deep resonant voice on the other end of the line still rings in my ears today, and I remember thinking that perhaps this was the way the Lord may sound if he were to communicate by telephone," recalled Knisely.[48]

The chief judge's law clerks continued to become members of the Garza family. The Garzas frequently invited clerks home for lunch, and if clerks were fortunate enough to arrive a few minutes early to drive the federal judge, Bertha treated them to a homemade Mexican breakfast. On holidays, such as Easter or Thanksgiving, the Garzas invited the clerks to meals with the entire family. The law clerks often viewed the Garzas as their second parents, and Garza, too, saw them as his children, and he never failed to call every former law clerk on his birthday.[49] For Garza the importance of familial ties that stemmed from his heritage resonated into his life on the court.

Garza remembered his humble, small-town origins. He instilled in his children a love for their community that by 1976 inspired eldest sons, Rey and David, to begin their own law firm in Brownsville, continuing a cycle begun more than thirty-five years earlier when Garza first hung out his shingle. Yet, the cycle was far from complete, as the next two decades brought even more opportunities to the chief judge of the district court.

CHAPTER 9

Toward the Fifth Circuit

1976–79

The devastating aftershocks of an era characterized by political and national traumas changed forever the nation's and Garza's perceptions of public service. Haunting questions of governmental trust, coupled with America's failing economic health, added to the strain on the nation's consciousness. Garza was hopeful that Democratic leadership could restore America's faith in government. He never suspected that this leadership would elevate him to the second highest federal court in the land. Indeed, the presidential election of 1976 opened up a period of great hope and opportunity in Garza's life that exemplified the pinnacle of his success.

Although fascinated with the current political scene, Garza was still busy with the court and his family. With two years now as chief judge, he had acquired the skills needed to keep the docket running smoothly and to address administrative duties with little difficulty. Enthralling cases, such as *Turner v. American Bar Association* or *Partida v. Castaneda*, no longer frequented Garza's court by this time. After fifteen years on the district bench, Garza found little novelty.[1]

Regardless of the routine nature of the district court docket, the process of adjudication continued to occupy Garza, primarily because of the sheer volume of cases. Particularly in Brownsville, Garza carried an unusually heavy docket of criminal cases, typically returning an astounding seven hundred indictments on average per year during the mid-1970s. As other federal judges throughout the country struggled with traditional federal criminal cases, the added load of drug and immigration issues continued to burden the United States District Court for the Southern District of Texas.[2]

Garza's civil docket was just as challenging. Clerks and court personnel remembered one case, humorous because of its name—*United States v. 76,552 Pounds of Frog Legs*. The case did not serve to define Garza as a jurist but, instead, illustrated the diversity of cases coming before the court. In this particular case the original claimants, Manuel Sánchez and Progressive Seas Products, Inc., moved for release of their condemned frog legs for reconditioning after the government forfeited the merchandise. At issue was whether the frog legs violated custom statutes and the Federal Food and Drug and Cosmetic Act. According to the prosecution, the plaintiffs willfully hid the fact that the frog legs, many of which were contaminated, failed to meet government standards.[3]

After a great deal of procedural wrangling, Garza held that the claimants were not entitled to a statutory exemption that would allow exportation of the frog legs. He also ruled that the government condemn the frog legs. He allowed the claimants a conditional repossession of the frog legs if they brought them into compliance with customs laws and if they paid all the fees incurred as a result of the customs violations. Clerks joked about the trial with the humorous name for years, reminding Garza to avoid frog legs when he dined out.[4]

Family life for the chief judge changed as his young children began to reach adulthood. Garza's youngest son, Nacho, began an accounting partnership with Garza's brother, seventy-three year old, Ygnacio, Jr. Nacho heralded the opportunity to benefit from his elder uncle's experience and to begin a faster route towards financial freedom. Garza was extremely pleased at his twenty-three-year-old son's decision. The proud father instilled in his children the importance of family interdependence, and Nacho was following the lessons learned in childhood.[5]

In November, 1976, Jimmy Carter defeated President Ford with a lukewarm 50 percent of the popular vote. It was a thin electoral win, diminished by the large portion of citizens who refused to vote. Regardless of the slim statistics, Garza was optimistic about the new administration. He hoped that the president-elect could fill the void left after the deaths of the Kennedy brothers and Lyndon Johnson. Garza believed the country needed a leader that would bring back citizens' faith in America's institutions and hoped Carter could mend the beleaguered presidency.[6]

One of the president-elect's first reconstructive steps was staffing the new administration. With the aid of longtime confidants Charles Kirbo, a Georgia attorney, and Griffin Bell, a former Fifth Circuit federal judge, Carter spent three weeks at his home in Plains, Georgia, researching prospective candidates for each key governmental position.[7]

Selecting an attorney general soon became Carter's top priority. He pressed advisor Griffin Bell to find a prospective candidate, and Bell considered Texas Attorney General John Hill. Before proposing Hill's nomination, though, Bell telephoned a few of his contacts in Texas, including Garza, to question them about Hill's qualifications. Garza and Bell had befriended each other at Fifth Circuit judicial conferences, and both Garza and Hill had attended many legal functions throughout Texas. The chief judge respected Hill's legal prowess and enthusiastically discussed Hill's many strengths with Bell.[8]

In relating Garza's remarks about Hill to the president-elect, Bell told Carter of Garza's own legal qualifications and of the way Garza's docket patterned the country's new agenda under Carter. As chief law officer of the federal government, the new attorney general would represent the United States in general legal matters, and Bell believed it was imperative that the individual have as diverse a legal experience as Garza's. Carter's interest was instantly piqued. He had repeatedly stressed his desire for an attorney general with a judicial background. More notably, Carter had also made a campaign pledge to appoint more minorities and women to federal positions and viewed Garza as a perfect opportunity to fulfill his promise. "Maybe Garza ought to be considered for attorney general," Carter suggested to Bell.[9]

That statement touched off a sequence of events that affected Garza's career. In December, 1976, a few days before Garza's annual hunting trip, Carter telephoned Garza's office and asked the chief judge whether he would consider the attorney general job. Garza, believing the call was a prank from his court personnel, promptly hung up on the next leader of the free world. Bell long remembered the humorous incident and relayed it in his autobiography. The presidential advisor was standing next to Carter during the short-lived telephone conversation. Through Carter's urging, Bell attempted the telephone call again. Once Bell convinced Garza of the seriousness of the offer, the chief judge politely told Bell he was not interested in the position.[10]

Attempting to persuade Garza to change his mind, Bell began addressing the many positive aspects of being attorney general. He discussed the prestige involved in the position and the enormous impact an attorney general wielded. Aware of Garza's close relationship with his children, Bell also told the federal judge that he could join his sons' law firm after his tenure ended. Garza need not worry that he was giving up a lifetime position as a federal judge, Bell insisted, for opportunities would abound after the four- to eight-year position ended. "When he seemed to warm up some, and it appeared to me that he might take the post, Charles Kirbo made a few calls checking on him," related Bell.[11]

Immediately after speaking to Bell, Garza telephoned Bertha. He told her he was both overwhelmed that the president would choose him for the crucial post and excited about the challenging prospect. After dealing with practically every type of case in the district court, the novelty of the attorney generalship was appealing to Garza. "I began to consider the idea. It was another way I could do something for my country," said Garza. Bertha was just as thrilled by the idea. But the couple questioned the personal consequences of the decision. It would be difficult to abandon their secure life-style, and they had become accustomed to the influences of living in a border town. Additionally, Garza truly enjoyed serving on the district court. Garza decided to use his upcoming hunting trip to contemplate his decision.[12]

Three days after speaking to Bell, Garza departed with his clerk, Charlie Lewis, to the Yzaguirre ranch in nearby Starr County. Garza was a childhood friend of Lalo and Luis Yzaguirre, owners of the twenty-thousand-acre ranch. Largely isolated from the rest of the county, the ranch possessed no modern-day facilities. The closest telephone was five miles north at a run-down gas station. As Garza and Lewis began their hike down to their favorite hunting range by the mouth of a small river, the sounds of a honking automobile horn distracted them. A young messenger ran towards the pair. Panting frantically, he delivered his urgent message: the president of the United States was on hold for Garza at the nearby gas station. Garza, with the messenger in tow, immediately ran to the truck, and sped toward the gas station.[13]

Reaching the telephone ten minutes later, Garza found that Carter was still on hold. This was the first time Garza would actually speak to Carter, excluding the time he hung up him. Carter pushed hard. Garza needed to recognize his duty to the South, to the law, to the country, Carter said. With a cigarette in hand, Garza paced as he spoke to the president. He thanked Carter for considering him as attorney general but told the president-elect he did not yet have an answer for him. He politely told Carter that he was seriously considering the attorney general job, but he would need a few more days to make a decision. Even as Garza said it, he realized it would be difficult to turn the president down. Garza assured Carter he would call him within the week, and then hung up the phone, tossed his cigarette, and returned to the hunting range.[14]

Directly after speaking to Garza, Carter asked Charles Kirbo to continue his unofficial investigation of the prospective attorney general nominee. Kirbo contacted attorneys throughout South Texas, many of whom were close friends of Garza. They notified the federal judge of the investigation after Garza returned from his hunting trip. When Garza learned of the probe into his personal and professional life, he decided he would make a decision within the next twenty-four hours. If he refused President Carter's offer, he did not want any time wasted on his investigation.[15]

Garza had contemplated the matter throughout his three-day hunting expedition and now discussed it with his wife and three sons. He also consulted his brothers, Ygnacio, Jr., and Leonel, along with his past law partner, now a state district judge, Gilbert Sharpe. Much like his decision fifteen years earlier to become a federal district judge, the weighty issue generated diverse opinions. Bertha told her contemplative husband that it would be difficult to uproot themselves from their quiet, insular hometown community and move to Washington, D.C. Through the Garzas' longtime friendship with Congressman Eligio (Kika) de la Garza and his wife, however, the Garzas had learned about many aspects of life in the nation's capitol. They could move to a suburban Virginia or Maryland area that would more closely mirror their ideal small-town living environment. Garza's sons also believed the family could quickly adjust to the new surroundings but also examined the prospect of Carter losing the presidency in 1980. Garza would be giving up a lifetime appointment to the federal bench, and there was only a small possibility that a new president would appoint a person Garza's age to fill a vacancy on a federal court. Garza's brothers and Sharpe also vacillated between the pros and cons of leaving a lifetime appointment and uprooting a family to take a position that may only last four years.[16]

Garza listened intently to the opinions of his loved ones and long-time friends. He finally came to the difficult conclusion that he would not accept Carter's offer. At most, Garza believed, he would be attorney general for eight years, and then he would have to search for new employment at the age of seventy. He did not want to begin a new career that late in life nor did he ultimately feel comfortable at the thought of leaving his hometown. He would undoubtedly face a culture clash moving to the more cosmopolitan Washington, D.C., area. Brownsville was the city that had nurtured his development into a young man, that had allowed him to pursue his potential, and that he cherished deeply. The latter reason may have been the most powerful motive Garza felt he had to refuse the prospect of becoming attorney general.[17]

Garza immediately telephoned Griffin Bell and told him that although he was honored to be considered, he had decided not take the position. "If I had been ten years younger, my decision may have been different," Garza told Bell and then directed the Carter advisor to drop his name from consideration.[18]

The attorney general position would have made Garza the highest-ranking Mexican American official in the history of the nation, also making him a recognizable figure. If Carter were to serve two terms, as many political analysts predicted, a Supreme Court appointment might have been Garza's next career move. But that was speculative. As it turned out, Carter did not have the opportunity to make any appointments to the Supreme Court. What is more notable, however, is that Carter's consideration of Garza for a cabinet post attested to the degree of acceptance the chief judge had garnered in the United States.

In the ensuing months Garza continued his hectic court schedule, dealing with cases that illustrated the full range of the law. In November, 1977, Garza ruled in *González v. Texas Employment Commission*, one of the few class action suits before the court in the 1970s. Limited numbers of this type of litigation existed in the docket. At issue was the constitutionality of Texas Employment Commission compensation policies denying benefits to women in the last trimester of pregnancy and in the first six weeks after giving birth.[19] *González* was the first women's rights issue to come before Garza's court, and it allowed him an opportunity to make an impact.

Although Garza had grown up in a traditional environment scattered with remnants of Mexican machismo, he held a liberal policy regarding women's rights. Garza had stressed to both his daughters the importance of achieving a college education and professional careers. Therefore, Garza held in *González* that the commission's lack of benefits to women denied due process. Garza believed in a strong sense of equity, but equity within the confines of law. Therefore, he granted hundreds of Texas women their first form of maternity leave. The Texas Employment Commission later appealed the case, but the Fifth Circuit dismissed it. This meant that Garza's holding stood.

In November, 1977, members of the Brownsville Independent School District Board spearheaded an effort to name a new school after Garza, Brownsville's most famous citizen. They allowed Garza to decide whether his name should be designated for an elementary, junior high, or high school. Aware of the intense rivalries that occurred in junior high and high school sports, Garza often quipped that he chose an elementary school because he feared hearing the condemnation, "Garza stinks," during the football season.[20]

In an elaborate ceremony held at the newly opened Reynaldo G. Garza Elementary School, the chief judge spoke of his path to the judiciary. As in many of his speeches, he praised education and credited his achievements to the encouragement of his long departed father, Ygnacio. Garza related to those in attendance that on Ygnacio's deathbed, his beloved father had explained to his children: "I am not leaving you much wealth, but I have provided you with something worth millions of dollars—education. Something no one can ever take away from you."[21] Typically, Garza did not accept praise, undoubtedly due to lessons of humility learned at church and at home.

Although he was not boastful regarding his professional or academic achievements, he did enjoy inflating his hunting and fishing successes. "If you heard him describe his marksmanship, it was no less that of the legends of the Old West," said hunting partner and now-federal judge, Filemón Vela. "He told tales of his fishing expeditions where with a machete in shallow water he would strike the largest red fish that have been recorded in the near-Mexican beach." Young incoming attorneys were unwilling to questions Garza's tall tales, and law clerks related the stories year after year.[22]

Within months after the naming of the Reynaldo G. Garza Elementary School, members of a Mexican American civil rights organization in Brownsville paid tribute to Garza by hosting a banquet in his honor to commemorate National Hispanic Heritage Week. During the banquet, discussions turned to the illegal alien issue and Carter's commitment to ensure "that all people within our borders, no matter how they may have got here, are treated with dignity and justice." Pleased that the president recognized the plight of illegal aliens, Garza hoped for presidential action on behalf of legal Mexican Americans requiring governmental support.[23]

In many Texas cities Garza's native group remained mired in the racial intolerance of the past. By the mid-1970s the median income of Mexican American families was 71 percent that of Anglos, and the census classified over a quarter of all Mexican Americans as poor. According to a United States Catholic bishops' committee, during the decade of the 1970s only 5 percent of Mexican Americans succeeded in reaching the highest levels of education and business. For the most part, Garza's status as a middle-class Mexican American continued to elude the ranks of his minority group.[24]

Many scholars attributed Mexican Americans' conditions to the economic downfall in the country. The 1960s and its climate of economic well-being begat sympathy for reform. With the economic erosion of the middle class in the 1970s, sympathy vanished and a conservative backlash emerged. The backlash hit twelve million Hispanics, 60 percent of them of Mexican origin.[25]

Mexican Americans fought this backlash both through the media and in federal courts, such as Garza's United States District Court, where Garza heard various civil rights suits related to Mexican Americans. The majority were valid legal actions. Some civil rights suits, however, were questionable. One such ambiguous case was *Hernández v. Western Electric Company, Inc.*, a civil action suit based on the Civil Rights Act of 1964. The case questioned whether Western Electric Company discharged the plaintiff, Rogelio E. Hernández, based on his Mexican American national origin. After the evidence failed to demonstrate a prima facie case of discrimination, meaning the evidence was insufficient to sustain a judgment, Garza ruled that he found no evidence of discrimination based on national origin. The chief judge ruled that Hernández did not meet the standards of the company, which fired him based on deficient skills.[26]

The chief judge, however, addressed the treatment the company afforded Hernández. Garza reprimanded Western Electric for its handling of the matter. He partly blamed management oversights on Hernández's inability to meet the company's standards. Aware of a personality dispute between Hernández and a supervisor trainer, the company failed to remedy the situation. Garza suggested that Western Electric's failure to assign the plaintiff a different supervisor trainer would have aided Hernández's ability to learn his task. Although Garza felt compassion for Hernández, he strongly believed in following the letter of the law. Finding no civil rights violations, he ruled accordingly.[27]

The chief judge ran his courtroom with utmost precision, retaining a common-sense approach to the law. "He had a knack of cutting to the core of an issue. He knew the law, he was intelligent, but he also knew how to apply all of that to the real world," said law clerk Ted Campagnolo. Unlike state judges, federal judges could comment on evidence, and Garza freely espoused his beliefs in the courtroom. Louisiana attorney Henry A. Politz, who later became chief judge of the Fifth Circuit, immediately developed respect for Garza after he read the chief judge's admonition to a jury during a trial, "Ladies and gentleman of the jury, you believe what you want to believe, but I believe this guy is a liar."[28]

Garza controlled the courtroom. "When you walked into his courtroom, you knew Reynaldo Garza was a federal judge, and I promise you that you conducted yourself commensurably," said Filemón Vela. Garza's booming voice remained his most powerful tool in accomplishing proper decorum. There was no audio system in the large, high-ceilinged courtroom during Garza's tenure as a district judge. For the chief judge normal volume was sufficient, and, commonly when admonishing attorneys or defendants, he exceeded normal volume.[29]

Although perceived as hard core in the courtroom, Garza still retained ultimate devotion for family. On June 9, 1978, the day of Garza and Bertha's thirty-fifth anniversary, David wed Diane Milliken in Dallas. Garza was so jubilant about his second son's marriage that he rented a bus to take his entire family, along with dozens of friends and family, from Brownsville to the wedding. Three months later, on September 16, 1978, youngest son Nacho married Marla Groth in Brownsville. Again, Garza celebrated the occasion with friends and family.[30]

But grief also touched Garza's life when eldest brother Ygnacio, Jr. died of cancer in February. The family had known of his prognosis for only a few weeks, as doctors had diagnosed his condition during an earlier hospital stay. When Ygnacio, Jr., returned from the hospital, the entire family kept vigil at his home during the night hours. On February 24, 1979, the seventy-six-year-old died. A tribute to the "longtime civic leader" appeared on the front page of the next day's *Brownsville Herald.* Garza deeply missed the brother who had advised him from childhood to adulthood. And as he had done with past tragedies, Garza delved into his court work soon after Ygnacio, Jr.'s funeral.[31]

Two months after Ygnacio, Jr.'s death Garza was again faced with a choice that would drastically affect his career. Unknown to Garza, United States Senator Lloyd Bentsen had singled him out as a candidate for a vacancy on the Fifth Circuit Court of Appeals. Garza would replace Judge Homer Thornberry, who was taking senior status from the higher court. After Bentsen suggested Garza's name to President Carter, the president readily agreed to the nomination.[32]

Carter was intent on appointing a greater number of women and minorities to the federal judiciary, but it was a difficult task to accomplish since the candidate pool was not as large as the representation of those groups in the total population. The numbers of minorities and women in the judiciary were dismal: only 3.8 percent were African American, 1 percent were Hispanic, and 1 percent were female. Carter planned on doubling the percentages. Appointing the first Mexican American to the federal Appeals Court would help accomplish the president's goal.[33]

Unlike previous administrations, Carter had implemented the use of screening commissions in the judicial selection process. The president had set up one commission in each state composed of eleven members. Commission members sent each candidate a questionnaire and evaluated their qualifications. Traditionally, the state commissions would then send a list of candidates to President Carter, whose advisors rated the potential appointees. Carter then selected one to two candidates and initiated an American Bar Association investigation of the individuals. Carter's advisors also consulted special interest groups, such as the Black Lawyer's Association. The new selection process was not as party-oriented as in previous years as it removed much of the power of United States senators in choosing federal judges.[34]

In mid-April, 1979, Garza learned from President Carter he was being considered for Thornberry's post. The president telephoned the chief judge in his chambers and spoke with Garza about his desire for the chief judge to serve on the Fifth Circuit. The president then ended the conversation by ribbing Garza, "You turned me down once; don't turn me down twice." Garza laughed heartily and thanked Carter for considering him. He voiced his enthusiasm for the position, and then agreed to go through the screening process.[35]

Garza was extremely happy about his prospective move to the second tier of the three-tiered federal court system. He had long regretted his hesitation when President Johnson offered to appoint him to the same court fourteen years earlier. He knew the position would mean more time away from home and a loss of courtroom action. Now that his children were older, however, the time spent away from Brownsville would not seem as detrimental. Appeals judges could choose their home base as long as they kept an office out of a federal building, so moving away from Brownsville would not be a concern. Additionally, Bertha was now free to join him on his out-of-town venues. Garza thrived from the excitement of trials, watching attorneys litigate, and instructing jurors about legal statutes. Appeals judges, however, rarely tried large cases; they did not sentence criminals and their names rarely appeared in newspapers. For that reason, some observers termed the position a "ticket to dignified obscurity." The Fifth Circuit promised a more relaxing atmosphere with less immediate time pressures than the district court. Garza would miss the trial action, but the attractions he saw on the Fifth Circuit far outweighed the losses.[36]

Again, Garza brought a serious decision to the attention of his family, his longtime confidants, and his peers on the district court. All agreed that an elevation on the Fifth Circuit was a wise move for the chief judge. As a Fifth Circuit judge, Garza would no longer deal with sentencing, the aspect of adjudication he found most disturbing. He would also lose much of the autonomy he possessed as chief judge of the district court. Garza pointed out that as a new member of the Fifth Circuit court he would again become a novice judge acclimating to a new task. He was willing, however, to give up his status to become a member of the second highest court in the land.[37]

In the spring of 1979, Garza received the screening commission's questionnaire from the Republicans on the judiciary committee. The questionnaire addressed issues such as each nominee's public interest legal work and views about criminal justice sentencing. The tenor of the questions suggested that the committee sought to determine one's propensity to follow a liberal or conservative stance on fundamental issues. "I considered this type of political litmus testing most inappropriate to engage a sitting federal judge," said Garza. He contemplated his answers for a few days and in many blanks he replied, "I have cases pending covering most of these questions, and I do not think it would be a good idea to answer any issue before a trial." Garza believed a federal judge should maintain an apolitical image and refused to compromise his adamant belief for a coveted position on the Fifth Circuit. Two weeks after sending in his questionnaire, the Senate judiciary committee scheduled a confirmation hearing, which meant that the screening commission had given him a favorable recommendation and would now go before the Senate—just as he had in 1961 for the district court appointment.[38]

It was while he was awaiting his confirmation hearing that Garza learned that his colleague, U.S. District Court judge for the Western District of Texas, John Wood, Jr., had been assassinated by a single rifle shot as he stood in his condominium parking lot in San Antonio. It was the first assassination of a federal judge in the nation, and the FBI put the case on its critical list. The FBI's main suspect in the killing was the Chagras family, known drug traffickers in El Paso. Wood possessed a reputation for his tough sentencing of drug dealers, and the FBI theorized retaliation had been the cause of his murder.[39]

Garza had established a warm relationship with Wood during their visits at various judicial conferences and was saddened by the loss of his congenial colleague. The crime also shocked him. Assassinations of federal judges occurred in Third World countries, not the United States, Garza believed. Although Garza had encountered occasional threats in the district court, until Wood's murder, he had never given much consideration to angry warnings from the many drug dealers he had sentenced.[40]

By June, 1979, the FBI was still unable to capture the assassins, and Garza vocally condemned the message of Wood's killing. There was little to stop others from attempting the same crime, Garza often told his courthouse personnel. Garza thought about Wood's murder, especially after attending a swearing-in ceremony of five new federal judges in Houston. Senator Bentsen, also present at the event, initiated the investiture with a silent prayer for Wood and promised that the assassins would be brought to justice. Garza, who led the investiture ceremony, felt the event was "one of gladness but a gladness tempered with sadness because of the death of our colleague." The chief judge concluded the ceremony by asking for a moment of silence for Wood.[41]

Three weeks after the investiture ceremony, Garza flew to Washington, D.C., to make his second appearance before the Senate judiciary committee. To expedite the hearings, committee members interviewed six other Fifth Circuit nominees along with Garza. The hearing was held at the Dirksen Senate Office Building near the Capitol, with Democratic Senator Howell Heflin of Alabama presiding. Senator Bentsen and Congressmen Eligio "Kika" de la Garza and Chic Kazen gave Garza nothing but high praise. In his remarks Bentsen extolled Garza's virtues, stating, "This man is revered in South Texas, . . . he is rendering a great public service in allowing his name to be placed here." Bentsen then endorsed the other two Texas nominees, Carolyn Dineen King and Thomas Reavley.[42]

After several other senators spoke on behalf of the other candidates, Senator Heflin noted that Garza received a "well qualified" rating from the American Bar Association's Standing Committee on the Federal Judiciary. Heflin then read the ratings of the other seven nominees and asked Garza to make the first statement. Garza thanked Bentsen, de la Garza, and Kazen for their praises and stated that he hoped he would make a contribution to the Fifth Circuit. Heflin then told Garza, "If confirmed, you will have the distinction of being the first judge of Hispanic origin to serve on the Fifth Circuit Court of Appeals." Heflin referred to the underrepresentation of women and minorities on the federal bench and asked the chief judge, "What recommendation do you have to remedy the situation?" Garza pointed out he was the first Mexican American appointed to the district bench and stated, "He [Kennedy] told me at that time that my actions on the bench would mean a lot toward whether other Hispanics like myself would have this opportunity." Garza then quipped, "It took eighteen years to get one on the Fifth Circuit, so I do not know what kind of job I did, Senator." The hearing room erupted in laughter.[43]

With that statement Garza had alleviated the somewhat tense nature of the confirmation hearings. "Everyone in the room was taken aback. He just told it like it was, and I'll never forget that moment," said fellow Fifth Circuit nominee Henry Politz, who later became chief judge of the circuit.[44]

Garza then lapsed into a serious statement. He told the committee that he foresaw a better future for Hispanic appointments, stating, "I think we are getting more and more qualified people." Garza pointed out that President Carter had recently appointed another Mexican American to his court, James De Anda, and ended with an optimistic statement regarding future Mexican American appointments. The Senate judiciary committee then questioned the other two candidates. The committee adjourned after two and a half hours, and Garza took the first plane home to Brownsville.[45]

A *Washington Post* article a few days later described Garza and the other two Texas candidates as "breezing through their confirmation hearing without any serious objections raised by the Senate judiciary committee." In Brownsville a local newspaper reporter interviewed Garza regarding the appointment and editorialized that "the man should be a member of the United States Supreme Court." Actually, the writer mirrored the sentiments of many Brownsville citizens.[46]

Once the nation heard of Garza's prospective appointment to the Fifth Circuit, groups such as the Mexican American Assembly and La Raza National Bar Association voiced their support of the candidate. In a laudatory letter to the president, the Mexican American Assembly described the "myriad . . . opportunities" in the administration to be responsive to the "nation's total community" through federal appointments. The group concluded the letter with the statement, "we laud your appointment of the Honorable Reynaldo G. Garza to the Fifth Circuit Court of Appeals."[47]

Just three days after Garza's sixty-fourth birthday in July, the Senate Judiciary Committee approved his nomination to the Fifth Circuit. As Garza was about to attend his morning Mass, Senator Bentsen called to tell him of the Senate confirmation. Garza thanked Bentsen, then Garza telephoned his entire family to share the good news. That evening they celebrated at a downtown Matamoros restaurant.[48]

Garza immediately made accommodations in Brownsville for his new chambers. Garza would move to the third floor of the federal court house, and Judge Filemón Vela, later appointed to the district court, would occupy Garza's old chambers. The judiciary had allotted Garza one extra clerk on the Fifth Circuit. Since his present clerk, Ted Campagnolo, had agreed to stay until 1981, Garza hired two more clerks to begin in the fall of 1979.[49]

In July, 1979, Fifth Circuit Chief Judge John Brown swore in Garza at the Fort Brown Hotel during an elaborate evening ceremony hosted by the Cameron County Bar Association and the Brownsville Clearing House Association. Because the FBI still had not captured Judge Wood's assassins, security at the event was tighter than usual. Hundreds of city, state, and federal officers surrounded the grounds of the aptly termed Fort Brown Hotel's Fortress Room. Security guards escorted Garza in front of a capacity audience, composed of his wife, children, family, friends, members of the media, and the general public. Nineteen federal judges attired in black robes were seated at the flag-draped speakers' table as Garza entered, followed by Fifth Circuit Chief Judge Brown.[50]

The ceremony began as Bishop John Fitzpatrick gave the invocation, followed by expressions of admiration and friendship in both English and Spanish from Garza's colleagues. Judge Brown then read telegrams from notables unable to attend, including Senator Bentsen and President Carter. The highlight of the program was a presentation of a formal portrait of Garza that was to hang permanently outside the second-floor courtroom he had presided over for eighteen years.

After the presentation Judge Brown read Garza's commission. The new appeals judge solemnly raised his right hand to take his judicial oath. Judge Brown ended the elegant ceremony with wit. "I am empowered to give you the rest of this day off. Report in tomorrow morning." Applause filled the auditorium. As the applause died down, Garza introduced Bertha and the children to the audience. Garza's good friend Sam Perl, rabbi emeritus of Brownsville's only synagogue, closed the event with a solemn benediction.

Immediately following the ceremony the Bar Association hosted a lavish dinner for more than two hundred attorneys, judges, and public officials and their spouses at a restaurant across the border in Matamoros. The festivities were replete with mariachis, Mexican food, and good cheer. Throughout the evening, Garza beamed with happiness, greeting his many guests.

The symbolism of celebrating this greatest of American accomplishments in a Mexican border town was powerful. Garza seemed to have reached the pinnacle of his career, but the next decade would be a culmination of bicultural fusion in Garza's career.

CHAPTER 10

The Fifth Circuit
1979–86

Although he was sixty-four years of age when he joined the Fifth Circuit in July, 1979, Garza easily adjusted to the new court. In the preceding eighteen years, the daily grind of presiding over a sprawling district with a crushing docket had become taxing. He knew he would not miss the district court's pressing deadlines or yearn for the burdensome administrative duties he had undertaken as chief judge. The Fifth Circuit indeed kept him busy, but it provided a quieter life. Instead of dealing with the theater of the courtroom filled with live testimony and dueling attorneys, he could now lead a tranquil existence, tucked away in his chambers with briefs, legal references, his secretary, and his law clerks. The transition signified more than just adapting to a placid adjudication pace. Garza's tenure on the appeals court brought him additional honors and recognition, which, in turn, meant that he did not have to compromise either himself or his heritage in achieving success.[1]

Garza stepped into a court maintained by twenty-five judges with jurisdiction over six of the country's most populous states. With cases coming from Alabama, Florida, Georgia, Louisiana, Mississippi, and

Texas, the annual appeals were about to exceed four thousand. As an appellate judge, Garza saw his judicial colleagues on the few days monthly when they gathered to hear oral arguments or, more rarely, at monthly conferences to discuss pending cases. He would travel to the court's headquarters in New Orleans seven times a year. Besides New Orleans, he could hear cases in Atlanta, Jacksonville, Fort Worth, and Montgomery, these cities having been designated by Congress as the places terms of court could be held.[2]

The appellate process was traditionally slower than district court operations. Several steps occurred before the Fifth Circuit court could consider reviewing the judicial ruling of a lower court. The party bringing the appeal first had to submit a brief, a full written explanation of a party's legal position, then allow the other party time to respond. In 1968 the Fifth Circuit had pioneered a process consisting of a screening panel of three judges who determined whether each case was worthy of proceeding through the appellate process. If the judges on the screening panel agreed to hear oral arguments, the clerk of the court placed the case on the appeals calendar and then parceled it out on an equitable basis to a panel. While on a panel, Garza worked with his fellow jurists, reaching decisions though exchanges of written memoranda, drafts, and informal conferences. Although attorneys for both sides were present, there were no jurors or witnesses present, and the concerned parties were generally not present either. Occasionally, if requested by the parties, the judges would sit *en banc*—that is, the full complement of judges on the circuit would reconsider a panel's decision. Judges also sat *en banc* when they perceived the appeal would present an unusually important legal question the whole court should address.[3]

Panel members considered the brief before they allowed oral argument. Oral argument consisted of an attorney's verbal summary of the written brief, generally limited to fifteen or twenty minutes on each side. Garza would read each brief meticulously, writing notes to himself to ask during oral arguments. On their few monthly gatherings, Garza and the other Fifth Circuit judges worked Mondays through Thursdays, hearing oral arguments beginning at nine in the morning and concluding shortly after the noon lunch break. During oral arguments, judges interrupted attorneys and asked questions. The main function of oral arguments was to clarify uncertainties about the facts or the law. It also allowed attorneys to present the most compelling aspects of their case. Garza used the oral arguments to probe the strength of the conclusions he reached from analyzing briefs. As he did during his district court years, he expected professionalism and efficiency from attorneys arguing before his panel. If attorneys drifted towards obscure tangents, one stern "stick to the case at hand" from Garza's deep resonant voice quickly put the oral arguments back on course.[4]

After oral arguments, the panel judges met in chambers privately, without their law clerks, and discussed cases. Debate was often vigorous and divisive, as all three judges attempted to vie for a ruling based on their individual views of the case. During breaks in tense discussions, Garza often walked back to his chambers for a quick puff of his cigarette and a moment of quiet contemplation. Because of the congenial nature of the Fifth Circuit, however, heated conference debates usually ended with an amicable resolution. During the discussions judges decided who would write each opinion. Law clerks conducted most of the research and would collaborate with their judge to write the opinion. Once written, clerks circulated the opinion to the other members of the panel. Several months traditionally passed before the court issued a mandate and the ruling took effect.[5]

Like many appellate jurists, Garza drew from his experience as a trial judge. Because of his strong criminal trial background in the district court, when writing opinions dealing with criminal matters, his fellow Fifth Circuit judges often turned to Garza's expertise. "In criminal cases, invariably we looked to him [Garza] for advice and recognition and guidance. His justice barometer was always keenly tuned, and he had a particularly good feel for those cases," said fellow Fifth Circuit judge, Henry Politz.[6]

On the appellate level, Garza's past trial experience was especially evident during oral arguments. "He was well-studied and was familiar with the briefs and positions of the parties. He was an active questioner. Having been a trial judge, he seemed to be very interested in what took part during the trial," recalled an attorney who went before Garza during oral arguments. Another attorney remembered, "His eyelids sit at half mast, but just when you think he may be asleep, he'll slap you with a tough question." Garza's active involvement on the appellate bench during oral arguments allowed him to acclimate rapidly to the new court.[7]

During his first few months on the new court, Garza naturally gravitated to judges from Texas, including Chief Judge John Brown. The two had cemented a friendship a decade earlier when they began a tradition at judicial conferences of performing a brief comedic skit together. Garza served as the straight man to Brown's fanciful act. Socially, Brown's ebullience contrasted with Garza's serious, reserved personality. The two men's wardrobe best exemplified the contrast. Garza usually wore a conservative single-breasted suit, accentuated by a traditional, two-toned striped or geometric tie. Brown donned brilliantly colored sport coats, blue or gray slacks, and flamboyant ties that helped blend the distinct, but never garish, attire. Similar to Garza's relationship with Lyndon Johnson, the chief judge and the new appointee complemented each other's temperament.[8]

Garza also befriended Thomas M. Reavley, a fellow University of Texas at Austin undergraduate alumni who was six years Garza's junior. Reavley had a varied legal career before his appointment in 1979, including a stint as assistant district attorney in Dallas, an adjunct professorship at the law schools of Baylor and the University of Texas, and a Texas Supreme Court judgeship.[9] Like Garza, Reavley grew up in a small town. The two found a common ground in their rural upbringing and formed a close relationship.

Sam Johnson was the third Texan who built strong ties with Garza. Another University of Texas law school alumni, he entered the Fifth Circuit three months after Garza. Like Reavley, Johnson had also served on the Texas Supreme Court, a position he held before his appointment to the Fifth Circuit.[10] Garza and Johnson shared many of the same friends but knew each other only slightly before joining the court. On the Fifth Circuit they developed a fast friendship.

Garza's affability with the Fifth Circuit judges from Texas matched his harmony with Louisiana-born John Minor Wisdom. During judicial conferences Garza had met hundreds of federal jurists, including members of the United States Supreme Court, but none could match the personal and intellectual admiration Garza felt for Wisdom. He was a revered judge and legal philosopher more than ten years older than Garza with two decades experience on the bench. First in his class at Tulane law school, Wisdom was an integral member of this group, known as The Four. Although Wisdom was most renowned because of his civil rights decisions, Garza's respect for the elder judge superseded issues of civil rights. It was Wisdom's daily scholarly dealings with legal precepts that heightened Garza's esteem for the Southern judge. The two shared a similar temperament and bonded together based on their common judicial philosophy. "I read many of Reynaldo's opinions when he was a district judge, and I found he possessed a keen sense for the law, especially concerning issues of civil rights," said Wisdom.[11]

Among the other judges, Garza formed a strong bond with Henry A. Politz, a jovial Southerner from Shreveport. He possessed a colorful personality, intensified by his heavy Cajun accent. Politz met Garza during the Senate confirmation hearings where both men were confirmed as appellate judges. Politz had received his judicial commission at the same time as Garza. Politz affectionately referred to Garza as El Jefe, recalling Garza's tenure as chief judge on the district court. Although Politz told many a colorful tale, he thoroughly enjoyed Garza's story-telling abilities and constantly asked him to retell his favorite humorous anecdotes. "His facial intonations, his gestures, no one could tell a tale like El Jefe," said Politz, who would later become chief judge of the appellate court.[12]

The nickname El Jefe was a subtle indication of both Politz's and the other Fifth Circuit judges' consciousness of Garza's biculturalism. Garza, too, used opportunities to make the judges aware of aspects of his Mexican heritage. For example, many of Garza's anecdotes reflected characteristics of his border hometown, and he often intermingled English with Spanish when describing incidents. These lessons on Garza's heritage were mutually beneficial. The judges became more understanding of cultural diversity, and the Brownsville judge demonstrated how effectively his two cultures could be interwoven.

During Garza's first year on the Fifth Circuit, he became embroiled in the court's long-standing interconflict—splitting the mammoth court. At twenty-five judges, and with an exploding Sun Belt population, the docket became unwieldy. The region's population growth directly affected the brimming docket. Increased commercial activity had resulted in expanded federal regulation. With the expansion, more attorneys and district courts had inevitably produced a greater number of appeals. By 1980 the number of appeals had increased 10 percent from the previous year to a staggering 4,236. This directly contrasted with the 3,900 appeals filed in 1960 in the entire federal appellate system. With the growth in appeals, more petitions for rehearing *en banc* flooded the court, meaning up to twenty-five judges, all with divergent opinions, could consider a case.[13]

Along with the difficulty in finding consensus within the large court, the time constraints inherent in *en banc* sessions quickly became a problem. If each judge spoke only five minutes, which was atypical, as there was an informal rule that judges would never interrupt each other when discussing their legal position on a case, deliberations could take hours. Frequently, Garza and the other Fifth Circuit judges stayed up most of the night during *en banc* sessions.[14]

En banc sittings were also problematic because of the many physical obstacles to such a large judicial body. Accommodating the populous court required a two-tiered bench. "I believe there were more than twenty judges, and the bench was only built for seven or nine at the most. It was quite a sight, and something that will probably not be seen again," said Ted Campagnolo, Garza's law clerk at the time.[15]

The urgent need to divide the court into two circuits was best illustrated by *Jurek v. Estelle,* a death penalty case. With twenty-two judges sitting *en banc* for the trial, debate was intense and fiery. *Jurek* was concerned with the acceptance or denial of a petition for writ of habeas corpus based on a defendant's claim that law enforcement officials did not voluntarily obtain his confession used at trial. The purpose of the writ was to release from prison the petitioner, whom in this case, the state court had convicted of capital murder and sentenced to death.[16]

Garza's opinion became the court's decision; yet, the four other opinions written in the case illustrated the problem of a large *en banc* court. Garza held that the defendant gave his first confession voluntarily and the court properly admitted it at trial, but he gave his second confession involuntarily and its use at trial was improper. In his ruling Garza reversed the lower court's denial of habeas corpus relief. Of Garza's closest acquaintances on the court who took part in the *en banc* decision, Judge Frank Johnson, Jr., concurred, Judge Brown concurred in part and dissented in part, and Judge Reavley dissented.[17] Evident by the five opinions, establishing consensus with twenty-plus jurists was nearly impossible.

After the case Garza and the majority of the other judges took an adamant stand for splitting the court. "At first we wanted to allow a year to pass before we would decide to split the circuit. It soon became clear that a split was inevitable," said Garza. To encourage legislative action, Garza and four of his fellow judges, including Frank Johnson, Jr., formed a committee to adopt a resolution urging Congress to divide the circuit into two circuits. The states of Louisiana, Mississippi, and Texas would compose one circuit, while the other circuit would include Alabama, Florida, and Georgia.[18]

Garza and the rest of the committee followed stringent guidelines to remain within the confines of their positions as judicial officers while advocating the split in Congress. They testified before a House judiciary committee and attended a dinner in Washington, D.C., to explain their position to members of the Senate. At the dinner Garza sat next to Senator Strom Thurmond of South Carolina. Although members of the Senate such as Thurmond favored a circuit split, it would be another year before there was a resolution to the issue.[19]

In March, 1980, Garza was in the nation's capital teaching a course for newly appointed judges at the Federal Judicial Center, when he and Bertha attended a reception hosted by the National Women's Political Caucus. The purpose of the affair was to celebrate the historic number of women, ten of them, on the United States Court of Appeals. Garza attended the event to honor fellow judge, Carolyn Dineen Randall (formerly King), whom Carter had appointed to the Fifth Circuit at the same time as Garza. Garza and Bertha arrived by taxi to the Georgetown home of W. Averell Harriman, former New York governor. Priceless antiques and flowering azaleas adorned the quarters. Of the more than one hundred and seventy-five guests, Garza was one of the few men present at the soiree. As Garza admired an original Picasso in the expansive mansion, a reporter asked his comments regarding female jurists. "I was one of those lawyers that didn't want women on juries. That was a long time ago. But now women make very fine jurors, and we're pleased with the two [women] judges in the Fifth Circuit," said Garza.[20]

In October, 1980, Garza was notably relieved when Congress approved the passage of the Fifth Circuit Court of Appeals Reorganization Act of 1980. The act officially split the Fifth Circuit. A day after Congress approved the act, President Carter signed it into law. The law mandated that Louisiana, Mississippi, Texas, and the Panama Canal Zone comprise the Fifth Circuit, with headquarters in New Orleans. The jurisdiction in the Canal Zone expired shortly after the split of the circuit because the Republic of Panama resumed control over the area. Congress authorized fourteen active judges as members of the Fifth Circuit. The remaining states of Alabama, Florida, and Georgia were now part of the Eleventh Circuit, headquartered in Atlanta. Twelve active judges presided over the new circuit court. The act would take effect a year later.[21]

A month after signing the historic act, President Carter made a trip to Garza's hometown. Presidential election activity was at its height, and Carter was attempting to gain the vote of Mexican Americans in South Texas. Carter's trip to Brownsville marked the first time a president had visited the city, with the exception of Zachary Taylor, who, as a general, brought the United States Army to the area in the 1840s. Thrilled to have the United States president in their midst, hundreds of Brownsville citizens attended a campaign rally in the city.[22]

During his address to the Brownsville community, Carter boasted of his pride at appointing the greatest number of Hispanic judges in America's history, and then told the audience of his offer to Garza of the attorney generalship. Carter said, "I regret very much . . . that the United States did not have the benefit of his service in that Cabinet post of attorney general," then he elaborated on Garza's judicial prowess. The crowd exploded with applause after Carter's remarks about their most famous citizen. Carter was undoubtedly using Garza's popularity to benefit his presidential campaign. Although Garza was out of town during the president's visit, youngest son Nacho, then a city commissioner, was part of the president's welcoming committee to the town.[23]

Unfortunately for Carter, his campaign efforts could not help him win another term as president, and Ronald Reagan's election as the fortieth president began twelve long years of Republican presidential power. Garza was naturally disappointed at the Democratic Party's loss, but his interest in politics was no longer nearly as consuming as it had been before his appointment to the appellate bench. With a deep respect for any individual assuming the presidency, Garza sent a letter to the new president wishing him success.[24]

During his second year on the Fifth Circuit, Garza wrote 135 opinions, more than any other judge on the court. He adjudicated a steady flow of cases involving the whole range of the law, including admiralty, employment discrimination, federal habeas corpus, labor, and taxation. His three law clerks slightly lessened his judicial burden. He continued, however, keeping the same hours as during his district court days. Every Saturday morning Brownsville citizens traveling through Elizabeth Street, a major downtown thoroughfare, saw Garza's vehicle parked outside the Federal courthouse. He came to work on Saturday to check his mail, pay his bills, and look over any pending matters, such as motions or presentence reports.[25]

In April, 1981, Garza celebrated two decades on the federal court.

His three clerks planned an elaborate ceremony in Brownsville to honor the judge. They invited over one thousand people to a seated dinner. Garza's fellow district judges, past law clerks, and district attorneys all joined in tribute. Former United States congressman, Joe Kilgore, who had advised Garza during his first Senate judiciary committee hearing in 1961, acted as master of ceremonies for the affair. Law school friend Joe Greenhill, chief justice of the Texas Supreme Court, delivered a moving speech and reminisced about law school years. Chief judge of the United States District Court, John Singleton, and former chief judge of the Fifth Circuit, John Brown, flew in for the special occasion. Former Fifth Circuit judge and attorney general, Griffin Bell, spoke admiringly about Garza. It was an evening filled with reverence for the federal judge from Brownsville, and Bell was himself awed by the devotion expressed by the community. "It was one of the nicest occasions I have ever been to. It was grand to see the community pay tribute to a sitting federal judge," stated Bell.[26]

As part of the ceremony Garza's clerks arranged for the Reynaldo G. Garza Elementary School twirling team to perform. Garza seemed noticeably touched by the presentation. He gave a heartfelt speech thanking those in attendance for making time to attend the event, proclaimed his happiness and closed his remarks with a brief prayer. It was a fitting tribute to Brownsville's native son.

A month after the anniversary celebration, Garza ruled on a school desegregation case coming before the Fifth Circuit. Notably irritated with the fact that desegregation cases were still being addressed in the 1980s, Garza put the issue in perspective in *Valley v. Rapides Parish School Board* with this statement: "Twenty-seven years after *Brown v. Board of Education* and sixteen years after the commencement of this litigation, we are confronted with yet another set of appeals arising from implementation of the command to desegregate public schools in Rapides Parish, Louisiana."[27] School desegregation cases continued to plague the court for the next decade.

In October Garza and Bertha attended the historic ceremonies commemorating the split of the Fifth Circuit. All active and senior judges, except for three, were present. They, along with court scholars, attorneys, and family members filled the imposing Italian Renaissance–style federal courthouse in New Orleans. After announcing its *en banc* decision in *Estate of Bright v. United States*, the Fifth Circuit court closed in final adjournment. The speeches then followed. Tulane Law School Professor Harvey Couch first delivered a brief historical review of the court, then former attorney general and Fifth Circuit Judge Griffin Bell traced the history of the Fifth Circuit split. As the Eleventh Circuit judges symbolically departed the building, Garza smiled contentedly. He was optimistic that the court would now function efficiently, the way it was meant to perform.[28]

Garza received another honor in May, 1982, when Houston Mayor Kathy Whitmire paid tribute to him, along with seven past United States district judges, by proclaiming May 24 as Federal Judicial Day. The highlight of the event was the unveiling of oil portraits of each judge. In a ceremony hosted by Whitmire, Garza's son, David, spoke of his father's position and of his district court days. David eloquently captured the emotional toll of sentencing that afflicted his father daily on the district bench. He then presented Garza with the portrait.[29]

Painted from recent photographs, the artist captured the mellowing that had taken place in the federal judge. In the portrait Garza appeared relaxed, in his judicial robe, but his green eyes were vivacious and bright as usual. Undoubtedly, the portrait would have depicted a tenser, older image if Garza had still been on the district court. Law clerk Campagnolo later spoke of the change he had seen in Garza after his elevation to the Fifth Circuit. The federal judge seemed younger, with a more relaxed composure. The clerk speculated that the elimination of the sentencing task that so weighed on Garza's emotions precipitated the change. "When he went to the Fifth Circuit, he no longer had to sentence people, and that seemed to take years off him," explained Campagnolo.[30]

Regardless of Garza's relatively youthful appearance as he approached his sixty-seventh year, he realized that he needed to ease his judicial pace. He wrote a brief letter to President Reagan detailing his decision to retire from active service beginning on his birthday, July 7, 1982. It by no means ended his court life, however, for in taking senior status, a judge continued to serve on the court but only with a reduced workload. He still heard oral arguments and written opinions, but he no longer served on summary panels or sat *en banc*. For Garza one of the benefits of taking senior status was creating an opening on the court and, thus, increasing the court's resources. Unlike many of his contemporaries on senior status, Garza continued to carry nearly a full workload.[31]

Garza's retirement from active service spawned a series of newspaper and magazine articles tracing his career. One theme seemed to span all the stories: Rio Grande Valley citizens considered Garza a folk hero. Although he constantly shunned such accolades, stories of his legendary status persisted, prompting one acquaintance to joke, "I knew Reynaldo Garza before he could walk on water." Garza, with his keen sense of humor, truly appreciated the quip.[32]

It was inevitable that Garza would see many of his old friends die with advancing age, yet he found new ones. The Garzas befriended the younger generation of Brownsville's old pioneer families along with rising city leaders. The Cardenas, Gavitos, Guerras, Lizkas, Longorias, Silvas, and Zavaletas were among the couples that replaced many of Garza's longtime friends. He kept his poker buddies, such as Jack Schnabel, Joseph Calapa, and Sylvano Christiano, and some of his former law clerks remained his hunting partners. He stayed active in the Knights of Columbus and considered many of its members his dearest friends. As in Garza's earlier years in Brownsville, social class not ethnicity dictated relations, and his friends represented members of the middle upper-class of the city's Anglo and Mexican American societies.[33]

Two weeks after his official retirement, Garza delivered one of his most noteworthy rulings, which was later appealed to the Supreme Court. Supreme Court justices hear only those cases that raise important issues involving federal law or the United States Constitution. Individuals desiring an appeal first file a petition for certiorari, which is a plea for the court's attention. In the 1982 term, there were more than four thousand petitions for certiorari. Of these petitions, the Supreme Court accepted only one hundred seventy-nine. Legal scholars view any case going before the Supreme Court as monumental, since it usually involves intricate issues of federal law that divide judges around the country.[34]

Wiggins v. *Estelle* brought to the Supreme Court's attention such issues. In *Wiggins* Garza's three-judge panel ruled whether the unsolicited interjections of a defendant's court-appointed standby counsel were inherently prejudicial, and thus denied the defendant his constitutional right to self-representation. Garza led the debate on the issue, one which was "never previously addressed" in the courts. He brought fellow judges to consensus, establishing the rule that standby counsel should, according to the court brief, "be seen but not heard." In his opinion Garza held that the standby counsel's participation in the defendant's defense was prejudicial because it violated the defendant's Sixth Amendment right to conduct his own defense.[35]

The Supreme Court later reversed Garza's decision. In an opinion written by Justice Sandra Day O'Connor, the majority held that the interference by standby counselor was reasonable and did not undermine the defendant's defense. In the dissenting opinion, Justices Byron White, William J. Brennan, and Thurgood Marshall sided with Garza stating "an accused who knowingly, intelligently, and voluntarily elects to do so is constitutionally entitled to refuse the service of a government-appointed attorney." Court scholars opined that in rejecting Garza's standard that standby counsel should "be seen but not heard," the Supreme Court majority created "an important tool to be used by the States to deprive defendants of their rights to self-representation." Further, scholars praised Garza's ruling and angrily postulated that the Supreme Court's majority decision would now force court-appointed counsels upon unwilling defendants, thus denying citizens the right to conduct their own defense.[36]

Two months after ruling on *Wiggins*, Garza dealt with an antitrust case that later was also appealed to the Supreme Court. At issue in *Hyde v. Jefferson Parish Hospital District No. 2*, was whether an exclusive contract between a hospital and a professional medical corporation for provision of anesthesiological services constituted an illegal tying arrangement under the Sherman Act. A tying arrangement was an agreement by a party to sell one product but only on the condition that the buyer also purchase a different or tied product. The hospital required patients wanting an operation to use the hospital anesthesiologists. The operation rooms were considered the tying product, but the anesthesia service was the tied product market.[37]

An excluded anesthesiologist sued, alleging that the tie prevented him from obtaining privileges of practice. The federal district court rejected the anesthesiologist's claim that the hospital arrangement represented an illegal tie under the antitrust laws. The lower court ruled that the hospital did not have sufficient market power over the tying product in the market in which it competed. The Fifth Circuit reversed the lower court's ruling. In the opinion Garza held for the anesthesiologist. He stated that the hospital possessed sufficient market power in the tying market to coerce purchase of hospital anesthesiologists, and rendered the arrangement illegal.[38]

The Supreme Court later unanimously reversed the Fifth Circuit and ruled that the hospital had insufficient market power to coerce its patients into buying the tied service. The Supreme Court split five to four, however, on the applicable legal standard to apply. The majority affirmed that tying arrangements "should be condemned" only where there was a "substantial threat that the tying seller will acquire market power in the tied-product market." The Supreme Court did not agree with Garza that the issue in *Hyde* constituted a threat.[39]

The ruling illustrated Garza's proconsumer stance. In most areas, Garza wrote moderate to liberal opinions. He invariably sided with employees in labor cases and against business in antitrust cases as he did in *Hyde*. On issues such as religion, he worked to fashion a responsible yet conservative position. "I would classify him as a liberal, but moderately liberal," said one attorney going before the appeals court. Garza was prone to follow his generation's stance and that of other middle-class Mexican Americans rather than the bent of liberal Chicano organizations. In general, Garza avoided the ideological extremes of the right or the left.[40]

Garza could not avoid, however, the dangers intrinsic in his position dealing with federal criminals, especially drug dealers. In the fall of 1982, a man donning army fatigues and wielding a high-powered rifle kicked the front door off Garza's home and ran through the house screaming to see the judge. The only person in the home was Garza's housekeeper, who escaped the intruder by running out of the house into the safety of a neighbor's home. Police never caught the perpetrator nor uncovered the motives for his violent action, although law enforcement officials suspected the influence of drugs in the case. Fearing that widespread publicity regarding the incident might prompt others to imitate the crime, officials played down the incident. Two United States marshals were immediately assigned to protect Garza, providing a tense setting for the next few months. The only light moment occurred at the New Orleans airport when a United States marshal, accompanying Garza, registered his gun with airline personnel. The woman registering the weapon, quietly leaned over toward the marshal and asked him whether Garza was his prisoner. Although the incident revealed the stereotyping and biases that were prevalent in the 1980s, Garza saw only humor in the fact that someone mistook him for a prisoner.[41]

In November, 1982, Supreme Court Chief Justice Warren Burger honored Garza by appointing him to the Temporary Emergency Court of Appeals. Burger appointed only five other circuit judges and three District Court judges to the prestigious post. Garza would hear all appeals taken from the federal district court arising under the Economic Stabilization Act. The court's purpose was to provide nationwide uniformity in price controls. The court met only a few times a year, usually in Washington, D.C., but occasionally in other locations the chief justice designated. It operated under its own rules, and Burger assigned cases based on the caseload of individual judges and the location of the case. The court allotted Garza one additional law clerk, as a result of his expanded duties, giving him three law clerks. After he retired from active service four months earlier, Garza had been allotted two clerks by Congress. He decided that managing one person would create more problems than it would solve by reducing the load, so he kept only two law clerks. A few years later, Supreme Court Chief Justice William Rehnquist appointed Garza chief judge of the Temporary Emergency Court of Appeals.[42] Garza's appointment to lead this prestigious court testified to the degree of acceptance he had garnered from all levels of the legal community.

Throughout the mid-1980s Garza's lifetime devotion to educational achievement spawned a series of honors. The first occurred when Garza's junior college, renamed Texas Southmost College, commended the federal judge with the naming of the Reynaldo G. Garza Lecture Series. Shortly thereafter, the Rio Grande Valley city of McAllen named an elementary school after the federal judge. Another honor came a few months later when a group of attorneys founded the Rio Grande Valley's only law school in Edinburg and named it the Reynaldo G. Garza School of Law. That same year St. Mary's University law school in San Antonio presented Garza with the Rosewood Gavel Award, recognizing him as an outstanding jurist.[43]

In late 1984 the American Association of Junior and Community Colleges designated Garza as National Alumnus of the Year. Garza and Bertha both attended the ceremony in Washington, D.C., where Garza delivered an address. In his classic unassuming style, he deferred the honor to the members of the association, stating that it was they who had enabled thousands of individuals to attend colleges close to home at affordable costs. Thus, he claimed, they deserved the recognition. He also used his time on the platform to deliver what would become his constant refrain—"give South Texas good colleges and professional schools and the people do the rest." For close to a decade Garza had advocated a doctoral program for his hometown's university, and he hoped that the association would help support his efforts.[44]

In the spring of 1985 Garza received a stronger voice for his mandate when Governor Mark White appointed him to the Select Committee on Higher Education. The committee met a few times a year and voiced its recommendations to the Texas legislature for higher education improvements. Garza became one of the committee's advocates for allotting funds to community colleges. Through his membership in the committee, Garza developed a warm friendship with White, and on several occasions the governor dined in Garza's home while attending gubernatorial activities in the Rio Grande Valley. Through this position, Garza would further his dream of advancing educational opportunities in South Texas, thus maintaining his ideological message of success through education.[45]

In April, 1986, all of Garza's former law clerks flocked to Fort Brown Auditorium to commemorate Garza's completion of twenty-five years of service on the bench. It was an intimate affair. Garza had requested that only his law clerks be present. Twenty-five men and one woman surrounded the federal judge as he spoke extemporaneously. The younger law clerks marveled at the stories told by the earlier clerks. Most of the clerks knew the tales well, for they had heard them dozens of times from the gifted storyteller who could speak both in somber judgment and animated levity. Undergraduate and law school memories at the University of Texas, the political years with Lyndon Johnson, meeting President Roosevelt during World War II—all phases of Garza's full life were among the stories told.[46]

During the ceremony a fellow appellate judge asked Garza if he was enjoying himself. Garza quipped, "With all these honors and tributes, I think people keep thinking it will be my last celebration."[47] He was now seventy-one. His strong stocky body no longer reached its full six feet. Although slightly stooped, he was still an imposing figure, weighing close to 185 pounds. He walked slower. His rich and deep voice was deeper. But Garza still had many more accomplishments ahead of him.

CHAPTER 11

Twilight

1986–96

Reynaldo G. Garza never thought of himself as extraordinary. Despite his path-breaking accomplishments, he viewed his career simply as the fulfillment of the American dream. He credited his success to a system that allowed any citizen to rise as long as he was willing to work hard and gain an education. Although he knew that without his Mexican American heritage, he would likely not have been considered for a federal judgeship, he believed that he had succeeded by taking responsibility for his legal career. Unlike some successful immigrants, Garza advanced without completely assimilating into the dominant Anglo culture. Throughout the later years of his life, however, he continued to close the gap still prevalent between the two cultures.

In the spring of 1987, Nacho, Garza's youngest son, an active civic participant and partner in a Brownsville accounting firm, ran for mayor of the city. The race was a difficult one for Garza because, as federal judge, he could not campaign for him. Always cautious about judicial ethics, Garza made no public comment during the race. The rest of the family, on the other hand, ran an effective mayoral campaign. Bertha canvassed the city's neighborhoods, encouraging people to vote for her son. The other brothers and sisters distributed fliers and made dozens of phone calls. During the campaign Garza queried Bertha nightly about the ebb and flow of the race's activities. By election day, Nacho gained a large popular mandate, and unsurprisingly, he won the race.[1]

Commenting on the mayoral victory years later, two Brownsville historians declared that Nacho's victory symbolized a return to elite control in the city.[2] Ironically, eighty years after the first Garza entered Brownsville with little financial resources and no political power, historians now considered this second-generation American a member of the elite. Nacho's political position demonstrated the progress the Garza family had made in three generations.

Nacho's tenure as mayor also illustrated a slight generation gap between father and son. Nacho held a more conservative view than his father, especially regarding the problem of illegal immigration. When asked by a *U.S. News and World Report* reporter about the Immigration and Naturalization Service, a group notorious for its alleged unfair treatment of illegal aliens, Nacho credited the agency for successfully switching from "tenaciously hunting down illegals [to offering] the olive branch of peace and amnesty." Moreover, the Brownsville mayor advocated limiting illegal immigration to "gain back control of the border."[3]

In contrast, however, in a National Public Radio interview, Garza made it clear that he was against setting immigration limits. He suggested that in South Texas political officeholders would never campaign for illegal immigration quotas, especially since most of these politicians' constituents were former illegal aliens, Garza explained. The elder Garza long remembered his own parent's move to the United States from Mexico and believed any individual willing to leave his country to make a new life in America deserved entrance into the United States. Nacho, though, was far removed from immigrant memories, which may have explained his ultraconservative view regarding the issue.[4]

In June, 1989, Garza presided over a controversial case with wide public interest. The case illustrated Garza's common sense and legal reasoning after more than two decades as a federal judge. In *Brock v. Merrell Dow Pharmaceuticals,* the parents of a child born with Poland's Syndrome brought liability action against Merrell Dow, the manufacturer of the drug Bendectin, which the mother took during pregnancy. A lower court entered judgment on jury verdict in favor of the plaintiffs. Merrell Dow appealed to the Fifth Circuit.[5]

While studying the evidence, Garza found it unusual that the plaintiffs had called to the stand an expert conducting research in Australia. The judge followed his hunch that the evidence was "nothing more than unproven medical speculation." After a careful review of the case, Garza ruled that there was a lack of conclusive epidemiological proof of causal relationship between the birth defect and Bendectin. Through his ruling, Garza set the precedent used by subsequent courts faced with toxic tort cases: to scrutinize "the basis, reasoning, and conclusiveness of studies" presented as evidence. Law schools throughout the country later used the case, dubbed by academics as a "mass toxic tort," as a teaching tool.

Three months after ruling on *Brock*, Garza received one of his most cherished honors. His alma mater inducted him, along with five others, to a prestigious group of distinguished alumni. Every year the university honored no more than five of its graduates with an elaborate ceremony in Austin, choosing only those individuals who had made a substantial contribution to society. Texas Southmost College President Juliet García had nominated Garza by writing a letter boasting that "Judge Garza stands as a model to any professional in the United States who understands commitment to public service, to justice, and to one's country." She closed by stating, "His is also a special source of pride to the Hispanic community that he so ably represents." García, who became the first Hispanic woman president of a university, had looked to Garza as a role model.[6]

Two days of events in Austin highlighted the festivities. Former Texas Governor John Connally, a 1961 Distinguished Alumnus and master of ceremonies for the affair, welcomed Garza with a beaming smile. All of Garza's children and their spouses also celebrated their father's triumph. They radiated with pride as journalist Bill Moyers, a graduate of UT, narrated a biographical film detailing Garza's life. As Garza accepted the award, he jokingly remarked to his children that he possessed enough medals and awards "to sink a ship." He then added, as he winked to Bertha, "We Article III judges are not known for our humility." It seemed fitting that the university that had educated him to pursue a legal career now celebrated his accomplishments. Donning the burnt orange blazer with the university seal traditionally awarded to Distinguished Alumni designees, Garza posed for a photograph with his family. It was one of his proudest moments.[7]

More accolades followed. In the spring of 1991, thirty-six of Garza's present and former law clerks gathered in South Padre Island to pay tribute to the seventy-six-year-old judge with thirty years of service on the bench. At the weekend gala law clerks arranged parties in Brownsville and South Padre Island. Distinguished guests included United States District Judges James DeAnda, Filemón Vela, and Ricardo Hinojosa. Brothers, sisters, children, grandchildren, and close friends of Garza joined the clerks and their families. More than half had worked for Garza on the appeals court. As a gift to the revered judge, the law clerks presented him with a Rolex watch, a gift he would never have bought for himself but that he treasured fondly because of its personal significance.[8]

In the summer of 1991 Garza's longtime efforts to improve his hometown's educational situation culminated with Texas Governor Ann Richards's signing of Texas Senate Bill 1050. The bill officially approved the merger of Texas Southmost College with the University of Texas System and changed the school's name to the University of Texas at Brownsville. Garza's public relations efforts on the Select Committee on Higher Education helped initiate the merger, and he was among the dignitaries present at the signing ceremony. Through its association with the University of Texas, the Brownsville university would now be privy to a greater share of state funding for higher education. The merger also gave the school the prestige of the more established Austin-based university. Garza celebrated the event with a small cocktail party at his home attended by Governor Richards.[9]

Just as the tributes increased in the next several years so did the effects of age. Although he remained sharp on the bench, the gait in Garza's step became increasingly slower. He continued to attend morning Mass daily but arrived at church at eight in the morning instead of six. Similarly, he was at the courthouse by ten every morning and left in the late afternoon instead of the early evening. He also followed his doctor's advice and stopped smoking. Seven times a year he heard oral arguments in New Orleans. He had no intention of stepping down from the Fifth Circuit, a court that by the 1990s was in critical need of all of its resources, including senior judges.[10] He now preferred to stay at the Royal Sonesta, an elegant French Quarter hotel, a few blocks closer to the federal courthouse. Many of the older judges were gone, but remarkably some, including ninety-year-old John Minor Wisdom still remained.

On holidays and occasionally after Sunday Mass, the entire family, now numbering more than twenty-two and growing steadily, descended upon their childhood home. Children's toys, swings, and slides filled the Garza's backyard as grandchildren played with their doting grandparents. Garza's children, now grown, each flourished in the Brownsville community. Rey and David continued their respected legal partnership. Nacho was the managing partner of a successful Brownsville accounting firm, and in 1991 and 1993 Governor Ann Richards appointed him chairman of the Texas Parks and Wildlife Commission. In 1994, President Clinton appointed Nacho to the board of directors of the Border Environment Cooperation Commission, established as a by-product of NAFTA. Bertita, a former schoolteacher, was a housewife raising three children; and Monica was an accountant for a major manufacturing company. Only two of Garza's siblings remained, elder sister María Rosa and younger sister Argentina. They both lived less than a block from their brother. Dozens of nephews, nieces, cousins, and in-laws, most living in Brownsville, were also part of the extended Garza family.[11]

On July 7, 1995, Garza turned eighty. Hundreds of birthday greetings poured in, but for Garza the mere passage of time was not as significant as it was for his clerks, who did not let the landmark go unnoticed. They planned a lavish surprise birthday weekend for the federal judge in South Padre Island. More than one hundred guests attended a Friday night cocktail party, and Garza's family and former court staff joined him for an intimate seated dinner the next evening. As their gift to the man whom many felt had changed their lives, the thirty-nine living law clerks each wrote a touching letter expressing their sentiments about the judge and reminiscing about their clerkship. They presented the leather-bound book to Garza at the Saturday night gala. The federal judge choked back tears as he embraced his clerks. He graciously thanked the hundreds in attendance and spent most of the weekend reminiscing with his wife, his children, and his court family.[12]

Although the 1990s for Garza was a time of much celebration, for many Brownsville residents, the decade remained mired by the realities of poverty and depravity. Mexico's continuing currency crises, along with Mexican consumers' heavy debt burdens, assumed after the signing of the North American Free Trade Agreement, contributed greatly to the misery in South Texas. Conditions were further aggravated by a public health dilemma. A cluster of infants was born with anencephaly, a mysterious birth defect, which brought worldwide attention to the living and working conditions of Brownsville area residents. Many residents and health workers believed that untreated waste flowing from the Rio Grande and from *maquiladoras* in Matamoros was responsible for the crisis. No official government agency, however, linked the *maquiladoras* to the birth defect. Brownsville was classified as one of the country's poorest cities.[13]

Mexican Americans throughout the nation did not fare much better. Only 44 percent of Mexican Americans completed high school in the early 1990s, compared to 79 percent of Anglos. By the beginning of the decade, there were only 55,000 professional degrees awarded to Hispanics. In Garza's own field, Article III federal judgeships, Hispanics filled approximately 27 of the more than 800 positions available by the mid-1990s.[14]

Garza never claimed that his path into the judiciary would increase the number of Mexican American appointments. He only asserted that he would do his best and would always be willing to work hard so that he could prove to legislators that Mexican Americans could, in fact, be effective jurists. His modest self-evaluation proved to be an accurate one, as his diligent efforts on the bench, combined with his perseverance, led to the appointment of dozens of Mexican American federal jurists. As Justice Raul A. González of the Supreme Court of Texas affirmed: "His lifetime of firsts, his efforts in the area of education, and his love for and contributions to the community are things we should all try to emulate. . . . Judge Garza, an eminent jurist, opened new paths."[15]

The numbers of Mexican American appointments would undoubtedly be greater, except that federal judicial appointments represent a considerable financial sacrifice for any top attorney. Mexican American attorneys cannot solely be lured by the position's prestige nor its opportunity to enhance the law's development. Most attorneys are well aware of the paradox of Article III judicial power. Alexander Hamilton early explained that the sole power inherent in a federal judgeship came from legal mandates, not the sword or the purse. Accordingly, many Mexican American attorneys delve into the political arena. Other federal judges, including Garza's own successor on the district bench, James DeAnda, left the court for the financial security of private practice.[16]

In April, 1996, Garza celebrated the completion of thirty-five years on the federal bench. The selection of his new law clerks for the 1997 term awaited his attention. As usual, he planned to show prospective applicants his beloved city, urge them to taste some spicy Mexican fare, and then judge from their reaction to his border hometown and the amount of spices they could endure whether they would become his new clerks. He has decided he will serve the federal bench until he is no longer physically or mentally fit for the task.[17]

As he approaches his eighty-first birthday, adjournment has not yet come for the federal judge from Brownsville. Instead, he continues along his normal path, one that has been illuminated by his immigrant parents' faith in their son and in the hope of the American dream.

Notes

Preface

1. The late Harold Medina, who was appointed in 1947 as federal judge to the Southern District of New York, was the son of a Mexican father and an English mother. Political figures, however, were unaware of his Mexican roots. Mexican American historians and legislators acknowledge Reynaldo G. Garza as the first Mexican American federal judge because of the ethnic implications of his appointment in 1961. See Joan W. Moore, Mexican Americans, p. 107; John Mashek, "Judge Garza's Appointment Makes Courtroom History," *Dallas Morning News*, Apr. 16, 1961, p. 2; "Garza Named U.S. Judge: First of Mexican Descent," *Houston Post*, Mar. 24, 1961, p. 3.

2. Ramsey Clark, interview by Larry Hackman, July 7, 1970, transcript, pp. 74–75; U.S. Senate, Committee on the Judiciary, Nomination, 87th Cong., 1st sess., Apr. 12, 1961, D146.

3. See James W. Vander Zanden, *American Minority Relations*; Leo Grebler et al., *The Mexican-American People: The Nation's Second Largest Minority*; Raymond H. C. Teske, Jr. and Bardin H. Nelson, "An Analysis of Differential Assimilation Rates among Middle-Class Mexican Americans," *Sociological Quarterly* 17 (Spring, 1976): 218–35.

4. St. John de Crèvecoeur, Letters from an American Farmer: Sketches of Eighteenth Century America.

5. Garza's ability to balance his identities epitomized the idea of cultural pluralism, the current attitude toward the immigrant experience set in motion by Kallen in Horace M. Kallen, *Culture and Democracy in the U.S.*

6. David Brion Davis, "Some Recent Directions in Cultural History," *American Historical Review* 73 (Feb., 1968): 705.

Chapter 1: Heritage and Youth, 1901–35

1. The Rio Grande Valley consists of the counties of Cameron, Hidalgo, and Willacy. Examination of the topography of the area shows that the geographical region termed the Rio Grande Valley is not a valley, but rather a delta. *Resacas* are excavations used to drain an overflow of water. In several Rio Grande Valley towns, *resacas* served as irrigation canals (Antonio N. Zavaleta, "Resacas and Bancos in Brownsville History," p. 3). Brownsville as an agricultural service center is documented in Antonio N. Zavaleta, "The Twin Cities: A Historical Synthesis of the Socieo-Economic Interdependence of the Brownsville-Matamoros Border Community," p. 149. For an account of this agricultural community and its hardships, see Ralph G. Bray, "Valley Growers Face the Future," *Texas Weekly*, Sept. 16, 1933, p. 4.

2. Matt S. Meier and Feliciano Ribera, *Mexican Americans/American Mexicans: From Conquistadors to Chicanos*, pp. 110–14; W. H. Chatfield, *The Twin Cities of the Border: Brownsville, Texas, and Matamoros, Mexico*, pp. 1–5. Although these Mexican immigrants were not from Texas, many considered themselves true Texans. From their historical perspective, their Spaniard and Mexican ancestors first settled in Brownsville in the late 1700s, and, thus, Texas remained their birthright (William Madsen, *The Mexican Americans of South Texas*, p. 4).

3. Meier and Ribera, *Mexican Americans/American Mexicans*, pp. 103–110; For information on immigration in the Rio Grande Valley, see Frank C. Pierce, *A Brief History of the Lower Rio Grande Valley*; Paul S. Taylor, *An American-Mexican Frontier*; Florence J. Scott, *Historical Heritage of the Lower Rio Grande*; Ozzie G. Simmons, "Anglo-Americans and Mexican-Americans: Images and Expectations," pp. 193–205.

4. Reynaldo G. Garza, interview by author, Brownsville, May 29, 1993.

5. Ibid.; Nola Martin Harding and Dorothy Abbott McCoy, "Francisco Yturria and Heirs," pp. 91–92.

6. María Rosa Dosal, interview by author, Brownsville, July 24, 1993.

7. Dosal interview; Reynaldo G. Garza, interview by Marc Knisely, Mar. 11, 1992.

8. R. G. Garza interview, May 29, 1993; "Longtime Civic Leader Ygnacio Garza is Dead," *Brownsville Herald*, Feb. 25, 1979, p. 1.

9. Brownsville's population statistics are cited in Department of Commerce, Bureau of the Census, *Thirteenth Census of the United States Taken in the Year 1910, Volume II*, pp. 779, 810. Brownsville's population severely declined toward the end of the nineteenth century because of hurricanes, border banditry, a cholera epidemic, and other diseases (Zavaleta, "The Twin Cities," p. 143). Brownsville's focus on Mexican political events is documented in Gilmer Speed, "The Hunt for Garza," *Harper's*, Jan. 30, 1892, p. 103.

10. Zavaleta, "The Twin Cities," p. 127; Niles Hansen, *The Border Economy*, p. 156; Madsen, *The Mexican Americans of South Texas*, p. 25. Madsen also states that in later years, strict immigration laws curtailed the amount of border crossings in Brownsville.

11. Speed, "The Hunt for Garza," p. 103.

12. Milo Kearney and Anthony Knopp, *Boom and Bust: The Historical Cycles of Matamoros and Brownsville*, pp. 191–92; David Montejano, *Anglos and Mexicans in the Making of Texas, 1836–1986*, p. 107.

13. Outsiders' perceptions of ethnicity dictating city relations is in Montejano, *Anglos and Mexicans*, p. 114. For a discussion of social class divisions in Brownsville, see Zavaleta, "The Twin Cities," p. 146.

14. Madsen, *The Mexican Americans of South Texas*, p. 11.

15. The genesis of the Brownsville affair is described in John D. Weaver, *The Brownsville Raid*; and Robert V. Haynes, *A Night of Violence: The Houston Riot of 1917*, p. 55. Brownsville's African American population is included in Department of Commerce, *Thirteenth Census*, p. 810. For the city's account of the Brownsville affair, see "Black Soldier Assaults Local Woman," *Brownsville Herald*, Aug. 11, 1906, p. 1; William Neale, *Century of Conflict, 1821–1913: Incidents in the Lives of William Neale and William A. Neale Early Settlers in South Texas*, pp. 136, 139; Weaver, *The Brownsville Raid*; and Haynes, *A Night of Violence*, p. 55.

16. Accounts of the Garza family regarding the Brownsville affair are in U.S. Senate, *Affray at Brownsville, Texas*, p. 2750; and in R. G. Garza interview, May 29, 1993.

17. U.S. Senate, *Affray at Brownsville, Texas*, pp. 2749–59.

18. The Brownsville paper's and the War Department's confirmations of the soldiers' crime is documented in U.S. Senate, *Affray at Brownsville, Texas*, pp. 2749–2759; and in R. G. Garza interview, May 29, 1993. An account of soldiers firing shots is in "Negro Soldiers Raid Downtown," *Brownsville Herald*, Aug. 14, 1906, p. 1. Roosevelt's dismissal of the troops is described in Albert Bigelow Paine, *Captain Bill McDonald Texas Ranger: A Story of Frontier Reform*, pp. 315–16. Brownsville citizens' belief in the soldiers' guilt is documented throughout Weaver, *The Brownsville Raid*; and in "Negro Soldiers Raid Downtown," p. 1.

19. Dosal interview.

20. Ygnacio Garza's testimony documented in Dosal interview; and U.S. Senate, *Affray at Brownsville, Texas*, pp. 2750, 2752. Judge Garza's quote is from his interview, May 29, 1993. As a historic aside, concerns over the Brownsville affair and the resulting punishment of the soldiers festered until 1972. In September, 1972, the Secretary of the Army awarded the soldiers, most of whom were dead, honorable discharges. In 1974 Congress awarded $25,000 in compensation to Dorise W. Willis, the only living soldier involved in the incident. See "House United Hears Survivor's Case," *New York Times*, June 15, 1973, p. 31; Congress, Subcommittee on Compensation and Pension, *Hearings to Extend Veterans' Benefits Eligibility to 167 Soldiers, or their Heirs, Dishonorably Discharged as a Result of Involvement in an Alleged Disturbance at a Brownsville, Texas, Garrison in August, 1906*, 93rd. Cong., 1st Sess., H.R. 4382, June 14, 1973, pp. 1220–40; and "Soldier Receives $25,000 Check," *New York Times*, Jan. 11, 1974, p. 61.

21. Dosal interview.

22. R. G. Garza interview, March 11, 1992.

23. Dosal interview.

24. R. G. Garza interview, May 29, 1993.

25. Patriarchal family structure is discussed in Richard A. Garcia, *Rise of the Mexican American Middle Class: San Antonio, 1929–1941*, p. 131. Ygnacio Garza as patriarch is from Dosal interview.

26. Argentina Garza, interview by author, Brownsville, July 24, 1993; and Dosal interview.

27. That members of Garza's ethnic group and generation were immersed in a bilingual environment is documented in Madsen, *The Mexican Americans of South Texas*, p. 52. Argentina Garza and Dosal interviews document the remaining ideas.

28. Dosal interview.

29. R. G. Garza interview, May 29, 1993.

30. Memories of walking to school are from R. G. Garza interview, Mar. 11, 1992. Poor attendance and other educational problems that affected Brownsville schools are documented in S. M. N. Marrs, state superintendent of public instruction, State Department of Education, *Twenty-Third Biennial Report, 1922–1924*, p. 187; and by Bruce Aiken, interview by author, Brownsville, June 8, 1993.

31. Aiken interview.

32. For information on school segregation of Mexican American students, see Mario T. García, *Mexican Americans: Leadership, Ideology, and Identity, 1930–1960*, pp. 354–59.

33. Dosal interview.

34. Betty Bay, *Historic Brownsville: Original Townsite Guide*, pp. 49–60; Argentina Garza interview.

35. Argentina Garza interview.

36. R. G. Garza interview, May 29, 1993.

37. Argentina Garza interview.

38. R. G. Garza interview, May 23, 1993.

39. Ibid.

40. Ibid.

41. Ibid.; discussion of social and class restrictions is from Carl Allsup, *The American G. I. Forum: Origins and Evolution*, p. 28.

42. R. G. Garza interview, May 29, 1993.

43. Garza's memory of his rank in school is from his interview, May 29, 1993. Literacy statistics are in Department of Commerce, Bureau of the Census, *Fourteenth Census of the United States Taken in the Year 1920, Volume III*, pp. 1016.

44. Dosal interview; Lino Pérez, interview by author, South Padre Island, July 25, 1993.

45. R. G. Garza interview, May 29, 1993.

46. Ibid.

47. Brownsville Junior College's student body is described in Chet Rebok, "Southmost College Founding Inspired by Local Civic Leader," *Brownsville Herald*, May 24, 1979, p. 11B; Garza's disappointment in not attending UT is in his interview, May 29, 1993.

48. Maurice Pipkin, interview by author, Austin, Mar. 28, 1994.

49. Argentina Garza interview; R. G. Garza interview, July 23, 1993.

50. Bertha Garza, interview by author, Brownsville, July 23, 1993.

51. Bertha Garza interview, July 23, 1993. Information about the church parish is from Bay, *Historic Brownsville*, pp. 178–81.

52. Bertha Garza interview, July 23, 1993.

53. R. G. Garza interviews, July 23, 1993, and May 29, 1993.

54. R. G. Garza interview, May 29, 1993.

Chapter 2: The Longhorn Years, 1935–39

1. How Mexican Americans embraced the American culture while remaining loyal to their heritage is discussed in Arnoldo De León, *Ethnicity in the Sunbelt: A History of Mexican Americans in Houston*, p. 80; and Garcia, *Rise of the Mexican American Middle Class*, pp. 83–88. De León also explains that Mexican Americans fell back on Mexican traditions in response to the racism and discrimination they faced during the 1930s and the war years. Richard A. Garcia attributes middle-class Mexican Americans' changing culture to modernization. He defines a middle-class gestalt based on an attitude of *gente decente* versus *gente corriente*— "the high society of reason, manners and culture versus the mass society of emotions, ill manners, and no culture." This division "manifested only when they [Mexican Americans] spoke of moving to a better section of town, joining their own clubs, or playing sports only with their friends and others like them." Yet, Garcia also states that in spite of its Americanization, the middle class aided the Mexican community financially, thus demonstrating civic virtue. Anglos' unfavorable responses are discussed in Milton M. Gordon, *Assimilation in American Life: The Role of Race, Religion, and National Origins*, pp. 85, 89. Anglos' misconceptions are discussed in Moore, *Mexican Americans*, pp. 28, 100–102. As explained by a Mexican immigrant, "When Lázaro Cárdenas was elected president of Mexico [1934–40] and said that Mexicans with roots in the United States should become U.S. citizens and express loyalty to that country, we began to change our attitudes [toward naturalization]" (Moore, *Mexican Americans*, p. 28).

2. Margaret Catherine Berry, *UT Austin: Traditions and Nostalgia*, p. 51; Alex Murphree, "Texas Re-Discovers Its University," *Texas Weekly*, Apr. 14, 1934, p. 8; Scott Armstrong, "Austin," *Christian Science Monitor*, Mar. 31, 1982, p. B3.

3. David F. Prindle, "Oil and the Permanent University Fund: The Early Years," *Southwestern Historical Quarterly* 86 (Oct., 1983): 277–98; Anthony Champagne and Edward J. Harpham, *Texas at the Crossroads: People, Politics, and Policy*, pp. 187–88; Elizabeth A. Moize, "Austin," *National Geographic* 177 (June, 1990): 168; Berry, *UT Austin*, p. 51. The university's large endowment of more than four million oil dollars was greater than that of any other state-supported university (Moll, *The Public Ivys*, p. 117; Rupert N. Richardson et al., *Texas: The Lone Star State*, pp. 354, 374–76.

4. Herschel T. Manuel, *Spanish-Speaking Children of the Southwest: Their Education and the Public Welfare*, p. 61; Murphree, "Texas Re-Discovers Its University," p. 8.

5. Murphree, "Texas Re-Discovers Its University," p. 9; Manuel, *Spanish-Speaking Children of the Southwest*, p. 61. Manuel also indicates that enrollment or population counts were assessed through the number of Spanish surnames (p. 61).

6. Department of Commerce, Bureau of the Census, *Fifteenth Census of the United States: 1930, Volume VI*, p. 972; Anthony Orum, *The Making of Modern Austin: Power, Money, and the People*, p. 178.

7. "Their Best Friends," *Daily Texan*, Mar. 27, 1947, in Alonso S. Perales, ed., *Are We Good Neighbors*, p. 240.

8. R. G. Garza interview, July 23, 1993.

9. Ibid.

10. Ibid.

11. Garza's memories of the Saldívar house are from his interview, July 23, 1993. González's accomplishments are recorded in Richardson et al., *Texas*, p. 396. By 1970 Gonzalez, from San Antonio, and Eligio (Kika) de la Garza, from the Rio Grande Valley, were the only two Mexican American members of Congress (Montejano, *Anglos and Mexicans*, p. 291). Saldívar was one of approximately 10,000 to 12,000 American soldiers who surrendered at Bataan, of whom about 4,000 survived. Most of the prisoners of war died of illness, physical exhaustion, or at the hands of Japanese soldiers. The incident was one of the many atrocities of World War II ("Julian Saldívar," American Defenders of Bataan and Corregidor Records [Newbern, North Carolina]). For more information about Bataan, see John W. Dower, *War without Mercy: Race and Power in the Pacific War*, pp. 51, 328.

12. R. G. Garza interview, July 23, 1993.

13. Ibid.

14. Ibid.

15. Ibid.

16. Ibid.

17. The Chicano movement's basic tenets are described in De León, *Ethnicity in the Sunbelt*, pp. 62–63.

18. R. G. Garza interview, July 23, 1993.

19. De León, *Ethnicity in the Sunbelt*, pp. 62–63.

20. R. G. Garza interievw, July 23, 1993.

21. "Allred Attends Latin Meeting," *Austin American-Statesman*, Dec. 8, 1936, p. 5. In May, 1969, the Texas House and Senate passed five bills removing statutes providing for segregated facilities and schools and allowing sporting events among persons of all races. The bills are discussed in Montejano, *Anglos and Mexicans*, p. 286.

22. R. G. Garza interview, July 23, 1993.

23. John Barron to Reynaldo Garza, Jan. 3, 1937, Judge Reynaldo G. Garza papers, Garza's residence, Brownsville, Texas; R. G. Garza interview, July 23, 1993.

24. R. G. Garza interview, July 23, 1993. For insight into Johnson's personality, see Robert Dallek, *Lone Star Rising: Lyndon Johnson and His Times, 1908–1960*, pp. 151–54.

25. R. G. Garza interview, July 23, 1993; Dallek, *Lone Star Rising*, pp. 151–54.

26. R. G. Garza interview, July 23, 1993.

27. Ibid.

28. R. G. Garza interview, July 23, 1993; "What Price Good Citizenship," *LULAC News*, Mar., 1938, LULAC Collection, Benson Latin American Library of the University of Texas at Austin; "Johnson Campaigns in Bastrop County," *Austin American-Statesman*, Apr. 8, 1937, p. 1.

29. R. G. Garza interview, July 23, 1993.

30. R. G. Garza interview, July 23, 1993; Reston, *The Lone Star*, p. 16.

31. R. G. Garza interview, July 23, 1993.

32. Murphree, "Texas Re-Discovers Its University," p. 8; Moll, *The Public Ivys*, p. 119; Armstrong, "Austin," p. B3.

33. Berry, *UT Austin*, p. 51.

34. The number of Hispanic students in Garza's law school class was determined by counting the number of Spanish-surnamed students listed in *The University of Texas Law Alumni Association Alumni Directory, 1994*, p. 299.

35. Bertha Garza interview, July 23, 1993.

36. Joe Greenhill, phone interview by author, Jan. 25, 1995.

37. Ibid.

38. Greenhill's accomplishments are listed in Mary Reincke, ed., *The American Bench: Judges of the Nation*, pp. 1870–71. Common family backgrounds were discussed in Greenhill interview and in R. G. Garza interview, July 23, 1993.

39. Accounts of Garza's distress over his father's illness and subsequent death are from Argentina Garza interview.

40. R. G. Garza interview, July 23, 1993.

41. R. G. Garza interview, July 23, 1993.

42. Reston, *The Lone Star*, p. 26.

43. Connally's victory celebration is in the 1938 UT yearbook, *The Cactus*, p. 146; Connally's runoff election is in Reston, *The Lone Star*, p. 46.

44. R. G. Garza interview, July 23, 1993.

45. Student demonstrations are described in Dower, *War without Mercy*, p. 15; Hildebrand's war views are from R. G. Garza interview, July 23, 1993, and Greenhill interview.

46. R. G. Garza interview, July 23, 1993.

47. Mexican Americans' strong sense of patriotism is described in Benjamin Márquez, *LULAC: The Evolution of a Mexican American Political Organization*, p. 20.

48. R. G. Garza interview, July 23, 1993.

49. O'Daniel's eccentricities are documented in McKay, *W. Lee O'Daniel and Texas Politics*, pp. 48–49.

50. Bertha Garza interview, July 23, 1993.

51. Argentina Garza interview; Dosal interview.

52. R. G. Garza interview, July 23, 1993.

Chapter 3: Peace and War, 1939–45

1. R. G. Garza interview, July 23, 1993.

2. Ibid.; Argentina Garza interview.

3. Bertha Garza interview, July 23, 1993.

4. "Troops Mass on Border," *Brownsville Herald*, Feb. 6, 1940, p. 4; Dower, *War without Mercy*, p. 111. When the Japanese unexpectedly attacked Pearl Harbor on December 7, 1941, Western impressions of Japanese "personality disorders" were reinforced (Dower, *War without Mercy*, p. 111).

5. For a discussion of how prewar activities affected Brownsville, see Charles Daniel Dillman, "The Functions of Brownsville, Texas, and Matamoros, Tamaulipas: Twin Cities of the Lower Rio Grande," pp. 11–12. Recollection of the border harassment is from R. G. Garza interview, July 23, 1993.

6. "West, Garza Get U. of T. Degree," *Brownsville Herald*, Aug. 28, 1939, p. 2.

7. Ibid., p. 3.

8. R. G. Garza interview, July 23, 1993.

9. Ibid.

10. Ibid.

11. Details of the trial were reported in "Public Record," *Brownsville Herald,* Sept. 22, 1939, p. 2. Garza's reputation was confirmed by retired *San Antonio Express News* city editor and former *Brownsville Herald* editor Clarence La Roach, interview by author, San Antonio, Mar. 28, 1994.

12. Bertha Garza interview, July 23, 1993.

13. Ibid.

14. Betty Alley, "Girl Scouts of Brownsville to Launch Drive for $4,000 to Aid Year's Program," *Brownsville Herald,* May 14, 1947, p. 4.

15. García, *Mexican Americans,* p. 37. For further information on LULAC, see Márquez, *LULAC.*

16. Quotation on LULAC's efforts to gain equality is from Guadalupe San Miguel, Jr., *Let All of Them Take Heed: Mexican Americans and the Campaign for Educational Equality in Texas, 1910–1981,* p. 69. A discussion on maintaining the status quo is in Garcia, *Rise of the Mexican American Middle Class,* p. 259.

17. Márquez, *LULAC,* pp. 15–38.

18. Upwardly mobile Mexican Americans are discussed in Richard A. Garcia, "Class Consciousness and Ideology—The Mexican Community of San Antonio, Texas: 1930–1940," *Aztlán* 9 (1978): 42; Frank Alvarado, "The Solution to Our Problems," *LULAC News* 3, no. 1, p. 1.

19. "Reynaldo Garza to Head LULACs," p. 1.

20. R. G. Garza interview, July 23, 1993.

21. Aggressive forms of political activism in various Texas cities are discussed in García, *Mexican Americans,* p. 59; R. G. Garza interview, July 23, 1993 (quotation).

22. Garza's election and his accomplishments are reported in "Reynaldo Garza to Head LULACs," p. 1. Goals and desirable characteristics of LULAC leaders are discussed in García, *Mexican Americans,* p. 37.

23. LULAC activites are described in Márques, *LULAC,* p. 28. Garza's memories of Brownsville LULAC activites are from his interview, July 23, 1993.

24. Brownsville's Charro Days celebration and its traditional customs are explained in "Los Días Del Charro en Brownsville," *Brownsville Herald,* Jan. 23, 1941, p. 1; Ruby A. Woolridge and Robert B. Vezzetti, "The Founding of Charro Days," in *More Studies in Brownsville History,* pp. 390–91.

25. LULAC philosophies are discussed in García, *Mexican Americans,* p. 41.

26. Garza's recognition of the school board seat as a pivotal position is expressed in his interview, July 23, 1993. For details of his election platform, see "Garza Seeks Board Place: To Be Candidate in School Contest," *Brownsville Herald,* Mar. 13, 1941, p. 1; "Record Vote Polled in School Elections," *Star Monitor Herald,* Apr. 6, 1941, p. 1.

27. This incident is reported in "Record Vote Polled in School Elections," p. 1, and was confirmed by Bertha Garza interview, July 23, 1993.

28. La Roach interview. Garza's campaign is reported in "Garza Seeks Board Place," p. 1.

29. Garza's victory, Matamoros' reaction, and Garza's thank you are reported in "School Chiefs to be Seated," *Brownsville Herald,* Apr. 6, 1941, p. 1; "Microscopio," *El Bravo,* (Matamoros, Mexico), Apr. 6, 1941, p. 1; "Many Thanks," *Brownsville Herald,* Apr. 7, 1941, p. 2.

30. Anglo power hold in border towns is discussed in Roberto E. Villareal, *Chicano Elites and Non-Elites: An Inquiry into Social and Political Change*, p. 131. Garza's position as the first Mexican American school board member was verified through a survey of *Brownsville Herald* issues from January 1, 1939 to December 31, 1942. Also see "School Board Heads Named," *Brownsville Herald*, Apr. 8, 1941, p. 1.

31. Garza's support of the pension plan is in his July 23, 1993 interview. Details of the board's action on saluting the flag is in "Compulsory Flag Salute Voted by Schools Here," *Brownsville Herald*, May 9, 1941, p. 1.

32. R. G. Garza interview, July 23, 1993.

33. "Representative Johnson Raps Strikes in 1st Talk: Senatorial Campaign in Full Swing," *Star Monitor Herald*, May 4, 1941, p. 1; Reston, *The Lone Star*, p. 28; "FDR Picks Johnson to Defeat Dies," *Dallas Morning News*, Apr. 24, 1941, p. 1.

34. Reston, *The Lone Star*, p. 62; Joe M. Kilgore, interview by author, Austin, Jan. 13, 1995.

35. The LULAC newspaper is quoted in García, *Mexican Americans*, p. 29. For information on political bosses in the Rio Grande Valley, see V. O. Key, *Southern Politics in State and Nation*, pp. 271–74; Dudley Lynch, *The Duke of Duval*; George Norris Green, *The Establishment in Texas Politics*; Robert A. Caro, *The Years of Lyndon Johnson: The Path to Power*, pp. 720–23.

36. Predictions of Johnson's victory are in "Johnson with 5,152 Lead, Appears Elected," *Houston Post*, June 22, 1941, p. 1; "Only Miracle Can Keep FDR's Anointed Out," *Dallas Morning News*, June 22, 1941, p. 1; Caro, *The Path to Power*, pp. 733–40. Garza's predictions of Johnson's future success are from Bertha Garza interview, July 23, 1993.

37. Morris Atlas, phone interview by author, Nov. 10, 1994; Emilio Crixel, interview by author, Feb. 7, 1994.

38. Atlas interview; Aiken interview; Crixel interview; Jack Wiech, interview by author, Feb. 7, 1994.

39. R. G. Garza interview, July 23, 1993.

40. Details of the crime are in "Lerma Aguilar is Convicted," *Brownsville Herald*, Oct. 12, 1941, p. 1.

41. "Army Gets Fifteen in Past Week," *Brownsville Herald*, Dec. 21, 1941, p. 1; R. G. Garza interview, July 23, 1993.

42. Special school board election details are in "Dr. Toland Will Head School Board; Leonel Garza Succeeds His Brother," *Brownsville Herald*, Dec. 23, 1941, p. 2; Garza's departure is from Bertha Garza interview, July 23, 1993.

43. Reports of Garza's talented oratory are from Lino Pérez interview; and "Spanish Speaking Soldier Cheered by Large Crowd," *Brownsville Herald*, Dec. 21, 1942, p. 1.

44. Garza's invitation to translate is from R. G. Garza interview, Aug. 3, 1993. For details of the meeting, see Irwin G. Gellman, *Good Neighbor Diplomacy: United States Policies in Latin America, 1943–45*, pp. 170–71, 225; Bryce Wood, *The Making of the Good Neighbor Policy*, pp. 130–31, 203. Wood also explains that the alliance between the United States and Mexico created by the Good Neighbor Policy disintegrated after the war as the United States turned its concerns to European devastation, the Soviet Union emergence as a super power, and the consequences of atomic warfare (p. 203).

45. R. G. Garza interview, Aug. 3, 1933.
46. Bertha Garza interview, July 23, 1993.
47. Argentina Garza interview; Dosal interview.
48. Bertha Garza interview, July 23, 1993.
49. Ibid.
50. R. G. Garza interview, Mar. 11–12, 1992.

Chapter 4: The Professional, Family Man, and Politico, 1945–59

1. Richard Polenberg, *War and Society: The United States 1941–1945*, p. 244 details the nation's growing prosperity; Department of Commerce, Bureau of the Census, *Census of Population: 1950, Volume II, Part 43, Texas*, pp. 42–43.
2. Argentina Garza interview; Bertha Garza interview, July 23, 1993.
3. Lino Pérez interview.
4. "Local Bulletin," *Brownsville Herald,* Jan. 9, 1946, p. 3; "Garza Resumes Position in Mexican Consulate," *Brownsville Herald,* Jan. 12, 1946, p. 2.
5. Bertha Garza interview, July 23, 1993.
6. "$282,500 Damage Suits Filed Here," *Brownsville Herald,* July 8, 1946, p. 1; "Rail Firm Loses in Damage Suits," *Brownsville Herald,* Mar. 6, 1947, p. 1. Personal recollections of Garza's involvement in the case is from Bertha Garza interview, July 23, 1993.
7. La Roach interview; R. G. Garza interview, July 23, 1994.
8. "Public Record," *Brownsville Herald,* Jan. 2, 1950, p. 3; Bertha Garza interview, July 23, 1993.
9. Kearney and Knopp, *Boom and Bust,* p. 236. Other Mexican Americans initially opposed to Stokely were lawyer O. B. García, historian A. A. Champion, and physician Vidal Longoria. All of these men continued to serve in Brownsville civic affairs throughout the twentieth century (Kearney and Knopp, *Boom and Bust,* p. 236).
10. Commissioners' races in Brownsville are in "First Political Sombreros Tossed Into Local Ring," *Brownsville Herald,* Sept. 1, 1947, p. 1; Tom Sanford, "Stokely Heads City Ticket in Fall Election," *Brownsville Herald,* Aug. 19, 1949, p. 1. Information about Mexican Americans holding city offices in Brownsville and other South Texas cities is from a survey of *Brownsville Herald* newspapers from Jan. 1, 1939, to Jan. 1, 1948; Allsup, *The American G. I. Forum,* p. 27; Pauline Kibbe, *Latin Americans,* pp. 227–29.
11. "First Political Sombreros," p. 1; Sanford, "Stokely Heads City Ticket," p. 1; "Don Pedro Says," *Brownsville Herald,* Sept., 1947, through Sept., 1948, p. 1.
12. "City Commissioners Initiate Water Project," *Brownsville Herald,* Dec. 3, 1948, p. 3.
13. Bay, *Historic Brownsville,* p. 101.
14. Lyndon Johnson's 1948 Senate race is documented in Paul K. Conkin, *Big Daddy from the Pedernales: Lyndon Baines Johnson,* pp. 103, 115–17; Dallek, *Lone Star Rising,* pp. 294–96, 306–307; Robert A. Caro, *The Years of Lyndon Johnson: Means of Ascent,* p. 193. Garza's participation in Johnson's Senate race is from R. G. Garza interview, Aug. 3, 1993; Lloyd Bentsen, interview by author, Washington, D.C., Feb. 12, 1994.

15. Johnson's Senate opposition is described in Conkin, *Big Daddy from the Pedernales*, pp. 103, 115, 116–17; Dallek, *Lone Star Rising*, pp. 294–96, 306–07; Caro, *Means of Ascent*, p. 193.

16. Green, *The Establishment in Texas Politics*, pp. 112–13; Caro, *Means of Ascent*, pp. 193, 383 (quotation), 383–85. One legislator, describing Johnson's tactics stated that Johnson "had a better understanding of campaign organization than Coke Stevenson did—of the use of radio, of the use of the press, of the organizing of local people" (Caro, *Means of Ascent*, p. 383).

17. Reynaldo Garza, interview by Joe B. Frantz, Dec. 2, 1970, interview 1, transcript, Lyndon Baines Johnson Library Oral History Collection, Lyndon Baines Johnson Library, Austin, Texas; Raul Besteiro, phone interview by author, June 27, 1995.

18. First-hand accounts of Johnson's stop in Brownsville are from R. G. Garza interview, Dec. 2, 1970; and Besteiro interview. For descriptions of Johnson's oratorical style, see Caro, *Means of Ascent*; Conkin, *Big Daddy from the Pedernales*; and Dallek, *Lone Star Rising*.

19. Bentsen interview.

20. Ibid. Bentsen won the United States Congressional seat in 1948, and voters reelected him in 1950 and 1952. In 1970 he defeated incumbent Senator Ralph Yarborough in the primary and beat United States Congressman George Bush in the general election to become a U.S. senator. In 1988 Bentsen ran unsuccessfully as the Democratic vice presidential nominee. In 1992 President Bill Clinton appointed him secretary of the treasury. For election details, see "New Congressman Celebrates Victory," *Houston Chronicle*, Nov. 8, 1948, p. 2A.

21. R. G. Garza interview, Aug. 3, 1993.

22. Bertha Garza interview, July 23, 1993.

23. "Congressional Turnouts Announced in Selected States," *New York Times*, Nov. 9, 1948, p. 24. For details on Johnson's contested victory, see Conkin, *Big Daddy from the Pedernales*, pp. 115–18; and Dallek, *Lone Star Rising*, pp. 298–348.

24. A survey of "From the Public Record: Court House," *Brownsville Herald*, Jan. 10, 1950, to Jan. 1, 1956, shows the level of activity of the law firm; quotation is from R. G. Garza interview, Aug. 3, 1993; Garza's legal focus is from his interview, Aug. 3, 1993; and from "Three Attorneys Form New Firm in Brownsville," *Brownsville Herald*, Jan. 3, 1950, p. 2.

25. Crixel interview, Aiken interview. Garza's financial success is from R. G. Garza interview, Aug. 3, 1993.

26. "Shivers Chooses Sixteen Valleyites on Committee," *Brownsville Herald*, Mar. 12, 1950, p. 2. Insight on Garza's visibility is from his interview, Aug. 3, 1993.

27. "Amid Korea's Booming Guns and Roaring Planes," *Brownsville Herald*, Jan. 13, 1952, p. 6. Osbaldo's return is described in R. G. Garza interview, Aug. 3, 1993.

28. R. G. Garza interview, Aug. 3, 1993.

29. For information on Texas politics in 1952, see Green, *The Establishment in Texas Politics*; and Sam Kinch and Stuart Long, *Allan Shivers: The Pied Piper of Texas Politics*. The account of Garza's radio address is from Kilgore interview.

30. "Killed in Korea Action," *Brownsville Herald*, July 30, 1952, p. 2; Bertha Garza interview, July 23, 1993.

31. Bertha Garza interview, July 23, 1993.

32. Garza's participation in Democrats for Eisenhower is from Joe Kilgore's interview. Eisenhower's performance in Texas is from William S. White, "Eisenhower Cracks South, Heads for Victory in Texas," *New York Times*, Nov. 5, 1952, p. 1. In the same article the *New York Times* also reported that Eisenhower "smashed the traditionally Democratic Solid South in his national victory over Governor Adlai E. Stevenson" (p. 1).

33. R. G. Garza interview, Aug. 3, 1993.

34. 49th annual Knights of Convention pamphlet, State of Texas, 1953.

35. Bertha Garza interview, July 23, 1993.

36. Lyndon Baines Johnson to Reynaldo G. Garza, Oct. 15, 1953, Apr. 23, 1954, July 15, 1954 (quotation), Mar. 28, 1955, "President's Correspondence," Lyndon Baines Johnson Papers, Lyndon Baines Johnson Library and Museum, Austin, Texas.

37. Bishop Mariano Garriega to Reynaldo Garza, July 28, 1954, Archives Department, Diocese of Corpus Christi, Pastoral Center, Corpus Christi, Texas; R. G. Garza interview, Mar. 11, 1992.

38. Bishop Garriega to R. G. Garza, July 28, 1954.

39. "State Deputy R. G. Garza Will Preside at Convention," *Brownsville Knight,* May, 1955, vol. 1, p. 1.

40. "Republican Texan Wins," *New York Times*, Nov. 3, 1954, p. 23; "'Mister Sam' Takes Over House Reins," *New York Times*, Nov. 4, 1954, p. 25; Garza's reaction to Johnson's victory is from Bertha Garza interview, July 23, 1993.

41. R. G. Garza interview, Aug. 3, 1993.

42. Ibid.

43. Garza's service to civic groups is in "Child Welfare Clinic for County Supported by Group," *Brownsville Herald,* June 2, 1948, p. 1; Meritorious Service Award, presented by Planning and Zoning Commission, Sept. 1, 1957, copy on file with author. Johnson's position in Senate is in William S. White, "Congress to Open Today in Harmony with White House," *New York Times*, Jan. 5, 1955, p. 1. Garza as advisor to LBJ is in Lyndon Baines Johnson to Reynaldo G. Garza, Jan. 17, 1957, Lyndon Baines Johnson Papers, Lyndon Baines Johnson Library and Museum, Austin, Texas.

44. "It's War Among Texas Democrats," *U.S. News and World Report*, Apr. 27, 1956, pp. 45–46. For information on the fight between Shivers and Johnson in 1956, see Kinch and Long, *Allan Shivers*, pp. 168–69, 184–85; Green, *The Establishment in Texas Politics;* Rowland Evans and Robert Novak, *Lyndon B. Johnson: The Exercise of Power,* pp. 244–45.

45. Shivers's reaction to Garza's decision is from R. G. Garza interview, Aug. 3, 1993. Johnson's control of the state party convention is from Dallek, *Lone Star Rising,* p. 500.

46. R. G. Garza interview, Aug. 3, 1993.

47. Bertha Garza interview, July 23, 1993.

48. "Garza Appointed to Good Neighbor Commission," *Brownsville Herald,* Apr. 24, 1957, p. 1; Nellie Kingrea, *History of the First Ten Years of the Texas Good Neighbor Commission,* p. 11; George Little, "A Study of the Texas Good Neighbor Commission," pp. 7-8; Carey McWilliams, *North From Mexico: The Spanish-Speaking People of*

the United States, pp. 265–70, 275–76; George Norris Green, "The Felix Longoria Affair," *Journal of Ethnic Studies* 19 (Fall, 1991): 29.

49. Texas Supreme Court positions are discussed in Green, *The Establishment in Texas Politics;* quotations are from Greenhill interview; Garza's participation is from R. G. Garza interview, July 23, 1993.

50. "Governor Daniel Appoints Valleyites to Education Commission," *Brownsville Herald,* Oct. 24, 1957, p. 3.

51. Bertha Garza interview, July 23, 1993.

Chapter 5: Approaching the Bench, 1959–61

1. R. G. Garza interview, Aug. 3, 1993; "Judge Allred Rites Set in Corpus Christi," *Brownsville Herald,* Sept. 25, 1959, p. 1.

2. Harold W. Chase, *The Appointing Process;* Joel B. Grossman, *Lawyers and Judges: The A. B. A. and the Politics of Judicial Selection.*

3. Joseph C. Goulden, *The Benchwarmers: The Private World of the Powerful Federal Judges,* p. 23.

4. Garza's popularity is documented in "New Federal Judge Has Respect of Attorneys Who Know Him," *Houston Chronicle,* Mar. 31, 1961, p. 8. Federal law mandates that district judges reside in their appointed district. The district covers forty-five counties in South Texas and a population of approximately three million individuals. *Congressional Record,* 57th Cong., 1st sess. vol. 35, 2136–37. Qualities considered during the judicial selection process are discussed in Goulden, *The Benchwarmers.*

5. "Report of the Standing Committee on the Federal Judiciary," *Reports of the American Bar Association* 85 (1961): 455.

6. Kennerly's support of the Republican party is in U. S. Congress, Senate, Statement of Honorable Ralph W. Yarborough, Committee on the Judiciary, p. 3; Cameron County Judge Oscar Dancy to John F. Kennedy, Apr. 7, 1961, John F. Kennedy Papers; Cameron County Judge Oscar Dancy to Lyndon Baines Johnson, Nov. 30, 1960, John F. Kennedy Papers; Charles L. Zelden, *Justice Lies in the District: The U.S. District Court, Southern District of Texas, 1902–1960,* pp. 210–11. Garza's role in considering potential candidates is from R. G. Garza interview, Aug. 3, 1993.

7. For more about the G. I. Forum, see Allsup, *The American G. I. Forum,* pp. 132–33. Allsup documents that in 1947 Dr. Héctor García organized a group of Mexican American veterans in Corpus Christi, Texas, to hear their concerns about their people's plight. In 1948 the group called themselves the American G. I. Forum. One of the main activities of the organization became sending letters and telegrams to Texas congressmen and senators urging these elected officials to help Mexican Americans achieve greater state and governmental representation. The group is presently active in twenty-eight states and Washington, D.C. (pp. 33–34, 155) Dr. Héctor García to Dwight D. Eisenhower, Mar. 4, 1960, Dwight D. Eisenhower Papers, Dwight D. Eisenhower Presidential Library, Abilene, Kansas.

8. Lyndon Baines Johnson to R. G. Garza, Jan. 13, 1960, "President's Correspondence," Lyndon Baines Johnson Papers; R. G. Garza interview, Aug. 3, 1993.

9. Zelden, *Justice Lies in the District,* pp. 210–11.

10. For more about Johnson as Kennedy's running mate, see W. H. Lawrence, "Kennedy Nominated on the First Ballot; Overwhelms Johnson by 806 Votes to 409," *New York Times*, July 14, 1960, p. 1; W. H. Lawrence, "Johnson Is Nominated for Vice President; Kennedy Picks Him to Placate the South: Choice a Surprise," *New York Times*, July 15, 1960, p. 1; W. H. Lawrence, "Kennedy Calls For Sacrifices In U.S. to Help the World Meet Challenges of 'New Frontier,'" *New York Times*, July 16, 1960, p. 1. Garza's role in this campaign is described in "New Federal Judge," p. 8.

11. "Johnson Speaks at Harlingen Campaign Rally," *Brownsville Herald*, Oct. 21, 1960, p. 1; Kilgore interview.

12. Garza's reaction to election results are from Bertha Garza interview, Sept. 23, 1994; and R. G. Garza interview, Aug. 3, 1993. For details of election results, see O. Douglas Weeks, *Texas in the 1960 Presidential Election*, pp. 63–80; James Reston, "Kennedy's Victory Won by Close Margin; He Promises Fight for World Freedom; Eisenhower Offers 'Orderly Transition,'" *New York Times*, Nov. 10, 1960, p. 1.

13. Judge Oscar Dancy to John F. Kennedy, Apr. 7, 1961, John F. Kennedy Papers; Judge Oscar Dancy to Lyndon Baines Johnson, Nov. 30, 1960, Lyndon Baines Johnson Papers; U.S. Congress, Senate, Statement of Honorable Ralph W. Yarborough, United States Senator, Apr., 1961, p. 3.

14. Bentsen interview.

15. Allsup, *The American G. I. Forum*, p. 133; Ronnie Dugger, "Texas' New Junior Senator," *New Republic* 136 (Apr. 22, 1957): 8; William G. Phillips, *Yarborough of Texas*, pp. 102–104; Chandler Davidson, *Race and Class in Texas Politics*, p. xvi.

16. The administration's commitment to the appointment of a Mexican American is from Ramsey Clark interview, July, 7, 1970, transcript, pp. 74–75. Kennedy's intention to conquer discrimination through exective powers is from Allen J. Matusow, *The Unraveling of America: A History of American Liberalism in the 1960s*, pp. 62–63; "Freedom of Communications," part 1 (Kennedy speeches), Committee on Commerce, Senate Report 994 (1961), pp. 1010–12.

17. RFK's recruitment of minorities is in Arthur M. Schlesinger, Jr., *A Thousand Days: John F. Kennedy in the White House*, p. 934.; Arthur M. Schlesinger, Jr., *Robert Kennedy and His Times*, p. 375; Alonzo L. Hamby, *The Imperial Years: The U.S. since 1939*, pp. 280–81; and Ramsey Clark, interview by author, New York, May 30, 1995.

18. Kilgore interview.

19. Clark interview, May 30, 1995; R. G. Garza interview, Aug. 3, 1993. For example, in 1954, Garza supported Allan Shivers for a third term during his gubernatorial campaign. Shivers defeated Yarborough in August, 1954; "Shivers Is Victor in Texas Runoff," *New York Times*, Aug. 28, 1954, p. 1.

20. Kilgore interview; Clark interview, May 30, 1995.

21. Clark interview, May 30, 1995.

22. Clark interview, July 7, 1970, transcript, pp. 74–75.

23. The salary of a federal judge is documented in Administrative Office of the United States Courts, *Reports of the Proceedings of the Judicial Conference of the United States Held at Washington, D.C., March 13–14 and September 20–21, 1961*, p. 55. Family discussions and concerns are from R. G. Garza interview, Aug. 3, 1993; Bertha Garza interview, July 23, 1993.

24. Call from RFK to Garza is from R. G. Garza interview, Aug. 3, 1993. Johnson's and RFK's agreement on Garza's appointment is in Schlesinger, *Robert Kennedy and His Times*, pp. 402–403; Navasky, *Kennedy Justice*, p. 298; Dallek, *Lone Star Rising*, pp. 490–91, 580–83.

25. Clark interview, July 7, 1970, transcript, pp. 74–75.

26. Robert F. Kennedy to John F. Kennedy, Mar. 23, 1961, John F. Kennedy Papers, John Fitzgerald Kennedy Library, Boston, Mass.; Clark interview, May 30, 1995.

27. R. G. Garza interview, Aug. 3, 1993.

28. Ibid.; Clark interview, May 30, 1995.

29. Hay-Adams Hotel description is from Clark interview, May 30, 1995; Garza's thoughts are from R. G. Garza interview, Aug. 3, 1993.

30. R. G. Garza interview, Aug. 3, 1993.

31. Details of Garza's meeting are in Lyndon Baines Johnson, "Daily Diary of President Lyndon Baines Johnson, 1963–69," Mar. 24, 1961, manuscripts, Library of Congress, Washington, D.C.; R. G. Garza interview, Aug. 3, 1993; "Nominee for Judge, Garza Meets Kennedy," *San Antonio Express News*, Mar. 25, 1961, p. 2A; "Garza Says JFK Predicted More Latins Would Be Judges," *Brownsville Herald*, May 14, 1979, p. 2. Garza's official nomination is recorded in U.S. Senate, Committee on the Judiciary, *Nomination*, 87th Cong., 1st sess., Apr. 12, 1961, p. D146; "Nominations," *New York Times*, Mar. 25, 1961, p. 2.

32. R. G. Garza interview, Mar. 11, 1992.

33. Celia Martin, phone interview by author, Jan. 4, 1995; Kilgore interview.

34. Clark interview, July 7, 1970, transcript, pp. 78–79.

35. Ibid., 79; Conkin, *Big Daddy from the Pedernales*, pp. 134, 159.

36. Clark interview, May 30, 1995.

37. Ibid.

38. R. G. Garza interview, July 23, 1993.

39. Bertha Garza interview, July 23, 1993.

40. Pablo Gonzáles to John F. Kennedy, Feb. 25, 1961, John F. Kennedy Papers (quotation); J. E. Bauer to John F. Kennedy, Mar. 24, 1961, John F. Kennedy Papers.

41. Lino Pérez interview. Anglos as power brokers in South Texas is in Montejano, *Anglos and Mexicans*, p. 285.

42. Reactions to Garza's appointment are in David Hanners, "Garza Marks Twenty Years As U.S. Judge," *Brownsville Herald*, Apr. 26, 1981," p. 1; "Brownsville Attorney Named Judge," *Valley Morning Star*, Mar. 24, 1961, p. 1.

43. San Miguel, *Let All of Them Take Heed*, pp. 116, 165; Allsup, *The American G. I. Forum*, p. 133; Rodolfo Acuña, *Occupied America: History of Chicanos*, p. 26; Gómez-Quiñones, *Chicano Politics*, pp. 90–91.

44. Garza's meetings with Kilgore and Johnson are from Kilgore interview; R. G. Garza interview, Aug. 3, 1994; Lyndon Baines Johnson, "Daily Diary," Apr. 11, 13, 1961.

45. Kilgore interview.

46. An account of Garza's nomination hearing is in "New United States Judge Takes Office in Brownsville: Reynaldo G. Garza," *Texas Bar Journal* 24 (June 22,

1961): 87. Statements during Garza's hearing are in U.S. Senate, Statement of Honorable Ralph W. Yarborough, United States Senator from Texas, pp. 3, 4; U.S. Senate, Statements of Honorable Joe M. Kilgore and John Young, United States representatives from Texas, April, 1961, pp. 6, 8.

47. R. G. Garza interview, Aug. 3, 1993; Mashek, "Judge Garza's Appointment," p. 2; "Garza Named U.S. Judge," p. 3.

48. Obligations of presiding judges are discussed in American Bar Association, *Opinions of the Committee on Professional Ethics and Grievances with the Canons of Professional Ethics Annotated and the Canons of Judicial Ethics Annotated*; and Arthur T. Vanderbilt, *Minimum Standards of Judicial Administration*, pp. 32–64. Garza's activities following his appointment are from Bertha Garza interview, Sept. 23, 1994; and R. G. Garza interview, Sept. 23, 1994.

49. R. G. Garza, Sept. 23, 1994.

50. The appointment of Garza's court personnel is from Graham McCullough to Reynaldo G. Garza, Apr. 22, 1986, Reynaldo G. Garza Papers, Brownsville, Texas; "Lalo Sanchez," *Brownsville Herald*, Aug. 21, 1961, p. 4; "Federal Judge Garza Takes Office Saturday," *Houston Chronicle*, Apr. 27, 1961, p. 4.

51. The hiring of law clerks is discussed in Paul R. Baier, "The Law Clerks: Profile of an Institution," *Vanderbilt Law Review* 26 (Nov., 1973): 1138, 1146. Garza's clerks are mentioned in "Federal Judge Garza Takes Office Saturday," *Brownsville Herald*, Apr. 27, 1961, p. 1.

52. Installation ceremony is described in "Federal Judge Garza," p. 1; Kilgore interview; Anderson, "Judge Garza Is Installed," Apr. 30, 1961, p. 1. When Garza joined the court, the other judges had already spent several years on the bench: Hannay, eighteen years; Connally, eleven years; and Ingraham, six years (Zelden, *Justice Lies in the District*).

53. Anderson, "Judge Garza Is Installed," p. 1; John F. Kennedy to R. G. Garza, Apr. 29, 1961, John F. Kennedy Papers; Lyndon Baines Johnson to R. G. Garza, Apr. 29, 1961.

54. Speeches are described in "Garza Takes Judge's Oath," *Dallas Morning News*, Apr. 30, 1961, p. 7; "Honored by His Country: Latin-American Judge," *Houston Chronicle*, Aug. 20, 1961, p. 8.

55. Anderson, "Judge Garza Is Installed," p. 1; Besteiro interview.

Chapter 6: Early Years on the Bench, 1961–63

1. "Changing the Mix," *Houston Post*, Aug. 18, 1979, p. 8B; "Hispanic Federal Judge 'Does What Law Requires,'" *El Paso Times*, May 13, 1979, p. 14B; John Mashek, "Judge Garza's Appointment Makes Courtroom History," *Dallas Morning News*, Apr. 16, 1961, p. 8.

2. Kennedy's goals are outlined in John F. Kennedy, *Public Papers of the Presidents of the United States*, p. 470. Mexican American participation in sociopolitical processes is in Montejano, *Anglos and Mexicans*, pp. 276–77, 218–87; Carlos Muñoz, Jr. *Youth, Identity, Power: The Chicano Movement*, pp. 38–39, 265.

3. Montejano, *Anglos and Mexicans*, pp. 285–87. A survey of the *Brownsville Herald* from 1960 to 1964 showed a majority percentage of Anglo representation in various economic, social and political activities. Other cited statistics are from Department of Commerce, Bureau of the Census, *Eighteenth Decennial Cen-*

sus of the United States: Census of Population: 1960, Part 45, Texas, p. 56; Department of Commerce, Bureau of the Census, *1970 Census of Population, Part 45, Texas,* pp. 187, 673.

4. Juliet García, interview by author, Brownsville, July 26, 1993; Federico Peña, interview by author, Washington, D.C., Feb. 7, 1995.

5. *Congressional Record,* 57th Cong., 1st sess. vol. 35, pp. 2136–37. A discussion of federal district judges' regional designations is found in 276 F. Supp. 479, 280 F. Supp. 554, and 407 F. Supp. 451.

6. Graham McCullough, phone interview by author, Oct. 17, 1994; R. G. Garza interview, Sept. 23, 1994.

7. Vanderbilt, *Minimum Standards of Judicial Administration,* pp. 32–64.

8. Regional culture of Corpus Christi is from Joe Cummings, *Texas Handbook,* pp. 377–78; population statistics are from U.S. Department of Commerce, Bureau of the Census, *Census of Population: 1960, Volume II, Texas,* p. 610. A discussion of segregation practices in Corpus Christi is in Montejano, *Anglos and Mexicans,* p. 286. In nine Texas cities, drugstores, restaurants, hotels, swimming pools, public schools, and cemeteries were closed to Mexican Americans until the late 1960s and early 1970s. In the 1990s for a majority of Texas cities, Anglos still retain economic control over Mexican Americans (see, for example, Jorge Rangel and Carlos Alcalá, "De Jure Segregation of Chicanos in Texas Schools," *Harvard Civil Rights–Civil Liberties Law Review* 7 [Mar., 1972]: 308; Clark Knowlton, "Patterns of Accommodation of Mexican Americans in El Paso, Texas," in *Politics and Society in the Southwest: Ethnicity and Chicano Pluralism,* p. 223).

9. G. McCullough to R. G. Garza, Apr. 22, 1986.

10. Ibid.

11. Fred Harper, "Judge Garza's 'Impossible Dream' Came True; Now Another Milestone," *Houston Chronicle,* July 14, 1974, p. 2.

12. William Mallet, phone interview by author, Brownsville, Oct. 19, 1994.

13. Bertha Garza interview, Sept. 23, 1994.

14. McCullough interview.

15. Ibid.

16. Griffin Bell, phone interview by author, Jan. 24, 1995.

17. "Garza, Scanlan Honored by Bar," *Brownsville Herald,* Aug. 18, 1961, p. 3.

18. Ramsey Clark interview, July 7, 1970, transcript, pp. 71–79.

19. Bay, *Historic Brownsville: Original Townsite Guide,* pp. 114–115; R. G. Garza interview, Sept. 23, 1994.

20. Bay, *Historic Brownsville,* pp. 114–15.

21. Number of court dockets is from *Annual Report of the Director of the Administrative Office of the United States Courts,* table C1.

22. Juan Ramón García, *Operation Wetback: The Mass Deportation of Mexican Undocumented Workers in 1954,* pp. 151–52.

23. U.S. House of Representatives, Committee of the Judiciary, Statement of the Honorable Lloyd M. Bentsen, 81st Cong., 1st sess., 1949, pp. 25, 27; Zelden, *Justice Lies in the District,* pp. 192–94.

24. On illegal immigration sentencing procedures in Brownsville, see *Criminal Docket Books,* Brownsville division, Federal Courthouse, Brownsville, Texas, 1961–64. Garza's expertise in handling illegal immigrants is from "Judge Garza

Clears Jail, To Return to Own Bench," *El Paso Times,* May 9, 1963, p. 2; Ramsey Clark interview, July 7, 1970, transcript, pp. 76–78.

25. Judgeship selections are discussed in Harvey C. Couch, *A History of the Fifth Circuit, 1891–1981,* p. 110. Noel's appointment is in Anthony Lewis, "President Names Seventeen to Judgeships," *New York Times,* Oct. 7, 1961, p. 10.

26. Bertha Garza interview, Sept. 23, 1994.

27. R. G. Garza interview, Sept. 23, 1994; Reynaldo Garza, Jr. interview, Sept. 22, 1994.

28. "Judge Garza Convention Speaker," *Brownsville Herald,* Apr. 30, 1961, p. 2; David C. Garza, interview by author, Brownsville, Sept. 22, 1994; Reynaldo Garza, Jr., interview; Nacho Garza, interview by author, Washington, D.C., Sept. 25, 1994.

29. Ruby A. Woolridge and Robert B. Vezzetti, *Brownsville: A Pictorial History;* "Rio Viejo," *Brownsville Herald,* June 21, 1956, p. 4; Bertha Garza interview, Sept. 23, 1994.

30. Milo Kearney et al., *A Brief History of Education,* p. 12.

31. Laredo celebration is described in Cummings, *The Texas Handbook,* p. 338. Garza's participation in George Washington celebration is in "City To Honor Federal Judge Reynaldo G. Garza," *South Texas Citizen* (Laredo), Feb. 21, 1963, p. 1; "R. G. Garza Named 'Mr. South Texas.'" *San Antonio Express News,* Jan. 23, 1963, p. 1; "One Hundred Thousand People View Fiesta Parade Saturday," *South Texas Citizen* (Laredo), Feb. 21, 1963, p. 1; Bertha Garza interview, Sept. 23, 1994.

32. "First Message to the Legislator," *Houston Chronicle,* Jan. 27, 1963, p. 1; "Give 'Em Education," *Texas Observer,* May 14, 1965; R. G. Garza interview, Sept. 23, 1994.

33. "Visiting Judge to Preside in U.S. Court," *El Paso Times,* Apr. 16, 1961, p. 2; "Judge Garza Clears Jail," p. 2; "Visiting Judge to Aid in EP Naturalization," *El Paso Times,* Apr. 26, 1963, p. 1.

34. Judge Reynaldo G. Garza Day, City of Kingsville proclamation, June 10, 1963, Garza Family Papers, Brownsville; Bertha Garza interviews, Aug. 3, 1993, Sept. 23, 1994.

35. "Tom Connally of Texas is Dead; Served in Senate for 24 Years," *New York Times,* Oct. 29, 1963, p. 1; "Connally Buried in Texas beside Grave of First Wife," *New York Times,* Oct. 31, 1963, p. 34; Lyndon Johnson, "Daily Diary," Oct. 30, 1963; William H. Mallet to R. G. Garza, Apr. 29, 1986, Reynaldo G. Garza Papers, Brownsville, Texas; R. G. Garza interview, Sept. 23, 1994.

36. Lyndon Johnson, "Daily Diary," Nov. 4, 1963; Reston, *The Lone Star,* p. 237.

37. U.S. Treasury Department, *Report of the U.S. Secret Service on the Assassination of President Kennedy: Exhibits,* pp. 1–2.

38. Reynaldo Garza, Jr., interview.

39. "Agents Close Border," *Brownsville Herald,* Nov. 23, 1963, p. 1; Mallet interview; Bertha Garza interview, Aug. 3, 1993; Robert E. Baskin, "Johnson Becomes President: Receives Oath on Aircraft," *Dallas Morning News,* Nov. 23, 1963, p. 1.

40. Aiken interview.

41. Ibid; Bertha Garza interview, Aug. 3, 1993.

42. Garza interview, Sept. 23, 1994; "Impact Shattering to World Capitals," *Dallas Morning News,* Nov. 23, 1963, p. 1.

Chapter 7: The Turbulent Sixties, 1963–69

1. Quotations are from Lyndon B. Johnson, *Public Papers of the Presidents of the United States*, p. 11. A discussion of the speech is found in John L. Steele, "The Texan Sits Tall in a New Saddle," *Life*, Dec. 13, 1963, pp. 26–27. Garza's support of Johnson is from Bertha Garza interview, Sept. 23, 1994.

2. Mallet interview.

3. Ibid.

4. Filemón Vela, phone interview by author, June 15, 1995.

5. Quote is from Mallet interview; Hanners, "Garza Marks Twenty Years," pp. 1A, 14A.

6. Hanners, "Garza Marks Twenty Years," p. 1A.

7. Bertha Garza interview, Sept. 23, 1994; P. T. Moore, Jr., phone interview by author, Jan. 4, 1995; Charles Lewis, interview by author, Brownsville, Mar. 30, 1995; Vela interview.

8. Census statistics are from Department of Commerce, Bureau of the Census, *The Eighteenth Decennial Census*, p. 56; and Department of Commerce, Bureau of the Census, *1970 Census of Population*, pp. 187, 673. Increased litigation in Texas is from Zelden, *Justice Lies in the District*. Garza's increased workload is from Bertha Garza interview, Sept. 23, 1994.

9. Mallet interview; Bertha Garza interview, Sept. 23, 1994.

10. Bertha Garza interview, Sept. 23, 1994.

11. Johnson's popular support is documented in Tom Wicker, "Johnson Swamps Goldwater and Kennedy Beats Keating; Democrats Win Legislature: Turnout is Heavy," *New York Times*, Nov. 4, 1964, p. 1; Garza's reaction is from R. G. Garza interview, Sept. 23, 1994.

12. Monica Garza, interview by author, Brownsville, June 1, 1995. Although Johnson won a decisive victory, the vestiges of the Kennedys remained: Robert F. Kennedy also won his election in November, 1964, to represent New York in the Senate (R. W. Apple, Jr., "Kennedy Edge 6–5: Keating's Defeat Is Termed a 'Tragedy' by Rockefeller," *New York Times*, Nov. 4, 1964, p. 1).

13. Bertha Garza interview, Sept. 23, 1994.

14. R. G. Garza interview, Sept. 23, 1994.

15. Eligio de la Garza, interview by author, Washington, D.C., Sept. 29, 1994.

16. Ibid.

17. R. G. Garza interview, Sept. 23, 1994. *Maquiladoras* are referred to by a number of names including *maquilas*, in-bond plants, and twin plants. The main border areas where *maquiladora* plants are located are Tijuana–San Diego, Nogales-Nogales, Ciudad Juárez–El Paso, and Matamoros-Brownsville.

18. Information about the Fifth Circuit can be found in Couch, *A History of the Fifth Circuit.*

19. R. G. Garza interview, Sept. 23, 1994.

20. Couch, *A History of the Fifth Circuit*, pp. 10, 124, 132–33.

21. Jack Bass, *Taming the Storm: The Life and Times of Judge Frank M. Johnson, Jr., and the South's Fight Over Civil Rights*, pp. 132–34 (quotation on p. 132); Fred P. Graham, "Johnson Names Two to Appeals Court," *New York Times*, June 18, 1965, p. 18.

22. Clark interview, May 30, 1995; R. G. Garza interview, Sept. 23, 1994.

23. "Seals, Singleton Approved," *Houston Post,* July 22, 1966, p. 20; R. G. Garza interview, Sept. 23, 1994.

24. David C. Garza, interview by author, Brownsville, Sept. 22, 1994.

25. Reynaldo G. Garza, Jr., interview.

26. Bertha Garza interview, Sept. 23, 1994.

27. R. G. Garza interview, Sept. 23, 1994.

28. Bertha Garza interview, Sept. 23, 1994, Mallet interview; Reynaldo Garza, Jr., interview, Dec. 21, 1994.

29. See "President's Correspondence," Lyndon Baines Johnson Papers for the following letters: Tony Bonilla to Ramsey Clark, July 28, 1965; Tony Campos to Lyndon Johnson, Mar. 8, 1967; County Judge Gus J. Strauss to Lyndon Johnson, June 26, 1968; Clifford H. Zirkel, Jr., to Lyndon Johnson, Mar. 13, 1964.

30. Bonilla to Ramsey Clark; quote is from Ramsey Clark interview, May 30, 1995.

31. Special Assistant to the President W. Marvin Watson to Reynaldo Garza, Mar. 29, 1968, "President's Correspondence," Lyndon Baines Johnson Papers; Lyndon Johnson to Reynaldo Garza, July 1, 1968, "President's Correspondence," Lyndon Baines Johnson Papers.

32. "Polls Show Opposition to Johnson," *Brownsville Herald,* Nov. 6, 1967, p. 6; Melvin Small, *Covering Dissent: The Media and the Anti-Vietnam War Movement,* p. 1, 32–48; R. G. Garza interview, Sept. 23, 1994.

33. "'Great Society' Faces Future—Changes Congress Is Making," *U.S. News and World Report,* July 10, 1967, p. 32; Fred P. Graham, "Senate Confirms Marshall as the First Negro Justice," *New York Times,* Aug. 31, 1967, pp. 1, 19; "Marshall Inducted in Closed Ceremony," *New York Times,* Sept. 2, 1967, p. 3; Fred P. Graham, "Johnson, as Clark Swearing-In, Vows Drive on Crime," *New York Times,* Mar. 11, 1967, pp. 1, 15.

34. Ellen Debenport, "Reynaldo Garza: Nation's First Mexican-American Federal Judge Eases Into Retirement," *Los Angeles Daily Journal,* July 28, 1982, p. 26.

35. Quotation is from Lyndon Johnson to Reynaldo Garza, Nov. 13, 1967, "President's Correspondence," Lyndon Baines Johnson Papers. For information about the Chamizal, see Phillip C. Jessup, "El Chamizal," *American Journal of International Law* 67 (1973): 423; After the Mexican War, Mexican and Americans agreed to set a boundary at the Rio Grande, from El Paso to Brownsville. Since the bed of the Rio Grande frequently changed through erosion or avulsion, Mexicans and Americans disputed the ever-shifting territory (Jessup, "El Chamizal"). Perception of Garza and sentiments expressed in following paragraph about *Sweatt v. Painter* are from R. G. Garza interview, Sept. 23, 1994.

36. David Halberstam, "Politics 1968," *Harper's,* March, 1968, p. 34.

37. Hanners, "Garza Marks Twenty Years," p. 1.

38. Garza interview, Sept. 23, 1994; predominance of drug cases is from *Annual Report of the Director of the Administrative Office of the United States Court,* U. S. District Court, Southern District of Texas, National Archives, Southwest Region.

39. U.S. Senate, Committee on the Judiciary, *Hearings before the Subcommittee on Improvements in Judicial Machinery of the Committee on the Judiciary on S. 3475,* pp. 1–3,

660; Craig R. Whitney, "Federal Courts to Get 'Magistrates,'" *New York Times*, Apr. 5, 1970, p. 62; Mallet interview.

40. Lyndon Baines Johnson, *The Vantage Point: Perspective of the Presidency, 1963–1969*, pp. 365–424.

41. Johnson's entire address is in *Public Papers of the Presidents of the United States, 1968–1969*, pp. 468–76; Garza's reactions are from Bertha Garza interview, Sept. 23, 1994.

42. R. G. Garza interview, Sept. 23, 1994.

43. Garza's reactions are from his interview, Sept. 23, 1994; details of the assassination are from Schlesinger, *Robert Kennedy and His Times*, pp. 1–2, 939, 942, 945, 982–83.

44. Clark interview; R. G. Garza interview, Sept. 23, 1994.

45. Johnson's departure is from Conkin, *Big Daddy from the Pedernales*, pp. 287, 290. Rio Grande Valley residents' memories of Johnson are from R. G. Garza interview, Sept. 23, 1994.

Chapter 8: The Chief, 1969–76

1. Garza's reputation is from Goulden, *The Benchwarmers*, p. 64. Quotations are from John Minor Wisdom, phone interview by author, July 13, 1994; Mallet interview. Garza's adjudication skills are from P. T. Moore interview.

2. P. T. Moore interview.

3. Ibid.

4. R. G. Garza interview, March 11, 1992.

5. Reynaldo G. Garza, Jr., interview, Sept. 22, 1994; Márquez, *LULAC*, p. 20.

6. R. G. Garza interview, Sept. 23, 1994; "Vietnam: The Long Way Home," *Newsweek*, June 23, 1969, p. 25.

7. R. G. Garza interview, Sept. 23, 1994.

8. George Bennett, phone interview by author, Feb. 8, 1995.

9. R. G. Garza interview, Sept. 23, 1994; Moore interview.

10. Bertha Garza interview, Sept. 23, 1994.

11. Bertha Garza interview, Sept. 23, 1994; Bennett interview.

12. Al Prince, "Garza to Preside at Biggest Civil Rights Trial of His Career," *Houston Post*, Mar. 23, 1970, p. 2; Fred Harper, "Longshoremen Unions Open Case For 'Segregation by Choice' Today," *Houston Chronicle*, July 15, 1970, p. 1.

13. "La Feria Student Exonerated," *Houston Chronicle*, Aug. 6, 1970, p. 8; "Judge: Rights Don't End at School Door," *Houston Chronicle*, Nov. 22, 1970, p. 6; Richardson et al., *Texas: The Lone Star State*, p. 450.

14. Fred Harper, "Judge Lashes ILA Chief on Mixing," *Houston Chronicle*, Sept. 15, 1970, p. 1.

15. *United States of America v. International Longshormen's Association*, 334 F. Supp. 976 (1971). The case's resolution is found in *Equal Employment Opportunity Commissioner v. International Longshormen's Association*, 511 F. 2d (1971).

16. Alfredo Cuellar, "Perspectives on Politics," p. 564. Also see De León, *Ethnicity in the Sunbelt*; and Garcia, *Rise of the Mexican American Middle Class*; and *United States of America v. International Longshormen's Association*, 334 F. Supp. 976 (1971).

17. Reynaldo G. Garza, Jr., interview.

18. "Judge Kills Five of Six Vote Indictments," *Houston Post*, Dec. 1, 1970, p. 6A; "Judge Orders Voters Named in Starr Case," *Corpus Christi Caller*, Dec. 1, 1970, p. 14C; "Vote Fraud Case Motions Denied to Hold Records," *Houston Chronicle*, Dec. 4, 1970, p. 5.

19. Discussions of political machines are found in Montejano, *Anglos and Mexicans*, pp. 245, 248, 251, 253, 279, 739–40.

20. "Fraternity Initiates Judge Garza," *Austin American-Statesman*, Dec. 6, 1970, p. 9A. David C. Garza interview, Sept. 22, 1994; Reynaldo G. Garza, Jr. interview.

21. R. G. Garza interview, Sept. 23, 1994.

22. Mallet interview.

23. Quotes are from John Hughes, "Drugs Flow Freely from Mexico," *Houston Post*, Dec. 1, 1970, p. 4C. For cases in which legal bounds were crossed, see *United States of America v. Alvarez-Gonzalez*, 401 F. Supp. 931 (1975); *United States of America v. Bates*, 398 F. Supp. 731 (1975); and *United States of America v. Zamora*, 364 F. Supp. 1170 (1973).

24. Catholic census of the Diocese of Brownsville, reprinted in *Valley Catholic Witness*, Sept. 3, 1967, p. 3.

25. For efforts to bring education to the Rio Grande Valley, see Kearney et al., *A Brief History of Education*, pp. 13–16; García interview.

26. Kearney et al., p. 260.

27. *Medrano v. Allee*, 347 F. Supp. 605 (1972).

28. Charles R. Chandler, "The Mexican American Protest Movement in Texas," pp. 231–52; Montejano, *Anglos and Mexicans*, pp. 284–85 (quotation on p. 284). Also see Reston, *The Lone Star*, regarding the strike.

29. R. G. Garza interview, Sept. 23, 1994.

30. Ibid.

31. Ibid.

32. Ibid.

33. Pipkin interview; Bertha Garza interview, Sept. 23, 1994. Details about Johnson's death are from Haynes Johnson, "Death Apparently Due to Heart Attack," *Washington Post*, Jan. 23, 1973, p. 1.

34. Garza's feelings about Johnson's death and about the abortion issue discussed in the following paragraphs are from R. G. Garza interview, Sept. 23, 1994.

35. David C. Garza interview; Reynaldo G. Garza, Jr., interview; Nacho Garza interview. President Nixon's sentiments about Johnson are in Stephen E. Ambrose, *Ruin and Recovery, 1973–1990*, p. 53.

36. Nacho Garza interview; Bertha Garza interview, Sept. 23, 1994.

37. Charles Lewis, interview by author, Brownsville, Mar. 30, 1995.

38. *Turner v. American Bar Association*, 407 F. Supp. 451, 456 (1975).

39. Quotations are from ibid.

40. Fred Harper, "Judge Garza's 'Impossible Dream' Came True; Now Another Milestone," *Houston Chronicle*, July 14, 1974, p. 2. Seniority has been the basis for the designation of the presiding judge of the circuit court since 1891, when the circuit court of appeals was created (26 Stat. 827 [1891]).

41. Marc Knisely, interview by author, Austin, Feb. 14, 1995; Harper, "Judge Garza's 'Impossible Dream,'" p. 2.

42. "Chief Judge Garza Honored at Bar Association Dinner," *Brownsville Herald,* Jan. 7, 1975, p. 1.

43. Knisely interview.

44. 28 U.S.C., sec. 1861–70.

45. Knisely interview; R. G. Garza interview, Sept. 23, 1994.

46. 384 F. Supp. 79 (1974).

47. The defendant appealed the case to the Fifth Circuit, who reversed Garza's ruling. The state then appealed the case to the Supreme Court. In a split decision, with Justices Warren Burger, Lewis Powell, William Rehnquist, and Potter Stewart dissenting, the Supreme Court affirmed the Fifth Circuit's ruling. Although the higher courts reversed Garza, the dissent by the four Supreme Court justices and the creation of a test for equal protection challenges resulting from the case attested to the evidence's ambiguousness. The evidence demonstrated that only 39 percent of those summoned for grand jury duty were Mexican American, even though Mexican Americans made up 79 percent of the population of Hidalgo County, where the trial took place. Regardless of the prima facie evidence, the courts faced the issue of whether the underrepresentation of Mexican Americans was the result of discriminatory practice or simply an accident of fate. To solve the dilemma, Justice Harry Blackmun adopted a scientific method to distinguish random occurrences from those caused by intent. Previous cases outlined no consistent method of determining when a disparity became strong evidence of discriminatory practices. The Partida case gave the federal courts an essential three-pronged test for determining discrimination that proved monumentally significant in subsequent cases brought under federal civil rights statues (*Partida v. Castaneda,* 384 F. Suppl 79 [1974], *Castaneda v. Partida,* 438 U.S. 482, 97 S. Ct. 1272 [1977]).

48. Knisely interview.

49. Knisely interview; Lewis interview.

Chapter 9: Toward the Fifth Circuit, 1976–79

1. "Garza Says JFK Predicted More Latins Would be Judges," *Brownsville Herald,* May 23, 1979, p. 16A.

2. *Annual Report of the Director,* table C1, p. 14; *United States of America v. 76,552 Pounds of Frog Legs,* 423 F. Supp. 329 (1976).

3. Allen Reid Tillson to Reynaldo Garza, Apr. 25, 1986, Reynaldo G. Garza Papers, Brownsville, Texas.

4. Ibid.

5. Nacho Garza interview.

6. Burton I. Kaufman, *The Presidency of James Earl Carter, Jr.,* p. 18; R. G. Garza interview, Sept. 23, 1994.

7. Kaufman, *The Presidency of James Earl Carter,* pp. 25–26.

8. Griffin Bell, phone interview with author, Jan. 24, 1995.

9. Ibid.

10. Bell interview; Griffin B. Bell, *Taking Care of the Law,* pp. 68–69.

11. Bell interview.

12. Bertha Garza interview, Sept. 23, 1994.

13. Lewis interview.

14. R. G. Garza interview, Sept. 23, 1994; Bell interview.

15. R. G. Garza interview, Sept. 23, 1994; Bell interview.

16. Bell interview; David Garza interview; Nacho Garza interview; Bertha Garza interview, Sept. 23, 1994.

17. R. G. Garza interview, Sept. 23, 1994.

18. Bell, *Taking Care of the Law*, p. 52; Bill Salter, "Possible AG Post Declined by Garza," *Brownsville Herald*, Dec. 22, 1976, p. 5; "Carter Says Hispanic American Was First Choice for Cabinet Job," *New York Times*, Nov. 3, 1980, p. 8.

19. *Gonzalez v. Texas Employment Commission*, 563 F. 2d. 776 (1977). Garza's sentiments about women's rights are from R. G. Garza interview, Sept. 23, 1994.

20. "School Named in Garza's Honor," *Brownsville Herald*, Nov. 24, 1977, p. 1; R. G. Garza interview, Sept. 23, 1994.

21. R. G. Garza interview, Sept. 23, 1994.

22. Vela interview.

23. Eutimio Ruedas to President Jimmy Carter, Aug. 28, 1978, White House Central File, Name File: Garza, R., Jimmy Carter Presidential Library, Atlanta, Georgia; "Memorandum," Sept. 17, 1978, White House Central File, Name File: Garza, R., Jimmy Carter Presidential Library; "Carter Running with the Rodriguezes," *Christian Science Monitor*, May 7, 1979, p. 24.

24. Department of Commerce, Bureau of the Census, Statistical Abstract of the United States: 1979 (Washington, D.C.: Government Printing Office, 1979), pp. 33, 398, 464; Tony Castro, *Chicano Power*, p. 5; Moises Sandoval, "Hispanics Have Potential for Great Contributions," *San Antonio Express News*, p. 3.

25. Castro, *Chicano Power*, p. 5. For more information on the conservative backlash, see Thomas Byrne Edsall and Mary D. Edsall, *Chain Reaction: The Impact of Race, Rights, and Taxes on American Politics*.

26. *Hernandez v. Western Electric Company*, WL 113 (1978).

27. Garza's ruling is in ibid.; Garza's feeling for the plaintiff is from Ted Campagnolo, phone interview by author, San Antonio, May 22, 1995.

28. Campagnolo interview; Henry A. Politz, interview by author, Shreveport, June 15, 1995.

29. Vela interview.

30. Bertha Garza interview, Sept. 23, 1994.

31. "Longtime Civic Leader Ynacio Garza is Dead," *Brownsville Herald*, Feb. 25, 1979, p. 1; Nacho Garza interview, Sept. 23, 1994.

32. Bentsen interview.

33. Bell interview; "Changing the Mix," *Houston Post*, Aug. 18, 1979, p. B8.

34. Discussions of the Carter Administration's judicial selection process are in Griffin Bell interview; and Jeffrey W. Stempel, "Symposium: New Paradigm, Normal Science, Crumbling Construct? Trends in Adjudicating Procedure and Litigation and Reform," *Brooklyn Law Review* 59 (Fall, 1993): 720 n. 219. Stempel adds: "The Carter administration championed deregulation and embarked upon a method of judicial selection much more favorable to the 'out-party' than was previously the case. The entire legal tone of the Carter years was different than the Kennedy and Johnson administrations. For example, no one would confuse Carter's Attorney General Griffin Bell with 1960s Attorneys General Ramsey

Clark or Robert Kennedy." Discussions regarding Garza's specific selection are found in "Houston Woman, Brownsville Man Nominated for Circuit Judgeships," *Houston Post*, Apr. 28, 1979, p. A20.

35. Bell interview; R. G. Garza, Sept. 23, 1994.

36. Bell interview; Bentsen interview by author; R. G. Garza interview, Sept. 23, 1994; U.S. President, *Public Papers of the Presidents of the United States*, pp. 733, 787; David G. Savage, *Turning Right: The Making of the Rehnquist Supreme Court*, p. 172 (quotation).

37. Bertha Garza interview, Sept. 23, 1994; Hanners, "Garza Marks Twenty Years," p. 14A.

38. R. G. Garza interview, Mar. 11, 1992.

39. Don Oldenburg, "Jack Lawn's War: The DEA Administrator and his Full Court Press against Drug Traffickers," *Washington Post*, Mar. 1, 1988, p. 1B; *United States* v. *Harrelson*, 754 F. 2d 1182; "Addenda," *Washington Post*, Mar. 12, 1986, p. 17A.

40. R. G. Garza interview, Sept. 23, 1994.

41. Ibid.; "Five New Judges Take Oath," *San Antonio Express News*, June 1, 1979, p. 1.

42. Quotation is in U.S. Senate, Committee on the Judiciary, *The Selection and Confirmation of Federal Judges*, 96th Cong., 1st sess., June 25, 1979, pp. 304 (quotation), 304–306.

43. Ibid., pp. 306–13 (all quotations appear on p. 313).

44. Politz interview.

45. Ibid. Quote from Garza is from U.S. Senate, Committee on the Judiciary, *The Selection and Confirmation of Federal Judges*, 96th Cong., 1st sess., June 25, 1979, p. 313.

46. Arthur Wiese, "Three Texas Nominees for Federal Bench Complete Hearings," *Washington Post*, June 29, 1979, p. 20A; Ward Walker, "Cuidado!" *Brownsville Herald*, June 29, 1979, p. 3.

47. Mexican American Assembly Education Task Force Chair Gustavo E. González to President Jimmy Carter, Aug. 1, 1979, White House Central File, Name File: Garza, R., Jimmy Carter Presidential Library; Arnie Miller to Gustavo E. González, Aug. 14, 1979, White House Central File, Name File: Garza, R., Jimmy Carter Presidential Library; "Lack of Minority Judges Hit," *San Antonio Express News*, May 2, 1979, p. 4.

48. "Garza Confirmed to Appeals Court," *Brownsville Herald*, July 14, 1979, p. 1; Arnie Miller to President Jimmy Carter, Apr. 23, 1979, Jimmy Carter Presidential Papers.

49. Campagnolo interview.

50. Descriptions of the ceremony here and in following paragraphs are from Eduardo Martínez, "Garza Becomes Appeals Judge," *Brownsville Herald*, July 14, 1979, p. 1; Walker, "Cuidado!" p. 3; Bell interview.

Chapter 10: The Fifth Circuit, 1979–86

1. R. G. Garza interview, Sept. 23, 1994. Quieter appellate court environment is described in Daniel John Meador and Jordana Simone Bernstein, *Appellate Courts in the United States*, p. 11.

2. Couch, *A History of the Fifth Circuit*, pp. 10, 175, 183, 186.

3. Meador and Bernstein, *Appellate Courts in the United States*, pp. 11, 16, 38,

70–79. Much of the statutory provisos regarding the operations of the United States federal courts are found in Title 28 of the United States code.

4. Procedures are discussed in ibid., p. 83. Garza's participation is from R. G. Garza interview, March 11, 1992. Recollections of Garza's courtroom manner are from Politz interview.

5. Meador and Bernstein, *Appellate Courts in the United States*; Politz interview; R. G. Garza interview, Sept. 23, 1994; Campagnolo interview.

6. Politz interview.

7. *Almanac of the Federal Judiciary*, 1993 ed., s.v. "Reynaldo G. Garza: Lawyer's Evaluation."

8. Bell interview.

9. *Judges of the United States*, 1978 ed., s.v. "Thomas M. Reavley."

10. Ibid., s.v. "Sam D. Johnson."

11. Information about John Minor Wisdom's life and career is in Jack Bass, *Unlikely Heroes*, pp. 15–18, 23, 24, 25–27, 46–51, 95, 100, 108–109; Bass, *Taming the Storm*, pp. 132–34; and J. W. Peltason, *Fifty-Eight Lonely Men*. Information about Garza's friendship with Wisdom is from R. G. Garza interview, Sept. 23, 1994; and Wisdom interview. Quotation is from Wisdom interview.

12. Information about Politz's career is in *Almanac of the Federal Judiciary*, 1993 ed., s.v. "Henry A. Politz." Quotation is from Politz interview.

13. Couch, *A History of the Fifth Circuit*, p. 189; Howell Heflin, "Fifth Circuit Court of Appeals Reorganization Act of 1980—Overdue Relief for an Overworked Court," *Cumberland Law Review* 11 (1980): 597, 613; Henry J. Friendly, *Federal Jurisdiction: A General View*, p. 31. Case filings increased tenfold from 1960 to 1990. The number of appeals court judges, however, merely increased from 68 to 179 (*Annual Report of the Director*, table S12).

14. Heflin, "Fifth Circuit Court of Appeals," pp. 593, 613; Couch, *A History of the Fifth Circuit*, pp. 10, 175, 183, 186; Bass, *Taming the Storm*, pp. 132–34.

15. Couch, *A History of the Fifth Circuit*, pp. 10, 175, 183, 186.

16. *Jurek v. Estelle*, 623 F. 2d 929 (1980).

17. Ibid.

18. Couch, *A History of the Fifth Circuit*, pp. 187–89. A history of the split is described in Bass, *Taming the Storm*, p. 409.

19. R. G. Garza interview, Sept. 23, 1994.

20. Elizabeth Bumiller, "Here Come the Judges," *Washington Post*, Mar. 12, 1980, p. D6. According to Bumiller, some guests at the reception speculated that the first woman justice on the Supreme Court may be in attendance (p. D6). Their speculations were not totally false as among the many jurists in the room was Professor Ruth Bader Ginsburg of Columbia's law school. In later years she become the second woman on the Supreme Court.

21. The Fifth Circuit Court of Appeals Reorganization Act of 1980, U.S. Code, Title 28, sec. 1 note, pp. 41, 44, 48.

22. Taylor's visit is described in John S. D. Eisenhower, *So Far from God*, p. 51; and Montejano, *Anglos and Mexicans*, pp. 42–43. Crowd reactions are from Nacho Garza interview. Carter's visit is described in U.S. President, *Public Papers of the United States*, pp. 2617–18.

23. Nacho Garza interview.

24. R. G. Garza to Ronald Reagan, Washington, D.C., Jan. 9, 1981, White House Correspondence, Ronald Reagan Library, Simi Valley, Calif.

25. Documenting the number of opinions written is *Clerk's Annual Report: Fifth Circuit Fiscal Year 1982;* Garza's schedule is from Campagnolo interview.

26. Bell interview; *Judge Reynaldo Garza, Twenty Years of Service* (program), Garza Family Papers, Brownsville.

27. *Valley v. Rapides Parish School Board,* 646 F. 2d. 925, 928–29.

28. *Estate of Bright v. United States,* 658 F.2d 999 (5th Cir. 1981); Couch, *A History of the Fifth Circuit,* pp. 195–98; R. G. Garza interview, Sept. 23, 1994.

29. "Federal Judicial Day Observed Here," *Houston Post,* Mar. 25, 1982, p. A14.

30. Campagnolo interview.

31. R. G. Garza to Ronald Reagan, Feb. 10, 1982, Ronald Reagan Library; Counsel to the President Fred F. Fielding to R. G. Garza, Mar. 19, 1982, Ronald Reagan Library.

32. David Hanners, "Judge Garza Going on Senior Status," *Brownsville Herald,* Feb. 17, 1982, p. 1A; "First Mexican-American Judge Retiring," *Times-Picayune* (New Orleans), Feb. 18, 1982, p. 24; "Thirty-Three Percent of Senior Federal Judges in Texas Do No Work," *Houston Post,* Feb. 21, 1989, p. A3. Quotation is from Ed Asher, "Garza's Career a Landmark," *Brownsville Herald,* Apr. 29, 1986, p. 1.

33. Monica Garza interview, June 1, 1995.

34. Herbert Jacob, *Justice in America: Courts, Lawyers, and the Judicial Process,* pp. 220–32; Statistical Sheet Compiled by the Clerks' Office of the United States Supreme Court, Oct., 1982, *Journal of the Supreme Court of the United States* (Washington D.C.: Clerk's Office, 1983). In the 1982 term, 183 cases were argued before the Supreme Court. The number included carryovers from the 1982 term. Sixteen cases were disposed without argument, and 151 opinions were written (Statistical Sheet).

35. *Wiggins v. Estelle,* 681 F. 2d. 266 (1982).

36. *McKaskle v. Wiggins,* 465 U.S. 168 (1984); Teresa A. Scott, "The Role of Standby Counsel: The Road from *Faretta* to *Wiggins,*" *Howard Law Journal* 27 (1984): 1799–1811.

37. *Hyde v. Jefferson Parish Hospital District No. 2,* 686 F. 2d. 286 (1982).

38. Ibid.

39. *Jefferson Parish Hospital District No. 2 v. Hyde,* 466 U.S. 2 (1984).

40. *Almanac of the Federal Judiciary,* 1993 ed., s.v. "Reynaldo G. Garza: Lawyer's Evaluation."

41. Keith Uhles to R. G. Garza, Apr. 17, 1986, Reynaldo G. Garza Papers, Brownsville, Texas.

42. James R. Elkins, "The Temporary Emergency Court of Appeals: A Study in the Abdication of Judicial Responsibility," *Duke Law Journal* 113 (1978): 114–15; Transcript of the Proceedings of the Final Session of the Court, United States Emergency Court of Appeals, 229 F. R. D. 1 (1961). Congress eventually decided to abolish the court.

43. David N. Rubin, "Judge Garza Given Award by Colleges," *Brownsville Herald,* Apr. 4, 1984, p. 1; Jorjanna Price, "Law School in Edinburg Gets Assist from Court," *Houston Post,* Jan. 17, 1988, p. 4B; "Law School Gets Special Consideration," *Dallas Morning News,* Apr. 7, 1993, p. 39A.

44. Rubin, "Judge Garza Given Award by Colleges," Apr. 4, 1984, p. 1 (quota-

tion); "Federal Judge Spending Little Time Looking Back: Valley Native Nearing Thirtieth Year on Bench," *Victoria Advocate*, Apr. 26, 1961, p. 6A.

45. Jorjanna Price, "Panel Backs 'Judicious' Education Budget Cuts, Tax Increase," *Houston Post*, Aug. 9, 1986, p. 19A; Nacho Garza interview.

46. McCullough interview; Mallet interview; Knisely interview; Campagnolo interview.

47. Knisely interview.

Chapter 11: Twilight, 1986–96

1. Kearney and Knopp, *Boom and Bust*, p. 263; Nacho Garza interview.

2. Kearney and Knopp, *Boom and Bust*, p. 263.

3. Joseph Shapiro, "Getting in Before the Gate is Locked," *U.S. News and World Report*, May 9, 1988, p. 23.

4. "Anti-Immigrant Sentiment on Rise in Southern Texas," *National Public Radio* manuscript, segment number 6, show number 1161, Aug. 30, 1993.

5. *Brock v. Merrell Dow Pharmaceuticals, Inc.*, 87 F. 2d 307 (1989).

6. Juliet García to Selection Committee Members, Mar. 1, 1989, University of Texas Alumni Center, Austin.

7. "Honors Planned for Judge Garza," *Brownsville Herald*, Sept. 28, 1989, p. 8B; Marc Knisely, "Profile: Reynaldo G. Garza," *Fifth Circuit Reporter*, vol. 7, no. 6, April, 1990, p. 471 (quotation).

8. Campagnolo interview.

9. Elise Ackerman, "TSC Joining University of Texas," *Brownsville Herald*, June 7, 1991, p. 1; Kevin Willmann, "Richards Signs College Bill," *Valley Morning Star* (Harlingen), June 9, 1991, p. A1.

10. By 1990 over five thousand appeals were filed in the circuit, far exceeding the number in the entire federal system only thirty years earlier (*Annual Report of the Director*, table S12); Crowded Fifth Circuit is documented in Michael C. Gizzi, "Perspectives of a Crisis," *Judicature* 78 (1994): 106, 109.

11. Bertha Garza interview, Sept. 23, 1994.

12. Knisely interview, Feb. 14, 1995; July 10, 1995.

13. For incidences of anencephaly in and around Brownsville, see Jerry Adler, "A Life and Death Puzzle," *Newsweek*, June 8, 1992, p. 52; Wayne Hearn, "Borderline Risks," *American Medical News*, Sept. 20, 1993, pp. 11–13; Sue Anne Pressley, "Years after Cluster of Birth Defects, Pain and Mystery Linger in Brownsville," *Washington Post*, Sept. 17, 1995, p. A3; Dan McGraw, "A Load of Trouble for Texas Border Towns: Mexico's Woes Spill across the Rio Grande," *U.S. News and World Report*, Oct. 2, 1995, pp. 64–67.

14. Department of Commerce, Bureau of the Census, *Statistical Abstract of the United States, 1993*, pp. 18–19, 154, 406–407; 28 U.S.C., sec. 44 (a) (Supp. V 1993) (listing the number of appellate judges for each circuit); 28 U.S.C., sec. 133 (a) (listing the number of district court judges for each district); "Database," *U.S. News and World Report*, May 3, 1993, p. 11; *U.S.–Mexico Border Health Statistics*.

15. Raul A. González, "A Life of Service: Reynaldo G. Garza," *Hispanic Law Journal* 1 (1994): 7.

16. Alexander Hamilton, *The Federalist Papers*, no. 78.

17. R. G. Garza interview, Aug. 8, 1995.

Bibliography

Newspapers

Austin American-Statesman. December 8, 1936; April 8, 1937; December 6, 1970.

Brownsville Herald. January, 1909–May, 1995.

Christian Science Monitor. May 7, 1979; March 31, 1982.

Corpus Christi Caller. December 1, 1970.

Dallas Morning News. April 24, 1941; June 22, 1941; April 16, 30, 1961; November 23, 1963; April 7, 1993.

El Bravo (Matamoros, Mexico). April 6, 1941.

El Paso Times. April 16, 1961; April 26, 1963; May 9, 1963; May 13, 1979.

Daily Texan. March 27, 1947.

Houston Chronicle. November 8, 1948; August 20, 1961; March 31, 1961; April 27, 1961; January 27, 1963; July 15, 1970; August 6, 1970; September 15, 1970; November 22, 1970; December 4, 1970; July 14, 1974.

Houston Post. June 22, 1941; March 24, 1961; July 22, 1966; March 23, 1970; December 1, 1970; April 28, 1979; August 18, 1979; March 25, 1982; August 9, 1986; January 17, 1988; February 21, 1989.

Los Angeles Daily Journal. July 28, 1982.

LULAC News. March, 1938.

New York Times. November 5, 1952; August 28, 1954; November 3–4, 1954; January 5, 1955; July 14–16, 1960; November 10, 1960; March 25, 1961; October 7, 1961; October 29, 31, 1963; November 4, 1964; June 18, 1965; March 11, 1967;

August 31, 1967; September 2, 1967; June 27, 1968; April 5, 1970; June 15, 1973; January 11, 1974; December 17, 1976; November 3, 1980.

San Antonio Express News. March 25, 1961; January 23, 1963; February 5, 8, 1978; May 2, 1979; June 1, 1979.

South Texas Citizen (Laredo). February 21, 1963.

Star Monitor Herald (Harlingen, McAllen, Brownsville). April 6, 1941; May 4, 1941.

Texas Observer. May 14, 24, 1965; May 9, 1969.

Texas Weekly. September 1, 1933–January 1, 1935.

Times-Picayune (New Orleans). February 18, 1982.

The Valley Catholic Witness. September 3, 1967.

Valley Morning Star (Harlingen, Tex.). March 24, 1961; June 9, 1991.

Victoria Advocate. April 26, 1961.

Washington Post. January 23, 1973; June 29, 1979; March 12, 1980; March 12, 1986; March 1, 1988; September 17, 1995.

Books and Other Sources

Acuña, Rodolfo. *Occupied America: History of Chicanos.* New York: Harper and Row, 1981.

Administrative Office of the United States Courts. *Reports of the Proceedings of the Judicial Confernce of the United States Held at Washington, D.C.,* March 13–14 and September 20–21, 1961. Washington, D.C.: Government Printing Office, 1961.

Aiken, Bruce. Director, Historic Brownsville Museum. Interview by author. Brownsville, June 8, 1993.

Allsup, Carl. *The American G. I. Forum: Origins and Evolution.* Austin: University of Texas Press, 1982.

Ambrose, Stephen E. *Ruin and Recovery, 1973–1990.* New York: Simon and Schuster, 1991.

American Bar Association. *Opinions of the Committee on Professional Ethics and Grievances with the Canons of Professional Ethics Annotated and the Canons of Judicial Ethics Annotated.* Chicago: American Bar Association, 1957.

Annual Report of the Director of the Administrative Office of the United States Courts. U.S. District Court, Southern District of Texas, National Archives, Southwest Region. Fort Worth: 1946–69.

Atlas, Morris. Telephone interview by author. November 10, 1994.

Baier, Paul R. "The Law Clerks: Profile of an Institution." Vanderbilt *Law Review* 26 (November, 1973): 1138–52.

Barron, John. Letter to Reynaldo Garza, January 3, 1937. Judge Reynaldo G. Garza Papers, Garza residence, Brownsville, Tex.

Barrow, Deborah J., and Thomas G. Walker, *A Court Divided: The Fifth Circuit Court of Appeals and the Politics of Judicial Reform.* New Haven: Yale University Press, 1988.

Bass, Jack. *Taming the Storm: The Life and Times of Judge Frank M. Johnson, Jr., and the South's Fight over Civil Rights.* New York: Anchor Books, 1993.

———. *Unlikely Heroes.* New York: Simon and Schuster, 1981.

Bauer, J. E. Letter to John F. Kennedy, March 24, 1961. John F. Kennedy Papers, John F. Kennedy Library, Boston, Mass.

Bay, Betty. *Historic Brownsville: Original Townsite Guide.* Brownsville: Brownsville Historical Association, 1980.

Bell, Griffin. Former U.S. Attorney General. Telephone interview by author. January 24, 1995.

———. *Taking Care of the Law.* New York: Morrow, 1982.

Bennett, George. Former deputy U.S. marshal. Telephone interview by author. February 8, 1995.

Bentsen, Lloyd. Former U.S. Treasury secretary. Interview by author. Washington, D.C., February 12, 1994.

Berry, Margaret Catherine. *UT Austin: Traditions and Nostalgia.* Austin: Shoal Creek Publisher, 1975.

Caro, Robert A. *The Years of Lyndon Johnson: Means of Ascent.* London: Bodley Head, 1990.

———. *The Years of Lyndon Johnson: The Path to Power.* New York: Vintage Books, 1981.

Castro, Tony. *Chicano Power.* New York: Saturday Review Press, 1974.

Champagne, Anthony, and Edward J. Harpham. *Texas at the Crossroads: People, Politics, and Policy.* College Station: Texas A&M University Press, 1987.

Chandler, Charles R. "The Mexican American Protest Movement in Texas." Ph.D. diss., Tulane University, 1968.

Chase, Harold W. *The Appointing Process.* Minneapolis: University of Minnesota Press, 1972.

Chatfield. W. H. *The Twin Cities of the Border: Brownsville, Texas and Matamoros, Mexico.* New Orleans: E. P. Brandao, 1893. Reprint, Brownsville: Brownsville Historical Association, 1959.

Clark, Ramsey. Former U.S. Attorney General. Interview by author. New York, May 30, 1995.

———. Interview by Larry Hackman. Transcript. July 7, 1970. Robert F. Kennedy Oral History Program, John F. Kennedy Library, Boston, Mass.

Clerk's Annual Report: Fifth Circuit Fiscal Year 1982. Washington, D.C.: Federal Judicial Center, July, 1982.

Conkin, Paul K. *Big Daddy from the Pedernales: Lyndon Baines Johnson.* Boston: Twayne Publishers, 1986.

Couch, Harvey C. *A History of the Fifth Circuit, 1891–1981.* Washington, D.C.: Bicentennial Committee of the Judicial Conference of the United States, 1984.

Criminal Docket Books. Brownsville division, Federal Courthouse, Brownsville, Texas, 1961–64.

Crixel, Emilio. Telephone interview by author. February 7, 1994.

Cuellar, Alfredo. "Perspectives on Politics," in *Chicano Studies.* Ed. Isidro Duran. New York: Macmillan, 1973.

Cummings, Joe. *Texas Handbook.* Chico, Calif.: Moon Publications, 1992.

Dallek, Robert. *Lone Star Rising: Lyndon Johnson and His Times, 1908–1960.* New York: Oxford University Press, 1991.

Dancy, Oscar. Letter to John F. Kennedy, April 7, 1961; May 2, 1961. John F. Kennedy Papers, John F. Kennedy Library, Boston, Mass.

———. Letter to Lyndon Baines Johnson, November 30, 1960. John F. Kennedy Papers, John F. Kennedy Library, Boston Mass.

"Database," *U.S. News and World Report,* May 3, 1993.

Davidson, Chandler. *Race and Class in Texas Politics.* Princeton: Princeton University Press, 1990.

Davis, David Brion. "Some Recent Directions in Cultural History." *American Historical Review* 73 (February, 1968): 705.

de Crävecoeur, St. John. *Letters from an American Farmer: Sketches of Eighteenth Century America.* London: 1782. Reprint, New York: Penguin Books, 1981.

De la Garza, Eligio (Kika). U.S. representative. Interview by author. Washington, D.C., September 29, 1994.

De León, Arnoldo. *Ethnicity in the Sunbelt: A History of Mexican Americans in Houston.* Houston: University of Houston Press, 1989.

Dillman, Charles Daniel. "The Functions of Brownsville, Texas, and Matamoros, Tamaulipas: Twin Cities of the Lower Rio Grande." Ph.D. diss., University of Michigan, 1968.

Dosal, María Rosa. Interview by author. Brownsville, July 24, 1993.

Dower, John W. *War without Mercy: Race and Power in the Pacific War.* New York: Pantheon Books, 1986.

Dugger, Ronnie. "Texas' New Junior Senator." *New Republic.* April 22, 1957, p. 8.

Eisenhower, John S. D. *So Far From God.* New York: Random House, 1989.

Elkins, James R. "The Temporary Emergency Court of Appeals: A Study in the Abdication of Judicial Responsibility." *Duke Law Journal* 113 (1978): 114–125.

Evans, Rowland, and Robert Novak. *Lyndon B. Johnson: The Exercise of Power.* New York: New American Library, 1966.

Friendly, Henry J. *Federal Jurisdiction: A General View.* New York: Columbia University Press, 1973.

García, Hector. Letter to Dwight D. Eisenhower, March 4, 1960. Dwight D. Eisenhower Papers, Dwight D. Eisenhower Presidential Library, Abilene, Kan.

———. Letter to John F. Kennedy, December, 1960. John F. Kennedy Papers, John F. Kennedy Library, Boston, Mass.

García, Juan Ramón. *Operation Wetback: The Mass Deportation of Mexican Undocumented Workers in 1954.* Westport, Conn.: Greenwood Press, 1980.

García, Juliet. President, University of Texas at Brownsville. Interview by author. Tape recording. Brownsville, July 26, 1993.

García, Mario T. *Mexican Americans: Leadership, Ideology, and Identity, 1930–1960.* New Haven: Yale University Press, 1989.

Garcia, Richard A. "Class Consciousness and Ideology: The Mexican Community of San Antonio, Texas: 1930–1940." *Aztlán* 9 (1978): 42.

———. *Rise of the Mexican American Middle Class: San Antonio, 1929–1941.* College Station: Texas A&M University Press, 1991.

Garriega, Mariano. Letter to Reynaldo Garza, July 28, 1954. Archives Department, Diocese of Corpus Christi, Pastoral Center, Corpus Christi, Tex.

Garza, Argentina. Interview by author. Brownsville, July 24, 1993.

Garza, Bertha. Interview by author. Brownsville, July 23, 1993; August 3, 1993; September 23, 1994.

Garza, David C. Interview by author, Brownsville, September 22, 1994.

Garza, Emilio. Federal judge, U.S. Court of Appeals. Interview by author. Tape recording. New Orleans, August 3, 1993.

Garza, Monica. Telephone interview by author. June 1, 1995.

Garza, Nacho. Interview by author. Washington, D.C., September 25, 1994.

Garza, Reynaldo. Interview by Joe B. Frantz. Transcript, interview 1. December 2,

1970. Lyndon Baines Johnson Library Oral History Colection, Lyndon Baines Johnson Library, Austin, Texas.

———. Interview by Marc Knisely. Transcript. March 11, 1992. Judicial Collection, Fifth Circuit Court of Appeals Library, New Orleans, La.

———. Interview by author. Brownsville, May 23, 1993, May 29, 1993, July 23, 1993, September 23, 1994.

———. Letter to Ronald Reagan, January 9, 1981. White House Correspondence, Ronald Reagan Library, Simi Valley, Calif.

Garza, Reynaldo, Jr. Interview by author. Brownsville, September 22, 1994; December 21, 1994.

Gellman, Irwin G. *Good Neighbor Diplomacy: United States Policies in Latin America, 1933–1945.* Baltimore: Johns Hopkins University Press, 1979.

Gómez-Quiñones, Juan. *Chicano Politics: Reality and Promise, 1940–1990.* Albuquerque: University of New Mexico Press, 1990.

González, Gustavo E. Letter to President Jimmy Carter, August 1, 1979. White House central file, name file: Garza, R., Jimmy Carter Presidential Library, Atlanta, Ga.

González, Raul A. "A Life of Service: Reynaldo G. Garza." *Hispanic Law Journal* 1 (1994): 6–7.

Gordon, Milton M. *Assimilation in American Life: The Role of Race, Religion, and National Origins.* New York: Oxford University Press, 1964.

Goulden, Joseph C. *The Benchwarmers: The Private World of the Powerful Federal Judges.* New York: Weybright and Talley, 1974.

"'Great Society' Faces Future—Changes Congress Is Making," *U.S. News and World Report,* July 10, 1967.

Grebler, Leo; Joan W. Moore; Ralph C. Guzmán; and Jeffrey L. Berlant. *The Mexican-American People, The Nations Second Largest Minority.* New York: Free Press, 1970.

Green, George Norris. *The Establishment in Texas Politics: The Primitive Years 1938–1957.* Westport, Conn.: Greenwood Press, 1979.

———. "The Felix Longoria Affair." *Journal of Ethnic Studies* 19 (Fall, 1991): 29.

Greenhill, Joe. Former chief justice, Texas Supreme Court. Telephone interview by author. January 25, 1995.

Grossman, Joel B. *Lawyers and Judges: The A. B. A. and the Politics of Judicial Selection.* New York: John Wiley, 1965.

Hamby, Alonzo L. *The Imperial Years: The U.S. since 1939.* New York: Longman, 1976.

Hamilton, Alexander. *The Federalist Papers.* No. 78 at 465. Clinton Rossiter ed., 1961.

Hansen, Niles. *The Border Economy.* Austin: University of Texas Press, 1981.

Harding, Nola Martin, and Dorothy Abbott McCoy. "Francisco Yturria and Heirs," in *Valley By-Liners: Roots By the River.* Mission, Tex.: Border Kingdom Press, 1978.

Haynes, Robert V. *A Night of Violence: The Houston Riot of 1917.* Baton Rouge: Louisiana State University, 1976.

Heflin, Howell. "Fifth Circuit Court of Appeals Reorganization Act of 1980: Overdue Relief for an Overworked Court." *Cumberland Law Review* 11 (1980): 597–613.

"It's War Among Texas Democrats," *U.S. News and World Report,* Apr. 27, 1956.

Jacob, Herbert. *Justice in America: Courts, Lawyers and the Judicial Process.* Boston: Little, Brown, and Company, 1978.

Jessup, Philip C. "El Chamizal." *American Journal of International Law* 67 (1973): 423.

Johnson, Lyndon Baines. "Daily Diary of President Lyndon Baines Johnson, 1963–69," March 24, 1961; April 11, 13, 1961; October 30, 1963; November 4, 1963. Manuscripts, Library of Congress, Washington, D.C.

⸻. Letter to Reynaldo G. Garza, October 15, 1953; April 23, 1954; July 15, 1954; March 28, 1955; January 13, 1960; April 29, 1961; October 10, 1961; November 13, 1967. Lyndon Baines Johnson Papers, Lyndon Baines Johnson Library, Austin, Tex.

⸻. *Public Papers of the Presidents of the United States.* Washington, D.C.: Government Printing Office, 1965.

⸻. *The Vantage Point: Perspective of the Presidency, 1963–1969.* New York: Holt, Rinehart, and Winston, 1971.

"Juan Saldívar." American Defenders of Bataan and Corregidor Records. Newbern, N.C.

Kallen, Horace M. *Culture and Democracy in the U.S.* New York: Boni and Liveright, 1924.

Kaufman, Burton I. *The Presidency of James Earl Carter, Jr.* Lawrence: University Press of Kansas, 1993.

Kazen, George Phillip. U.S. district judge. Telephone interview by author. January 24, 1995.

Kearney, Milo; Alfonso Gómez Arguelles; and Yolanda Z. González. *A Brief History of Education in Brownsville and Matamoros.* Brownsville: University of Texas–Pan American, Brownsville Press, 1989.

Kearney, Milo, and Anthony Knopp. *Boom and Bust: The Historical Cycles of Matamoros and Brownsville.* Austin: Eakin Press, 1991.

Kennedy, John F. Letter to Reynaldo G. Garza, April 29, 1961. John F. Kennedy Papers, John F. Kennedy Library, Boston, Mass.

⸻. *Public Papers of the Presidents of the United States.* Washington, D.C.: Government Printing Office, 1964.

Kennedy, Robert. Letter to John F. Kennedy, March 23, 1961. John F. Kennedy Papers, John F. Kennedy Library, Boston, Mass.

Key, V. O. *Southern Politics in State and Nation.* New York: Knopf, 1949.

Kibbe, Pauline. *Latin Americans.* Albuquerque: University of New Mexico Press, 1946.

Kilgore, Joe M. Former U.S. congressman. Telephone interview by author. January 13, 1995.

Kinch, Sam, and Stuart Long. *Allan Shivers: The Pied Piper of Texas Politics.* Austin: Shoal Creek Publishers, 1974.

Kingrea, Nellie. *History of the First Ten Years of the Texas Good Neighbor Commission.* Fort Worth: Texas Christian University Press, 1954.

Knisely, Marc. Interview by author, Austin, February 14, 1995.

Knowlton, Clark. "Patterns of Accommodation of Mexican Americans in El Paso, Texas," in *Politics and Society in the Southwest: Ethnicity and Chicano Pluralism.* Eds. Z. Anthony Krusewski, Richard L. Hough, and Jacob Ornstein-Garcia. Boulder: Westview Press, 1982.

LaFeber, Walter. "The Rise and Fall of American Power, 1963–1975," part 4, in *America in Vietnam: A Documentary History.* New York: W. W. Norton and Company, 1985.

La Roach, Clarence. Telephone interview by author. March 28, 1994.

Lewis, Charlie. U.S. attorney. Telephone interview by author. March 30, 1995.

Little, George. "A Study of the Texas Good Neighbor Commission." M.A. thesis, University of Houston, 1953.

Lynch, Dudley. *The Duke of Duval.* Waco: Texian Press, 1976.

McCullough, Graham. Letter to Reynaldo G. Garza, April 22, 1986. Reynaldo G. Garza Papers, Brownsville, Tex.

McGraw, Dan. "A Load of Trouble for Texas Border Towns: Mexico's Woes Spill across the Rio Grande," *U.S. News and World Report,* Oct. 2, 1995.

McKay, Seth Shepard. *W. Lee O'Daniel and Texas Politics, 1938–1942.* Lubbock: Texas Tech Press, 1944.

McWilliams, Carey. *North From Mexico: The Spanish-Speaking People of the United States.* New York: J. B. Lippincott Company, 1948.

Madsen, William. *The Mexican Americans of South Texas.* New York: Holt, Rinehart, and Winston, 1964.

Mallett, William H. Letter to Reynaldo G. Garza, April 29, 1986. Reynaldo G. Garza Papers, Brownsville, Tex.

———. U.S. magistrate. Telephone interview by author. October 19, 1994.

Manuel, Herschel T. *Spanish-Speaking Children of the Southwest: Their Education and the Public Welfare.* Austin: University of Texas Press, 1965.

Márquez, Benjamin. *LULAC: The Evolution of a Mexican American Political Organization.* Austin: University of Texas Press, 1993.

Mars. S. M. N. *State Department of Education.* Twenty-Third Biennial Report 1922–1924. Austin: State Printing Office, 1924.

Martin, Celia. Telephone interview by author. October 17, 1994.

Matusow, Allen J. *The Unraveling of America: A History of American Liberalism in the 1960s.* New York: Harper and Row, 1984.

Meador, Daniel John, and Jordana Simone Bernstein. *Appellate Courts in the United States.* St. Paul: West Publishing Company, 1994.

Meier, Matt S., and Feliciano Ribera. *The Chicanos: A History of Mexican Americans.* New York: Hill and Wang, 1972.

———. *Mexican Americans/American Mexicans: From Conquistadors to Chicanos.* New York: Hill and Wang, 1993.

Miller, Arnie. Letter to President Jimmy Carter, April 23, 1979. Jimmy Carter Presidential Papers, Jimmy Carter Library, Atlanta, Ga.

———. Letter to Gustavo E. González, August 14, 1979. White House central file, name file: Garza, R., Jimmy Carter Presidential Library, Atlanta, Ga.

Moize, Elizabeth A. "Austin." *National Geographic,* June, 1990, 50–71.

Moll, Richard. *The Public Ivys: A Guide to America's Best Public Undergradute Colleges and Universities.* New York: Penguin Inc., 1985.

Montejano, David. *Anglos and Mexicans in the Making of Texas, 1836–1986.* Austin: University of Texas Press, 1987.

Moore, Joan W. *Mexican Americans.* New Jersey: Prentice-Hall, Inc., 1970.

Moore, P. T., Jr. Telephone interview by author. January 4, 1995.

Muñoz, Carlos Jr. *Youth, Identity, Power: The Chicano Movement.* London, 1989.

Navasky, Victor. *Kennedy Justice.* New York: Atheneum, 1971.

Neale, William. *Century of Conflict, 1821–1891: Incidents in the Lives of William Neale and William A. Neale, Early Settlers in South Texas*. Eds. John C. Rayburn and Virginia Kemp Rayburn. Waco: Texian Press, 1966.

"New United States Judge Takes Office in Brownsville: Reynaldo G. Garza." *Texas Bar Journal* 24 (June 22, 1961): 87.

Opinions of the Honorable Reynaldo G. Garza, Chief Judge, United States District Court, Published in the Years 1970–1979. St. Paul: West Publishing Company, 1979.

Orum, Anthony. *The Making of Modern Austin: Power, Money, and the People*. Austin: Texas Monthly Press, 1987.

Paine, Albert Bigelow. *Captain Bill McDonald Texas Ranger: A Story of Frontier Reform*. New York: J. J. Little and Ives Co., 1909.

Peltason, J.W., *Fifty-Eight Lonely Men*. New York: Harcourt, Brace, and World, 1961.

Peña, Federico. U.S. Department of Transportation Secretary. Interview by author. Tape recording. Washington, D.C., February 7, 1995.

Perales, Alonso S. *Are We Good Neighbors?* New York: Arno Press, 1948.

Pérez, Lino. Interview by author. Tape recording. South Padre Island, July 25, 1993.

Phillips, William G. *Yarborough of Texas*. Washington, D.C.: Acropolis Books, 1969.

Pierce, Frank C. *Texas' Last Frontier: A Brief History of the Lower Rio Grande Valley*. Menasha, Wis.: Collegiate Press, George Banta Publishing Company, 1917; republished, 1962.

Pipkin, Maurice. Former Texas state representative. Telephone interview by author. March 28, 1994.

Polenberg, Richard. *War and Society: The United States 1941–1945*. Philadelphia: J. B. Lippincott Company, 1972.

Politz, Henry A. Chief judge, U.S. Court of Appeals, Fifth Circuit. Telephone interview by author. Shreveport, La., June 15, 1995.

Public Papers of the President of the United States. Washington, D.C.: Office of the Federal Register, National Archives and Records Service, 1965.

Public Papers of the Presidents of the United States. Washington, D.C.: Government Printing Office, 1970.

Public Papers of the Presidents of the United States. Washington, D.C.: Office of the Federal Register, National Archives and Records Service, 1980.

Ruedas, Eutimio. Letter to President Jimmy Carter, August 28, 1978. White House central file, name file: Garza, R., Jimmy Carter Presidential Library, Atlanta, Ga.

Rangel, Jorge, and Carlos Alcalá. "De Jure Segregation of Chicanos in Texas Schools." *Harvard Civil Rights–Civil Liberties Law Review* 7 (March, 1972): 308–21.

Reincke, Mary, ed. *The American Bench: Judges of the Nation*. Minneapolis: Reginald Bishop Forster and Associates, Inc., 1979.

Reston, James. *The Lone Star; The Life of John Connally*. New York: Harper and Row, 1986.

Richardson, Rupert N.; Ernest Wallace; and Adrian N. Anderson. *Texas: The Lone Star State*, 6th ed. New Jersey: Prentice-Hall, 1993.

San Miguel, Guadalupe, Jr. *Let All of Them Take Heed: Mexican Americans and the Campaign for Education Equality in Texas, 1910–1981*. Austin: University of Texas Press, 1987.

Savage, David G. *Turning Right: The Making of the Rehnquist Supreme Court.* New York: John Wiley and Sons, Inc., 1992.

Schlesinger, Arthur M., Jr. *A Thousand Days: John F. Kennedy in the White House.* Boston: Houghton Mifflin Company, 1965.

———. *Robert Kennedy and His Times.* New York: Ballantine Books, 1978.

Scott, Florence J. *Historical Heritage of the Lower Rio Grande.* San Antonio: Naylor Company, 1937.

Simmons, Ozzie G. "Anglo-Americans and Mexican-Americans: Images and Expectations," in *Racial and Ethnic Relations Selected Readings.* Ed. Bernard E. Segal. New York: Thomas Y. Crowell Company, 1966.

Sitkoff, Harvard. *The Struggle for Black Equality, 1954–1980.* New York, 1981.

Small, Melvin. *Covering Dissent: The Media and the Anti-Vietnam War Movement.* New Brunswick: Rutgers University Press, 1994.

Speed, Gilmer. "The Hunt for Garza." *Harper's Weekly,* January 30, 1892, p. 103.

Stempel, Jeffrey W. "Symposium: New Paradigm, Normal Science, Crumbling Construct? Trends in Adjudicating Procedure and Litigation and Reform," *Brooklyn Law Review* 59 (Fall, 1993): 659–760.

Takaki, Ronald. *A Different Mirror: A History of Multicultural America.* Boston: Little, Brown, and Company.

Taylor, Paul S. *An American-Mexican Frontier.* Chapel Hill: University of North Carolina Press, 1934.

Teske, Raymond H. C., Jr., and Bardin H. Nelson. "An Analysis of Differential Assimilation Rates among Middle-Class Mexican Americans." *Sociological Quarterly* 17 (Spring, 1976): 218–35.

Tillson, Allen Reid, Letter to Reynaldo Garza, April 25, 1986. Reynaldo G. Garza Papers, Brownsville, Texas.

U.S. Congress. *Congressional Record.* 57th Cong., 1st Sess. Vol. 35, 2135–37.

———. House of Representatives, Committee of the Judiciary. *Statement of the Honorable Lloyd M. Bentsen.* 81st Cong., 1st Sess., 1949, 25, 27.

———. House of Representatives. "The Tonkin Gulf Debate and Resolution," *Congressional Record.* 84th Cong., 1st Sess., 18132–33, 18406–18407, 18458–59, 18470–71.

———. Subcommittee on Compensation and Pension, *Hearings to Extend Veterans' Benefits Eligibility to 167 Soldiers, or their Heirs, Dishonorably Discharged as a Result of Involvement in an Alleged Disturbance at a Brownsville, Texas Garrison in August, 1906,* 93rd. Cong., 1st Sess., H.R. 4382, 1220–40.

U.S. Department of Commerce, Bureau of the Census. *Census of Population: 1950,* Volume II, Part 43, Texas. Washington, D.C.: Government Printing Office, 1952.

———. *Census of Population: 1960,* Volume II, Texas. Washington, D.C.: Government Printing Office, 1962.

———. *Eighteenth Decennial Census of the United States: Census of Population: 1960,* Part 45 Texas. Washington, D.C.: Government Printing Office, 1961.

———. *Fifteenth Census of the United States: 1930,* Volume VI. Washington, D.C.: Government Printing Office, 1933.

———. *Fourteenth Census of the United States Taken in the Year 1920,* Volume III. Washington, D.C.: Government Printing Office, 1922.

– – –. *Historical Statistics of the United States Colonial Times to 1970*, Part 2. Washington, D.C.: Government Printing Office, 1975.

– – –. *1970 Census of Population*, Part 45 Texas. Washington, D.C.: Government Printing Office, 1973.

– – –. *Statistical Abstract of the United States: 1979*. Washington, D.C.: Government Printing Office, 1979.

– – –. *Statistical Abstract of the United States: 1993*. Washington, D.C.: Government Printing Office, 1993.

– – –. *Thirteenth Census of the United States Taken in the Year 1910*, Volume I. Washington, D.C.: Government Printing Office, 1913.

U.S.–Mexico Border Health Statistics. 6th ed. El Paso: U.S./Mexico Border Field Office, Pan American Health Organization, 1990.

U.S. President. *Public Papers of the United States, Jimmy Carter, 1980–1981*. Washington, D.C.: Government Printing Office, 1982.

U.S. Senate. *Affray at Brownsville Texas*. Hearing, 60th Cong., 1st Sess., June 4, 1907.

– – –. Committee on the Judiciary, *Hearings before the Subcommittee on Improvements in Judicial Machinery of the Committee on the Judiciary on S. 3475*. 89th Cong., 2nd Sess. July 11–13, August 23, 1966.

– – –. Committee on the Judiciary. *Nomination*. Hearing, 87th Cong., 1st Sess., April 12, 1961.

– – –. Committee on the Judiciary. *The Selection and Confirmation of Federal Judges*. 96th Congs, 1st Sess., June 25, 1979.

– – –. "Freedom of Communications." Part I, Kennedy Speeches, Committee on Commerce, Senate Report 994, 1961.

– – –. Committee on the Judiciary. Statement of Honorable Joe M. Kilgore and John Young, U.S. Representatives from Texas. Washington: Ward and Paul, April, 1961. Unpublished CIS microfilm, Library of Congress.

– – –. Committee on the Judiciary. Statement of Honorable Ralph W. Yarborough, U.S. Senator from Texas. Washington, D.C.: War and Paul, April, 1961. Unpublished CIS microfilm. Library of Congress.

U.S. Treasury Department. *Report of the U.S. Secret Service on the Assassination of President Kennedy: Exhibits*. Washington, D.C.: Reproduced at the National Archives, 1965.

Vanderbilt, Arthur T. Minimum *Standards of Judicial Administration*. New York: Law Center of New York University, 1949.

Vela, Filemón. U.S. District Judge. Telephone interview by author. June 15, 1995.

Villareal, Roberto E. *Chicano Elites and Non-Elites: An Inquiry into Social and Political Change*. Palo Alto: R and E Research Associates, Inc., 1979.

Weaver, John D. *The Brownsville Raid*. New York: W. W. Norton, 1970.

Weeks, O. Douglas. *Texas in the 1960 Presidential Election*. Austin: University of Texas Press, 1961.

Wisdom, John Minor. Senior judge, U.S. Court of Appeals, Fifth Circuit. Telephone interview by author. July 13, 1994.

Wood, Bryce. *The Making of the Good Neighbor Policy*. New York: Columbia University Press, 1961.

Woolridge, Ruby A., and Robert B. Vezzetti, "The Founding of Charro Days," in

More Studies in Brownsville History, ed. Milo Kearney, 309–92. Brownsville: Pan American University Press, 1989.

———. *Brownsville: A Pictorial History.* Norfolk, Va.: Donning Company Publishers, 1982.

Zanden, James W. Vander. *American Minority Relations.* New York: Ronald Press Company, 1972.

Zavaleta, Antonio N. "Resacas and Bancos in Brownsville History," in *More Studies in Brownsville History.* Ed. Milo Kearney. Brownsville: Pan American University Press, 1989.

Zelden, Charles L. *Justice Lies in the District: The U.S. District Court, Southern District of Texas, 1902–1960.* College Station: Texas A&M University Press, 1993.

Index

NOTE: Pages with illustrations are indicated by italics.